Of Love,
Hope, & Rainbows

JUDIE MEISE

WESTBOW
PRESS®
A DIVISION OF THOMAS NELSON
& ZONDERVAN

Scripture quotations marked (NIV) are taken from the Holy Bible, New
International Version®, NIV®. Copyright © 1973, 1978, 1984, 2011 by Biblica,
Inc.™ Used by permission of Zondervan. All rights reserved worldwide. www.
zondervan.com The "NIV" and "New International Version" are trademarks
registered in the United States Patent and Trademark Office by Biblica, Inc.

Scripture taken from the King James Version of the Bible

WestBow Press books may be ordered through booksellers or by contacting:

WestBow Press
A Division of Thomas Nelson & Zondervan
1663 Liberty Drive
Bloomington, IN 47403
www.westbowpress.com
1 (866) 928-1240

Because of the dynamic nature of the Internet, any web addresses or
links contained in this book may have changed since publication and
may no longer be valid. The views expressed in this work are solely those
of the author and do not necessarily reflect the views of the publisher,
and the publisher hereby disclaims any responsibility for them.

Any people depicted in stock imagery provided by Thinkstock are models,
and such images are being used for illustrative purposes only.
Certain stock imagery © Thinkstock.

ISBN: 978-1-9736-1199-8 (sc)
ISBN: 978-1-9736-1198-1 (e)

Print information available on the last page.

WestBow Press rev. date: 01/12/2018

Contents

Dedication

To Ernie, my one in a million – miracle man

What an inspiration you have been to me and so many. Your courage, drive, determination, fight, all that you have displayed in your 20 years battling Multiple Myeloma – Bone Marrow Cancer - including two Bone Marrow Transplants has been phenomenal. You truly are the "Best Trouper Ever". We have celebrated over 57 years of marriage now and have known each other three and a half years in addition to that. For 60 years, we have shared our love for one another, and God could not have chosen a better person for me. You truly have been my Prince Charming. Thank you for being so kind, considerate, and giving, even when I know how difficult it is for you to go out of your way to make my life special. I am so grateful for your love. We've been through so many difficult days, but no matter what, we have stood by each other. God has blessed us with four awesome sons and our family has grown to 28 special people to love. We have so many memories to cherish. Although we both wish that big "C" word would have never come into your life, I truly believe we have both learned to appreciate our days together so much more. And, it is true, God gave us far more days than we thought would ever be possible. We don't know what the future has in store for us, but we do know what was in our past. God has been so good. For now, I will cherish every day that God gives us. The present is God's gift to us, and together we will unwrap each day with love and gratitude in our hearts. God Bless You, Honey. For all of your days, I will love you.

To Jeff – our firstborn son

My first memories of you as a baby were your never-ending smiles. Every time I would look your way, I was greeted with that precious smile. You were so happy and full of life. Growing up as the oldest, you took on the role of being the leader and responsible one. I will always cherish the time I had watching you grow. Being a part of the activities you were involved in – Little League Baseball, Cub Scouts, VBS, PTA and other activities at your school, all of these bring back many special memories. You had a great mind and memorized well. The plays you were in at Urban were very special. You were the star of "The Million Dollar Man". Because you played the trombone, I was able to attend many enjoyable concerts and parades. You have been blessed with skillful hands. Your artwork and now your work in Tool and Die have been extra special. You were always a hard worker and have provided well for your family. As an adult, I am so grateful you have taken part as a leader in your church. Your willingness to share the love of the Lord and His Word have been a blessing to many. Your expertise in home repairs and construction have also been a great blessing to many. You have been through some very tough times, but through it all, God was there. I am so grateful for your fight to lead a good life. You have many qualities that can bless the lives of others. I pray that you will continue to use your skills and knowledge to bring praise and honor to the God you love. Stand strong, and keep your mind on the goal. I am grateful you are my son, and I will always love you.

To Tim – our second son

You came into this world full of life and energy. From little on, you were a handsome little guy. Your drive and determination was amazing. You accomplished many things earlier than most children, and your love of sports and competition was evident at a very early age. You were a great Little League Baseball player. I was so proud of you. You were also involved with V.B.S., and Cub Scouts. I loved being able to attend your school activities and band concerts where you played the Baritone. You always excelled in Math, and your teacher always told me you were hitting all home runs when it came to Math. You took that skill into your adulthood and went on to achieve the honor of becoming a Certified Public Accountant. I am so proud that you established your own business – My-Z Financial & Tax Services. You have served the Lord with your teaching and leadership roles at your church. You have overcome difficult obstacles in your life, and you have become stronger in the fight. You have been a good dad to your three children, and a good husband to your wife. I pray that God will continue to bless you with strength and will keep you in His will as He directs you in the future. You have a special heart of giving. Your sincerity, empathy, and the special way you touch the lives of others has been commendable. I am so proud to call you my son, and I will always love you.

To Todd – our third son

From the time you came into this world, you were an amazing child. Your beautiful, big, brown eyes and blonde hair generated special comments from all those who saw you. Your calm, soft-spoken, loving spirit was there right from the start. You were a very content little guy. Having two older brothers, you were taken many places to attend their activities. You were so amazingly good and content wherever we went. I was grateful for the times we could share with V.B.S., Cub Scouts, and your school activities. You mastered the trombone and provided many great musical experiences that I will always cherish. Being a part of the Band in Jackson, Tennessee, was especially exciting. I'm so proud and grateful for all that you achieved with music. It took some very tough experiences for you to go through before God opened the door for your college experience. This brought you to getting your

Master's Degree in Social Work. You did an awesome job, and I am so proud of your accomplishments. Your employment has often been self-sacrificing, and you have carried on in an honorable way. Caring, compassionate service has been a gift that you have brought to so many. Your service to your heavenly Father has also been commendable. I am so proud that you have used your knowledge and abilities in serving the people that God has brought to you. The Spirit of God has been so powerful in your life. Your children have exemplified the good example that you have been to them. I pray that God will continue to bless you and guide you as you seek to serve those with special needs as well as all those who become a part of your life. May God bless you with strength, safety, and good health as you continue to use your special gifts. I thank the Lord for who you have become, and I will always love you.

To Scott – our fourth and youngest son

You were definitely God's special surprise to our family. Just when we thought our family was complete, God gave us you. What a wonderful blessing you have been to our family. Growing up with parents that were 40 plus years older than you could have been complicated, but that didn't happen with you. From day one, you had so many people around you to care for you and love you. I am so grateful you were there with me when we moved to Tennessee. You definitely helped me with the adjustment of moving to another state. You were blessed with siblings who helped teach you with academics and with sports at a very young age, and you learned so well. You were content and happy and full of smiles, enjoying life to the fullest. Your ability to memorize and retain information was incredible. This gift gave you special roles in plays, starting in grade school. You excelled academically and did so well with sports, especially with basketball, baseball, soccer, cross country running and volleyball. You have made us all so proud. One of my greatest memories was when you received the $10,000.00 scholarship at

North High the year you graduated. What a great honor that was. You went on to graduate from U. W. Madison with a double major in just four years. This was incredible. Your heart for caring for others has been amazing. You are a hard worker and are providing well for your family. You continue to study and grow in your line of work. You have also found a love for knowing your Lord and Savior Jesus Christ. We are so grateful for the leadership you are taking on, as others are being blessed by all that you are doing. You have brought so much joy into my life. It's been an incredible journey. I am so proud of who you are, and I know God has great plans for your future. I thank God that you are my son, and I will always love you.

To Debbie – our first daughter-in-law

You were the first female to become part of our family. I was so excited. You were accepted and loved by all of us right from the start. While you were still dating Jeff, you stepped in to help care for Scott when I was working. You were there for me when I was sick. I'll never forget your first dinner at our house. It was an impromptu invitation. We were having duck. When Jeff and his brothers started saying this was Daffy, you started to cry. I immediately came to your defense and told you it was okay if you didn't want to eat it. I never served duck to you again. Because of your marriage to Jeff, we have five awesome grandchildren – Ryne, Mark, John, and the twins, Kelsey and Kristin. It has been a blessing to see how you have grown in your faith and service to the Lord. I will always cherish the memories we have had in attending so many Women of Faith Conferences together. I also am so grateful for the years of Women's Bible Study that we shared. What a blessing to see you now, leading and sharing your knowledge and love of the Lord. I could not ask for anything more. We've gone through many difficult times together. I thank God for your willingness to be there for me when I needed support. I am grateful I was able to do the same for you. It brings me much joy to see you carry on some of the family traditions of acknowledging our Lord and Savior Jesus Christ. You are a strong leader, and your life has blessed the lives of many. You are a very hard worker, and you have definitely been a blessing to your family. God has brought you through many tough times, but He has always been there giving you strength and guidance to carry on. Many lives have been blessed by your kindness, insight, and love. I am so grateful to call you my daughter-in-law, and at times, I feel you have been far more than that. God bless you in all you do. I will always love you.

To Lisa – our second daughter-in-law

You are our first out-of-state daughter-in-law. Tim met you while living in Tennessee, after Ernie, Scott, and I had returned to Wisconsin. Thank you for your part in bringing me three very special grandchildren, Nicole, Micah, and Jared. You have used your technical skills to be a great blessing to many. May God continue to be with you and use you for His purpose. Your dedication to serving in your church has been amazing. I am thankful for times when I felt you were expressing thoughtfulness and love. My very first pedicure was a special time spent with Nicole and you. God bless you and guide you in all you do. I will cherish the good memories. Know that you are loved.

To Denise – our third daughter-in-law

Your story of meeting our son, Todd, is so amazing. After the second time sitting next to each other in church in Jackson, Tennessee, God had the two of you discovering His pathway to your future together. God is so good. We first met you in Chattanooga, Tennessee, for about an hour when we were returning from a vacation trip to Florida. Nine months later, we were heading back to Tennessee for your wedding. It was so clear that Todd had found the love of his life. You captured his heart with your beauty, gentleness, and sweet, sweet spirit. Over the years, we have grown to love you so much. I admire the awesome talents that you possess. Most of all, I am so grateful for the incredible mother that you are to your precious girls, Kaitlyn and Maddie. They are so fortunate to have you as their mom, and Todd is so blessed to have you as his wife. You are an awesome role model in all that you do. Your skills are amazing, and you are a top-notch homemaker. What a joy it is to experience your love for cooking, and what a delight it is to receive gifts that you have created. I am so grateful for your faith, and I love seeing you serve the Lord sharing your knowledge with others. Your dedication, devotion, and self-sacrificial nature are phenomenal. I am so blessed to call you my daughter-in-law. May God continue to bless you in all that you do. I will love you always.

To Debbi – our fourth daughter-in-law

You came into our lives most recently. God has allowed us to live close enough to be able to spend good time together. This has been a real blessing to me. I thank God that you are now living in Wisconsin. Scott first met you in this state, and after many years of living and working in Illinois, you are now a Wisconsinite. You have brought two grandchildren into our lives for which we are so thankful. We love them very much. God blessed your marriage by allowing Scott to father your precious little son, Barry. What an awesome blessing. Along with that you have given us the joy of bringing Orion into our lives. You have been an awesome, caring, fun-loving mother to our grandchildren. They are so blessed to have you. You have also been supportive in your marriage to Scott, and you have welcomed all of Scott's family into your life. You have an awesome gift of hospitality. You have many friendships, and your love and compassion for others is very special. Your dedication to God and your love of worship is commendable. I am so grateful for the good role model you have been. I pray that you will continue to learn and grow in your love of the Lord. Know that He loves you very much, and will care for all your needs. Rest in His loving arms when challenges come before you, and know that He will never leave you nor forsake you. Your special smile is a beacon for all those around you. May each day bring you the joy of the Lord as your life shines for Him in all you do. I feel so blessed to be able to call you my daughter-in-law. I will always love you.

To Ryne – our first grandson

You are an amazing grandson. Loved by many. Your friendly nature shines brightly. You have been blessed with special skills. Thank you for your darling little girl, Emma. I know that you love her, and you are an awesome daddy to her. Little Emma, our first great-grandchild, is absolutely a joy. She has an amazing, thoughtful, compassionate, honest heart. I am confident that God has great plans for her life. I am so grateful she is learning the love of Jesus, who she freely confesses is living in her heart. God's Spirit is so alive in her and is so evident when she prays. What a blessing. I am so glad you have continued to use your gift of playing the drums and are blessing the lives of many attending your church. You also continue to enjoy running and using your cross-country skills. You have brought a lot of enjoyment to my life. You were our first grandchild that helped me out with V.B.S. using your artistic abilities. Thanks to you we put together awesome paintings to decorate the classroom wall at church as you shared the skills you have been blessed with. I appreciate your willingness to help grandpa and me out when we need an extra hand. I feel grateful when I can be there to help you out as well. I pray that God will continue to bless you and provide for all your needs in the future. May your love for Him grow as you live your life in service for Him. I am proud that you are my grandson. I want you to remember that I will always love you.

To Mark – our second grandson

You have a heart that desires to reach out and give to others. Caring and sharing are qualities that you possess. You have a winning, beautiful smile that is definitely infectious. Your love of little children (and dogs), and the attention you give them is so special. You are very thoughtful in all you do. One of my favorite stories comes from when you were very young. The rains were pouring down in our city of Sheboygan. You were in your basement when you saw water begin to run through the brick wall. You put a bucket under the falling water flow, grabbed your huge stuffed Cookie Monster toy and ran upstairs. Shortly after, that wall gave way, and your entire basement was flooded to the top with water and mud. At that same time, I was in the mountains of Colorado praying that God would save all the people of Sheboygan. I had no clue what was happening at your house, but I do know this - I am so thankful that God heard my prayer, and you were safe, as were all the people of our city who battled through that terrible flood. God saved you for a purpose. You are so loved. My prayers are that you will use your special gifts to make a great difference in this world. God has great plans for your future. Run the race, and keep your eyes on the ultimate goal. I am so grateful that you are my grandson. I will always love you.

To John – our third grandson

You were the little blonde haired, blue-eyed wonder. Actually, coming into this world at 10 pounds and 2 ounces, you really weren't so little, but you definitely were amazing from the start. I realized you were going places with that inquisitive mind way back when you were very little. What fun you had unwinding all my music tapes when you stayed at our house when your mom was in the hospital having your twin sisters. Then at the age of four, you seemed to be the pro at the Memory Game. I didn't have a chance winning that game with you. You were gifted with an awesome mind and great abilities to write. Your kindness, gentleness, and patience are commendable. I will always cherished the many, many times that you used your skills to help me with my computer. You built and created many things, and also helped me out when I needed a big guy with strong muscles. You have many special qualities that have been so helpful to many. Our times together have always been so special. Many trips were made helping Scott move. Because of your love of Lauren, little Mason, our first great-grandson has been born. What a sweet, darling little guy he is. I've fallen in love with his soft, beautiful, brown eyes and gentle spirit. He is a precious gift from God. It is already evident he will be very intelligent. I know you love your family very much. God has blessed you. I pray that you will use your gifts to serve God in all you do. By your example, your children will grow in the love of the Lord. You have much to give. I also cherish the special times we had working together with V.B.S. We had so much fun. You were a great helper to me in so many ways. I am so grateful I can call you my grandson. I will always love you.

To Kelsey – our firstborn (twin) granddaughter

Yes, you were our first born girl. What a joy! You entered this world so, so tiny. Because of your Mom's difficult pregnancy, there were people who tried to tell me you would never make it. If you did, there would be big health problems. Not once did I ever believe them. God instilled in my heart right from the start that you would be just fine. You were. I'll never forget when I first saw you. Born at seven months, and just two pounds, five ounces in weight, you were a miracle. I'll never forget looking at your fingers. They were hardly as big around as a toothpick, and they were very long. As I stood there, amazed, God told me, Kelsey has piano fingers. When I went back into your mother's hospital room, I told her this news. I had great confidence that God would take care of you, and He has done this. I am so proud that you have worked so hard to get your degree in Nursing. Your hard work ethics has been so commendable. You have already achieved great things. I wish you all the best as you continue your education to pursue becoming a Nurse Practitioner. God has great plans for you as you continue to use your gift of mercy. Many people will be blessed as you use your knowledge and skills in caring for their health needs. God Bless You in your efforts. Remember to stay close to Him in all that you do. You are loved. Thank you also for all your help with V.B.S. I loved having you as my helper. I'll never forget that awesome Lab table scene you made for our wall hanging. I was very impressed by your artistic ability. I pray that God will continue to bless you in all you do. Keep following God's will for your life. I am grateful to say you are my granddaughter. I will always love you.

To Kristin – our second (twin) granddaughter

You came into our lives just a minute after Kelsey. At just three pounds, seven ounces, you were a precious sight. A special miracle from God. Not only did I have one baby girl in my life, now there were two. What an incredible blessing. I was so grateful for the years that I was able to care for you on days when your mom worked while you were growing up. Those are awesome memories. Our times together were always special. When you were three years old, I learned a very important lesson. Never take twins to the beach unless you have another adult with you. I'll never forget this experience. I had scarcely set the blanket down on the sand when you said, "I want to play in the water." Then I heard Kelsey say, "I want to play at the playground." You both ran, lickidy-split off in different directions, while I stood there yelling, "STOP, STOP, COME BACK!" – to no avail. I quickly decided that the water may be more dangerous, so I caught up to you first and together we went to catch up with Kelsey. My words to both of you were made clear – We have to stay together. Next time we went to the beach, I took a helper along. One of my favorite remembrances of you was when you were probably around seven or eight years old. I said to you and Kelsey, "Tomorrow is our last day together before school starts. You get to plan what you want to do and where we should go." Every now and then, I allowed the two of you to make the plans for our time together. Your words were so, so cute. You took a big breath, sighed, and said, "I just want to savor the day." That put a big smile on your Grandma's face. I was amazed that you even knew the word "savor". It really didn't take long to see, you were very intelligent, and driven to do well in all that you pursued. Along with that, you were always adventurous. I am so proud of your accomplishments. You have done amazing work in advancing your knowledge in getting your degree in Lab and Chemistry. You already had research papers published. What a great job you are doing. God has awesome plans for your future. You have great gifts to give to this world, use them wisely, and be blessed. I am so happy that John, JB has come into your life, and pray for God's blessings on your plans to marry. May God Bless your lives and allow you to be a blessing to many. I am so proud to call you my granddaughter. I will love you always.

To Nicole – our third granddaughter

You were my first Tennessee-born granddaughter. You are a free-spirited, bubbly, happy girl. It's always hard for grandmothers to be so far away, but we have done our best to have time together throughout the years. It's hard to believe you are already 20 years old. Having our connection on Facebook really helps me to feel closer to you. I am so grateful that your parents have raised you to know the Lord. You have a beautiful voice and gift for music. I love to see you playing your guitar and hear you singing your praise and heartfelt love to Jesus. Your life is just unfolding. I will always know you are God's child. I will always be assured that He loves you. You are an awesome, devoted friend and are loved by many. Your beautiful smile and loving, caring heart are so special. You have a gift of showing a special love for children. My prayer is that God will keep you close to Him and that you will seek to serve Him in all that you do and say. He has great plans for your life. Continue to seek His guidance, and you will be blessed to be a blessing. I pray that there will be good, positive people that will come into your life, and your future will be bright. I am so thankful that I can call you my granddaughter. Please remember, I will always love you.

To Micah – our fourth grandson

You are our first Tennessee-born grandson. You are growing up so fast, it is amazing. You are becoming a young adult, and have shown great talent with technology and creativity. It's been awesome to see you grow, and I truly enjoy our conversations. There have been many changes in your life, and you are definitely maturing. I know that you love the Lord and that means everything to me. I pray that you will continue to be faithful to your Lord and Savior Jesus Christ in all that you do. As you are growing physically, may you also be growing in your knowledge and love of the Lord. God has great plans for your future. Follow His guidance and use your gifts to bless all those around you. God will surely bless you. I am proud to say you are my grandson. I will love you always.

To Jared – our fifth grandson

You are an amazing young man already, even at the age of 13, so wise beyond your years. God has blessed you with great discernment at a very young age. Your wisdom is incredible. I truly hope you will use this special gift to bless all those around you. Your music ability of playing the drums and singing is also so special. May you continue to use these gifts for the Lord with joy. Your soft-spoken, gentle, and polite character are so commendable. God is preparing you for great things. You are a wise leader and with God's guidance, many will be blessed by your influence on their lives. I pray that your health will prevail, and God will grant you all you need to combat the diabetes you are dealing with. You have been a strong fighter. Stand tall and strong in the Lord. He will help you in all you do. I love your sweet smile. Continue to let your light shine. I am so thankful that I can call you my grandson. Know that I will always love you.

To Orion – our sixth grandson

You are our extra, added, gifted grandson. I am so happy you have come into our family. Your Mom brought you into our lives, and I am so grateful. You have a love for technology and a gift of being able to assemble and construct things. You waited a long time for a sibling. God finally provided. You have been a proud, big brother to Barry. I am grateful that your family loves the Lord. That is so important to me. Life can sometimes be challenging, but you can always know that you are loved. I love you very much and pray that God will bless you and help you to grow to be the man He has created you to be. Your family loves you, and God loves you even more. You are His child, and He wants you to stay close to Him and make decisions that will be right and good. Work hard to learn. Stay the course, and you will achieve great things. You are a loving child, and I am grateful for the times we can have together. God bless you, and keep you in His loving care. I am so grateful that you came into my life, and I am proud to have you as my grandson. I will always love you.

To Kaitlyn – our fourth granddaughter

You were the first grandchild to be born in Jackson, Tennessee, the city where I was able to live for four years. It didn't take long to realize what an awesome, intelligent girl you are. You truly are a special, gifted child of God. I loved having the chance to come to your school and have lunch with you when you moved to Lebanon, TN. I believe you were in first grade. We sat together at our own table, and you pointed out your special friend who was at another table. You told me that the two of you loved to talk about Jesus together. Wow! How proud I was of you. How grateful I was that your parents were teaching you well. You have continued to excel in reading, math, and all that you do, achieving levels far beyond your grade expectations. You are an amazing, beautiful girl. I love coming to Tennessee to visit you, and I especially enjoy having fun in the motel pool. How exciting it was to be able to help you learn to float on your back so beautifully. (March 2016) You did so well. Your sweet smile, gentleness, and soft-spoken ways are all so special. I know God has awesome plans for your future. You will be a great leader in whatever you do. I pray that God will always give you special people in your life that you will love to talk to about Jesus. This will bring great blessing to your life. Continue to do your very best, and then use your knowledge to make this world a better place to live in. God loves you so much. You truly are His special child. I am so grateful that I can call you my granddaughter. I will love you always.

To Maddie – our fifth granddaughter

You are our sweet, free-spirited, precious little girl. You were also born in Jackson, Tennessee. Your beautiful blonde hair and pretty blue eyes are so special. You are kind hearted and a great helper. You love to share. I love our times together. You have been blessed with confidence. Always remember to do your best and tell the truth. I love to hear you pray, and I know that Jesus listens to all you say. I know you are His special child. Jesus loves you very much, and he will help you in all that you do. You are doing very well in school and excelling beyond your grade expectations just like your older sister, Kaitlyn. Keep up the good work. I loved to see how well you are doing with your swimming when you came to Sheboygan last summer (2016). Your determination and drive will get you far. Always follow Jesus. I'm so happy you are my granddaughter. I will always love you.

To Barry – our seventh grandson

You are my little sweetheart, and the first of our Meise boys to be born in Illinois. Now you are just four years old. Your infectious smile captures the hearts of all of us. Every time I think of you, I smile. Already, I see your love for sharing. It is so sweet. Already, I see your desire to gift others. I can only imagine where God is going to take this all. From the time you were born, I saw your dad and mom teach you to pray. I saw them take you to church. I heard grown adults remark how amazed they were that at a very early age you folded your hands and were silent as a prayer was said. That means so much to me. Always remember you are God's special child. He loves you so much, and I know He has great plans for your life. Always keep that love in your heart, and never stop smiling. One of the fun stories I love to share happened when we had more than twenty people at our house for Thanksgiving dinner. Because there was so much chatter going on, I decided to pick up a bell that I had in a hutch and ring it in order to get everyone's attention. It was time for them to come to the table for dinner. You were only two and a half at that time, but you didn't forget the dinner bell, and you knew exactly where I had it. For a long time after that, when you came to our house, you headed for the hutch and brought out the bell. You looked for your special place setting on the dining room table, and set the bell down beside your plate. You wanted to be sure you were ready to be the bell ringer when it was time for dinner. If you arrived before the table was set, you looked at me wondering what was going on. For you, coming to Grandma's house meant, we would be having a good dinner together at the dining room table. You are just so cute. I am so grateful that we have more time together now that you moved to Wisconsin. I love watching you grow, and I love all those special hugs. I love telling people that you are my grandson. I am so proud of you. I hope you will always remember, I will always love you.

And to Jesse, Kirsten, Joseph, Benjamin, and Seth...You are so much a part of our family. Jesse, I am so grateful your friend and classmate, our grandson Mark brought you into his family when you were in second grade. Because of this you became our special grandson. How awesome it was to be able to have you join us for so many holidays and special occasions. You have been blessed with great intelligence. You were always willing to help me when I needed something constructed or when I needed your technical expertise. You helped Grandpa and me out in so many ways. I'll never forget the Thanksgiving dinner that you asked me if Kirsten could join us. When you got to our home, you announced that you became engaged the night before. We all fell in love with her right from the start. When we shared something special that we were thankful for that Thanksgiving, you said, "Grandma, I just want you to know that you have been a very strong influence on my life." How precious those words were to me. Praise God! The next year was your wedding and shortly after that the two of you were on your mission to Haiti. Not only did you and Kirsten bring three darling boys into this world, Joseph, Benjamin, and Seth, you also accomplished many amazing things in the course of just a few years. We watched on Facebook how you first started out living with another family. Then we watched you build your own home. High up in the mountains with no electricity, no refrigeration, no plumbing, you and Kirsten had much to learn and you were willing to sacrifice so much. You have continued to make home improvements to make life better for your family and others. Next we saw you using your engineering skills to build cisterns. Then we watched the construction of the church. For a special surprise, playground equipment was brought in for all the children. Next, we saw you building a school that was started in 2016. You also built a guest house, which was needed for all the guests that came to help you out. You built an incinerator and then added a second floor to the school. You and Kirsten have been incredible, amazing missionaries. You have sacrificed much for the work God has brought to you. You have done this all with joy and gladness. I am so grateful for Facebook. I get to keep in touch with you and see your smiling faces as you serve God and the people of Haiti. I thank God for the blessing you are. I am so proud of all of you. God bless you in all that you are doing. May He keep you strong, healthy, and safe. May He give you wisdom to share the story of salvation in Jesus to many. Take care, and know that I will always love you.

Rob, Laura, Erika, Kyle, and Hailee, you have come into our lives, and you are truly a part of our family. I feel so close to you. I am so grateful for our times together and have so many memories that I treasure. I love having you come to stay with us at our home. I love the times we were able to visit you and stay at your home both in Arizona and in Minnesota. Every moment has been so special and so much fun. Rob, I am so proud to see you succeed in your work. I am impressed hearing you speak. You have been blessed with wisdom and eloquence that has been a great asset in your role as a leader. Laura, you are the best thing that ever happened to Rob. I admire you for your many talents. You are an awesome, supporting wife, and your kids could not have a more loving, supportive mother. I am so happy you introduced me to the joy of painting. I am so grateful that your family is growing. Erika brought Jesse into your family and now you have become proud grandparents of your grandson Jorden. What a blessing! Thank you for your loving, caring ways. I am so glad that you are a part of my life. May God guide you and bless you in all you do. Please know that I will always love you.

For the many special people that God has put into my life, whether it was for a short time, a lifetime, or a season. It was for a good reason. All the wonderful women who were a part of the Bible studies I led, all the special Rainbow Kids volunteers and participants, Pastors and educators, and all the people I met and worked with on committees at church and in this community, I have been blessed beyond measure. My memories of you and our time spent together have been a great influence on my life and in who I have become. Whether we are near or whether we are far apart, you have remained very special to me, and close in my heart. I thank God for each and every one of you.

And most of all, with all my heart and soul, I dedicate this to my heavenly Father God, the King of my life, to my Lord and Savior Jesus Christ, you are my Rock and my Redeemer, and to the Holy Spirit – living and reigning in me. Without You, I am nothing. With you, I can rejoice in knowing that I am only a sinner, miraculously saved by your grace. May this be for your glory.

Introduction

The words – "You should write a book" – were spoken to me many times throughout my life. I have always loved writing, and I love sharing stories from my life with family and friends.

My initial intentions for writing this book were to document my life's story for my family. At times, I have been asked questions about the past, and although I was never really interested in genealogy, I was encouraged to seek out some information about my parents and grandparents. I was surprised to find out things I had never been told, things that my family will most likely find interesting. This book is a compilation of stories inspired by God with some topics being encouraged by the Sheboygan Senior Center "Life in Writing" class.

My main reason for writing this book is to tell "My Story". We all have a story to tell. Life is an adventure. I look at my life as a love story. As a child of God, I hope I will be able to convey God's amazing love. Through the challenges, trials, mountain tops, and valleys – no matter where I have been, I know that God was always there with me – leading the way, teaching me, holding me close, lifting me up, and loving me every single moment of my life.

In our lives, there will be hard times and good times. Jesus tried to teach us this. After Jesus rose from the dead, He met with His disciples. He showed them the wounds on His hands and feet. Because of His great love for us, we can know that His life and His suffering was not in vain. Jesus told His story so that the world will know of His Amazing Grace. God has shown me miracles that I know He would want me to share with many. I pray that I can do this – for His Glory.

My Ancestors

Grandpa & Grandma Vercouteren

My grandparents from my mother's side of the family, Karel Vercouteren and Dina Cornelia (Kamerik) Vercouteren were born in the Netherlands. Grandpa Vercouteren was born on April 19, 1875, and Grandma was born on September 22, 1876. They were married on February 17, 1898 in Terneuzen, Netherlands, in the province of Zeeland. My cousin, Karl, did some extensive work on our genealogy and said our lineage was traced back to Charlemagne. So I guess that would mean we have royalty in our genealogy.

My grandparents emigrated to the United States of America from Rotterdam, Holland, traveling on the ship Post Dam. Being on the rough waters of the Atlantic Ocean for so many days was extremely difficult. It didn't take long before everyone got sea-sick. It was a tough struggle trying to survive. They arrived in the State of New York on May 11, 1906. Traveling with my grandparents were three of their children - seven year old Catherine, five year old Magdalena (my mother), one year old Jacobus (Jim), and my Grandmother's mother, my Great Grandma Magdalena Kamerik. My grandma told the story of a traumatic experience at Ellis Island, when a black man led her mother away for some bureaucratic purpose. Grandma was not familiar with bureaucracy, black people, or an unfamiliar language. She feared that her mother was being taken away forever. Thank God, it turned out to be only a brief separation.

Most emigrants came to America for the economic opportunities that were abundant. My grandpa did have a good job with Water Works (the system of canals and dikes), so he may have just been adventurous, or he may have been lured to come to the United

States by others who had emigrated. At the time that he left Holland, his mother had already passed on. I've been told that he didn't feel accepted in his family after his mother had passed away, and his dad re-married.

Grandpa Vercouteren first brought his family to Sheboygan, Wisconsin, because they had friends living here from Terneuzen, Netherlands. There was a Dutch settlement in Sheboygan County. My grandparents lived at 2031 North 11ᵗʰ Street, and grandpa became employed at the Kohler Company.

Around 1913, my grandpa and grandma moved to Arpin, Wisconsin, in Wood County, with their four children – Catherine Magdalena, Magdalena Catherina, Jacobus Pieter, and Govert Jacobus - (Govert was their only child born in America). In Arpin, Grandpa tried his hand at farming for a short time.

Stories had been told that grandpa had been "taken for a ride" with misinformation about the farm. It was terrible land, not at all the quality of land they were told it would be. Grandpa did relate that they tried to grow potatoes and sugar beets. This is what they were familiar with from living in the old country. The ground in Arpin was hard, rocky, and difficult to work; and at harvest time, it was hard to tell the difference between the rocks and the crop to harvest.

In 1914, while the family was living in Arpin, WI, the whole family became American citizens.

By 1920, Grandpa moved his family back to Sheboygan where they lived in a house located in an alley at 716 ½ Erie Avenue. He went back to work at the Kohler Company until 1923. At that time, he started to work at the American Chair Company and was employed there for 25 years.

Later, my grandparents purchased a home at 2319 N. 20ᵗʰ St. in Sheboygan. This is the only home I remember visiting. It was a two bedroom home with a small kitchen, living room and dining room. The basement of their home was set up to be an additional apartment. My Uncle Jim and his son, Jimmy, lived there for a time after my Aunt Helen became ill and passed away. Jimmy, my cousin, was little when this happened so my grandparents stepped in to care for him.

My grandparents stored a lot of stuff in the basement. They were collectors, and some people may have called them "hoarders". There were many jars of preserved foods in the basement that my grandmother had made. I loved to go to Grandma's house. There was always a dish of candy on the dining room table. We all loved her homemade Babbelaars (a creamy butterscotch flavored hard candy). She often served us a small glass of milk and windmill cookies. I loved the small glasses with Scotty dogs, sailboats, and other colorful objects painted on them. At times, all the relatives (around 45 people) gathered for special occasions at this home. The house was over-loaded with people, but we always enjoyed being together.

I still have memories of us younger children going into the spare bedroom. We all sat up on the bed, turned out the lights, and listened to my cousin, Karl Vercouteren, tell ghost stories. They were harmless, silly stories that made us giggle. I still remember one of Karl's stories that had a spooky, scary, something coming up the stairs to get us. With an eerie tone, this mysterious thing was saying, "I float, I float". It turned out to be a bar of Ivory soap. For those of you too young to remember, Ivory soap was made into bars that floated in water. I loved how Karl told us ghost stories when we were just kids. I think God was giving him practice time for his future occupation. Karl's scary ghost stories later became the Bible's Holy Ghost stories. I am proud to tell you that this cousin became

Reverend Karl Vercouteren. We were all so proud that we had an ordained Pastor in our family.

We also played "hide and seek" at our grandparent's home. My favorite place to hide was in a walk-through closet located between the two bedrooms. When I think of this now, I cannot imagine what all got stomped down on in that closet. I'm afraid Grandma was very busy picking up after us all when we left. It's amazing that she always welcomed us to come back.

My grandma often used the phrase "Low and Behold" when she was expressing herself. One time she was very excited about something and instead of saying "Low and Behold", she said, "Holy and Blow". This brought laughter to all of us, and is still a favorite memory of her. Grandma was very special to all of us. With her Dutch accent, Grandma pronounced my name – U-T or Ewe-T. She was so sweet.

My grandpa liked to tease. He walked with a cane. When I was little, he loved to take his cane and hook my arm while I was walking past the chair where he sat. I guess I liked this attention, so I continued to walk past Grandpa's chair often. Grandpa had a special chair in their living room that had wooden arms that lifted up with storage compartments inside. Newspapers and other reading material were usually in front of him. A Statue of Liberty lamp was there to light up his area. Sometimes Grandpa would talk in Dutch. When we were eating dinner, he would ask us to pass something speaking Dutch, and we would have to try to guess what he wanted. I have fond memories of my grandparents. They were always kind to all of us and fun to be with. I truly do not have any negative memories of my Grandpa and Grandma Vercouteren.

My grandparents and their children were members of Hope Reformed Church while living in Sheboygan. The church was located on 10th Street and Ontario Avenue and later moved to the present location of 6th Street and Ontario Avenue.

Grandpa Vercouteren passed away when he was 80 years old, on March 24, 1956. I was 14 years old at that time, and this was the first funeral service I remember attending. Grandma Vercouteren passed away when she was 90 years old, on March 26, 1967. When grandma passed away, I was 25 years old, married, and had two sons. Grandpa and Grandma Vercouteren were the only grandparents that I got to know.

One of the treasured memories of my grandpa was a prayer that he wrote and passed on to all of us. Because my prayers are never the same as I allow the Spirit to speak through me, I don't use this prayer, but I often do find myself saying some of these words. It's quite amazing that recently (January 2016), I heard some of my nieces praying Grandpa's prayer. After all these years, that's quite a tribute to him.

This was Grandpa Karel Vercouteren's prayer:

Lord our God, we bring our humble thanks for the many blessings you have bestowed upon us. You have satisfied our bodily needs; you have given us more than we needed. Lord, we acknowledge your goodness and loving kindness with grateful hearts. And now, we pray that you will keep us the rest of this day. Cause your face to shine upon us and guide us by your Holy Spirit that we may walk in the fear of your Holy name. We pray this, Lord, not because we are worthy of it, but only through the merits of your Son, Jesus Christ our Savior. Amen

My Ancestors

Grandpa and Grandma Otte

My grandparents from my Dad's side of the family, Gerhardt Otte and Flora (Buteyn) Otte were born in 's-Heer Arendskerke, Zeeland, Netherlands. Grandpa Otte was born on February 13, 1871, and Grandma was born on April 15, 1866.

My Grandma Flora Buteyn was the oldest of 13 children. Her parents were Cornelius Buteyn and Maria (Kerkhoven) Buteyn. Flora had two sons, Cornelius Buteyn born April 24, 1887 and John, sometimes known as Jan Buteyn born September 18, 1889. Cornelius and John were raised by their grandparents and were accepted as brothers by their aunts and uncles. My grandma's family lived in a small brick house owned by a wealthy man. The children slept in a large attic room in small compartments in the wall, three children in a compartment. My great-grandfather worked as a hired man, known as a servant of farmers. He worked for a rich farmer for 24 years. For reasons unknown, he was told to leave the farm. Plans were made to come to America.

Before coming to America, my grandparents, Gerhardt Otte and Flora Buteyn were married in Nieuwdorp, Zeeland.

They emigrated to the United States of America boarding the ship "Rotterdam" on April 28, 1898. The trip took eight days to get across the Atlantic Ocean to New York. The trip was rough, and most everyone got sea-sick. It was a battle trying to survive. From New York they took a two day train ride and arrived in Sheboygan, Wisconsin on May 10, 1898. There were 23 members of the Buteyn family on this trip including my grandparents - Gerhardt and Flora

Otte, my dad, John Otte, born 11-29-1894, two younger brothers, Peter Otte, born 11-18-1895, and Cornelius Otte born 8-27-1897, and my Dad's two older half-brothers, Cornelius Buteyn and John Buteyn. My dad was three years old when they came to the United States, his brother Peter was two, Cornelius was eight months old, and his half-brothers Cornelius and John Buteyn were eleven and nine.

Grandpa Gerhardt and Grandma Flora Otte had five children. Three were born in the Netherlands, my dad John, Peter, and Cornelius Otte. Cornelius Otte lived less than a year, from August 27, 1897 to June 6, 1898. He died less than two months after arriving in the United States. The two children born in America were Christian, who lived to be only four months old - from May 21, 1899 to September 24, 1899, and Marie (Mary), born March 18, 1903.

Grandma Flora Otte became ill and passed away on June 18, 1911 at the age of 45. My dad was only 17 years old at the time. His brother, Peter, was 16 and his sister, Mary, was only eight. The loss of my Grandmother was hard on their family.

A year later in 1912, Grandpa Gerhardt Otte married Adriana Clarrisse, who had been the family's housekeeper. At that time, my dad decided to leave home. Grandpa Gerhardt & Adrianna (Jennie) had one son, William, and four daughters, Cornelia, Jeanette, Wilma, and Elsie. These were my Dad's step-sisters and step-brother.

Grandpa Gerhardt Otte was a janitor for the Water Works Company in Sheboygan.

Grandpa Gerhardt Otte passed away on May 25, 1946. He was 75 years old at that time. My step-grandma, Adrianna, was born June 18, 1893 and passed on December 19, 1955 at the age of 62. I never was acquainted with any of my dad's parents nor his step-mother. I thought they had all passed away before I was born. I found out that my dad chose to leave home and cut the ties with his dad after his mother passed away and his dad chose to marry Adrianna, who was only a year older than my dad.

My family probably knew and spent the most time with my dad's sister, Aunt Mary. I remember her from when she lived in Illinois and came to visit us fairly often. From what I can remember, she had a tough life.

In my research, I found many documents showing several different names and spellings for my grandpa – Gerard Otte, Gerard Otto, Geerard Otte, Gehard Otte, Geert Otte, Gerhardt Otte, and Harry Otte. Grandma's names – Fora Otte, Fora Otto, Forra Otte, Flora Otte, Florra Otte. My dad was listed different places as Johannes, Jan, Johannes Abbe Otto, and John Otte. I've been told that this was not unusual for emigrants due to the translation of the different languages.

To be honest, I never had an interest in Genealogy as many people do. I have relatives that traced back the Otte ancestry and have put together records. I guess what I enjoyed the most about our family history is that I saw that our faith in God has been there through the ages. It sparked my interest to see how my ancestors were involved in prison ministries and the teaching and instructing of God's Word on down through the centuries. It makes my heart glad to see this has continued to the present time. For this knowledge, I thank God for my heritage and for all the servants of the Lord who have come before me. As my story unfolds, you will see that my dad was a very strong Christian leader and a great example to follow.

My Ancestors
Dad & Mom

My parents, John Otte and Magdalena Catherina Vercouteren were both born in the Netherlands. My Dad was born November 29, 1894, and my Mother was born November 10, 1900. My Dad came to the United States with his parents Gerhardt and Flora Otte and three siblings in 1898, when he was three years old. My mother came to the United States with her parents Karel and Dina Vercouteren and two siblings in 1906, when she was five years old. Both my parents had other siblings who were born in America.

My dad served in the WW1-U.S. Army infantry in France and Germany from 1917–1919. He did not talk much about this experience, but he did tell us that he was on the front lines. They were fed – what he called – slumgullion stew. (A dictionary description of this is – "A cheap or insubstantial stew). At times my dad woke up to find snow on his bunk. He said very little, but we got the message – his service in the Army was an extremely tough experience. One that he preferred to put out of his memory.

On June 3, 1920, my parents were married. Over the next 21 years, they had ten children – Florence Cornelia, 11/25/1921; Carl, 6/24/1923; Ruth Marie, 7/27/1925; Robert John, 1/13/1928; Lois Mae, 2/9/1930; Gerald James, 3/11/1932; Donald Roy, 2/20/1934; Rachel Ann, 2/14/1936; Diane Faye, 12/27/1938; Judith Claire, 7/9/1941.

My dad was a machinist at Globe Manufacturing and Kohler Company. Later he did janitorial work at Kohler. After retiring in 1960, he worked part-time at H.C. Prange Company as a janitor.

My mother began working at Hills Department Store after I was born in the early 40's. She was the head of the Foundations Department (intimate apparel). She was on her own in this department so she was responsible for buying, selling, inventory, fitting – if needed, and all record keeping. This was quite an accomplishment as she only attended school through 8th grade. Her math and reading skills were definitely commendable considering that she never attended high school.

My dad's favorite sport was baseball. We did not have a TV in our home until around 1957, and at that time, the picture was in black and white only. When the baseball game was on, we were not allowed to use the vacuum cleaner, as this would block the TV picture from coming in, and that would upset my dad. He did not want to miss one minute of the Milwaukee Braves baseball games.

My dad and mother never owned or learned how to drive a car, so we either had to walk, or take the bus wherever we went. When I was older, my brothers had a car, and they often would transport us to church on Sundays. We attended First Christian Reformed Church (currently called Christ Community Church). We always attended two Sunday services – morning and evening.

My parents never owned their own home. Once they were married, they always rented homes in Sheboygan. When I was born, we lived above Stephani's Grocery Store at 1427A N. 8th Street. Then we moved to a three bedroom home with only one bathroom at 1414 North 7th Street. At that time, we still had all 12 of us living at home. Some of my siblings had to sleep in the dining room area. My siblings and I walked a little over a half mile to go to Sheboygan Christian School located on the corner of 3rd Street and Lincoln Avenue. Every day we walked, in all kinds of weather. Later the new Sheboygan Christian School was built next to our church parsonage on 5th Street and Geele Avenue. That made our walk just a little bit farther.

In 1949, the house we were living in was sold, so we had to move again. My parents and six of my siblings were split up living in the homes of four of my married siblings. My parents and I lived with my oldest sister, Florence, her husband, Don and their two children, Sandy and Donna. My two nieces and I slept crosswise in a full sized bed. None of us liked sleeping in the middle, so we had to take turns. After many months of searching, my family was blessed with finding a six bedroom, living room, dining room, kitchen, two-story house at 1601A South 12th Street. My parents rented this house until all the rest of us were married, and my dad had passed away. Somehow we survived with having only one bathroom in all the places we lived. Our last home was torn down along with two other homes on that block in order to widen a curve on South 12th Street. My older siblings remember living in homes where there was no bathtub nor shower. This was common at that time.

We were very fortunate that our South 12th Street house was on a corner where the bus stopped. When the weather was bad, we would watch for the bus from our kitchen window. When we saw the bus a block away from our house, we would run the length of our house through the kitchen, dining room, living room and then out the front door and down the front steps. We could be standing on the corner just in time to catch the bus. My dad took the bus to the Kohler Company, my mother took the bus downtown to work at Hill's Department Store, and my sister, Diane, and I took the bus to Sheboygan Christian School. We had to transfer to another bus in order to get from the Southside to the Northside to our church and school. On Saturdays, we took the bus to attend Catechism classes at our church.

My parents provided each one of us kids with a Christian education in our home, school, and church. We attended First Christian Reformed Church in Sheboygan until I was 15. Because our church congregation grew to be so large, it was necessary to start a second Christian Reformed Church. My parents were part of the 25 families that founded Calvin Christian Reformed Church. The old Zion Evangelical Reformed Church building on 6th Street and Erie Avenue was purchased. Later the new Calvin Christian Reformed Church was built on Saemann Avenue.

My dad was active in the church and served on the church governing board as an Elder. He also was active in Prison Ministry and preached to the Sheboygan County Jail inmates on Sunday afternoons. He loved serving the Lord and had a desire to touch the lives of those who were troubled. There really wasn't a quiet place in our home for him to study. I remember him practicing the messages that he would be preaching to the jail inmates. He would walk from our dining room into the kitchen – back and forth around the tables, speaking his message out loud. He read and studied his Bible every day, and he read from the Bible to all of us at dinnertime. He also led us in prayer before and after our meals. He lived out his faith and was a great example to us. Each week, sometime before we went to Catechism classes at church, he would check to see that we had all our memory work done by quizzing us to make sure we were ready with the right answers. I was so grateful for my good memorization skills. My dad worked extremely hard to provide for both the physical and spiritual needs of his family, and then he also went the extra mile by providing for the needs of others in our community. He always had a huge heart for the poor and less fortunate, and loved bringing the good news of salvation to so many.

Favorite fun-time memories of my dad were when the two of us would take the bus to Legion Park on Saturday nights to attend the Sheboygan Indian's baseball games. I was chosen to play on the Sheboygan Christian School's 7th and 8th grade softball team when I was only in 6th grade. My dad taught me the game of baseball and helped me with my pitching skills. If I wasn't pitching, I would be playing at third base. Although we never went on a vacation trip, we did go to Milwaukee to see Milwaukee Braves games with my older siblings. At that time, I could name all the players and their positions. Of course, Hank Aaron became a favorite of mine. Baseball was the sport my Dad and I enjoyed together.

My mother was kind and loving. Her calm, gentle spirit captured the hearts of us all. She was a hard worker. Working at a department store gave her opportunities to watch for good bargains. She always made sure I had nice clothes to wear. She took advantage of putting things on layaway and paid whatever she could from her paycheck until the item was paid for in full, and then she could bring it home. She did make good purchases, and I still remember some of the pretty clothes she bought for me. My parents did not own a credit card. My mother was an excellent cook and baker. I remember her putting the pan of bread dough in front of the big heating vents in our house to help the dough raise faster. Heating vents were often used to dry our hair and dry wet clothing and laundry as well. Cakes, cookies, and all other foods were made from scratch. There were no packaged, boxed foods for her to use.

My mother followed the tradition that her mother had set and always had a dish of candy on the dining room table. Working at Hill's Department Store gave her access to their awesome candy selections. Glass separated bins held many choices of candy that could be purchased by their weight. When I shopped for candy, I sometimes just asked the clerk for a nickel or dimes worth of the candy I wanted. Favorite candies at our house were chocolate covered raisins or nuts, chocolate malted milk ball candies, chocolate stars, tan colored candy raisins, orange circus peanut candy, gumdrops, candy corn, and flat chocolate circles with tiny, round, white sprinkles on the top called Non-Pareils.

Hill's Department Store's hair salon was located on the mezzanine. It was fun being able to watch the people shopping down on the first floor while you were getting your hair cut. I remember my mother setting up an appointment for me to have my hair permed there. Getting a permanent took many hours. In those days, hair was put in curlers that would be hooked up to a heated machine with a hood that was set directly above your head. The curlers would get extremely hot. One time the woman who did my permanent did something wrong, and my scalp got burnt by the hot curlers. I cried. The beauticians tried to console me by giving me a bag of chocolate candies from their store. I guess that good candy did help to stop my tears. I don't remember ever getting another permanent there after that experience. My family learned to use home permanents. Toni or Lilt brand perms became our favorites. For many years, my sisters and I gave each other home permanents. To this day, I still have some boxes of permanent curlers in my house. I really don't know why. I would guess that it's probably safe to throw them away now.

Even though we had a large family, my mother was always ready and willing to set another place at the dinner table for an unexpected guest. She taught us to share the little that we had. She was very talented in hand crafts and often made gifts for others. She loved to crochet, knit, tat, make jewelry, and arrange centerpieces. To this day, I am enjoying some of the treasurers that she made for me. My mother loved her children and grandchildren, and they loved her. My nieces and nephews love to recall stories of their very special grandmother.

At our house, we all had specific chores to do. On Spring break from school, we all worked together and cleaned the entire house. When my mother was working full-time, my sisters Rachel, Diane and I took care of the weekly cleaning and cooking. Rachel generally did the cooking. Diane and I argued over who was going to wash and who was going to dry the dishes. I would have to say my mother taught us well, as we all did become good housewives and mothers.

Getting through the years of the Depression had to be very difficult for my parents, but I feel they did an excellent job in raising their ten children. We learned to enjoy and appreciate the simple things in life. Picnics in the park, going to the beach in Lake Michigan, enjoying the beauty of nature, singing hymns around the piano, playing games, sitting together eating dinner, sharing our faith, going to church together, - these were some of the treasured memories that my parents gave to me. Some people may have considered us to be poor. I'd say they were wrong. We were rich, because we had all the important things that really mattered. Best of all, we knew we were loved. God was good, and we were blessed.

My dad passed away on February 9, 1970, at the age of 75. Parkinson's disease had him bedridden and in a nursing home for his last year of life. I was 28 years old when he passed. My mother passed away on July 8, 1983, at the age of 82. I was one day away from being 42 at the time of her death. I have this assurance, we will meet again in eternal glory. Until then, I will cherish the awesome memories and the blessings of being raised in a Christian home by loving parents. Thanks be to God.

Siblings

Not many people can say they are the youngest of ten children. I am. We were all born in Sheboygan. These are some of the special memories I have of my five older sisters and four older brothers.

FLORENCE, the oldest of my siblings was born on November 25, 1921. She married Don Jensema in 1943 when I was just two years old. Their daughter Sandy, was born a year later. That made me an Aunt at the age of three. Donna was born the following year. We were so close in age that we became good playmates. I don't remember Florence living at home with all of us as I was too little. I do remember Florence and Don taking my parents and me in to live with them when we had to move from the house we were renting after it was sold. I was only seven at the time. Later, Florence and Don had two more children, Larry and Patty.

Florence was a hard worker. Being the oldest, I think she took on the role of being the "responsible" one. At times, we probably thought she was being the "bossy" one. She was an excellent cook and baker. She made beautiful wedding and Bible cakes for many of our celebrations. She also made delicious Christmas cookies. She worked in the check-outs at the H. C. Prange Company for many years. Florence was 20 years older than I was. When I was 20, I had our first son, Jeff. Twenty years after that, I had our youngest son, Scott. So the two sisters and the two brothers, (my sons), were all twenty years apart. The four of us often got together for a photo when our families were all together. The last one taken was in 2011 when Florence was 90, I was 70, Jeff 50, and Scott 30. Florence passed away on June 3, 2014 when she was 92 years old. As of 2016, she has lived to be the oldest of my deceased siblings and parents.

My brother, **CARL,** was born on June 24, 1923. I do not remember living at home with him as he left home shortly after high school graduation to serve in the U.S. Army in World War II. Not long after he returned from active duty, he married Ethel Braatz. Carl and Ethel had four children, Allen, Jane, Julie, and Lynn. I babysat for their older children and later, their daughters Jane and Julie babysat for my children.

Carl worked for close to 20 years at Armour Leather Company (Armira). He was very active with the Union at Armour Leather and served in many leadership roles including that of Union President. He also became active in City Government and served as a County Board Supervisor for 17 years. In 1967, he was elected to represent Sheboygan in Madison as our Assemblyman and served until 1980. He was elected to be Sheboygan's State Senator in Madison in 1980, and served in that role for another four years. For 36 years he served Sheboygan County residents. These years were very memorable for me as my husband, Ernie, was Carl's Campaign Chairman, and I was his Campaign Secretary. We spent a lot of time together and became very close. My brother Carl, was 18 years older than me, but my husband and I became best of friends with Carl during his years of service in politics. Our families have great memories of weekend trips, dinners out, and going to many dances, and special events together. We worked diligently on Carl's election campaigns and saw great success. My brother's demonstration of great leadership was a huge influence on me and my future.

Carl was also known for his love of music and for his love of playing the Tuba. Campaign ads often included Carl playing his Tuba to the tune of "Born Free", and even "Dueling Banjoes". He was a member of the Sheboygan Civic Orchestra, Sheboygan Municipal Band, and the Sheboygan Wuerl Band now called the Sheboygan Pops Band.

Carl's faith was very important to him. He often expressed to me how blessed he felt he was. These words were expressed to me once again in our final conversation on January 1, 2011. By the end of that day, he slipped into a coma and later passed on January 13, 2011. Carl's Christian heritage meant so much to him. For many years he taught Sunday School at his church. He was a man of integrity, and I feel blessed and so proud to have had him as my brother. He was a good example, and I believe his life encouraged me to step up my own life of service to God and to others.

My sister, **RUTH,** was born next on July 27, 1925. After I was born, my mother went to work and my sister Ruth, took care of me. Ruth married Lester Klujeske in 1943 and moved back home when Les went to serve in the U.S. Navy. Ruth had their first child, Tom, in 1944. He was only a little over three years younger than I was so we grew up together. Later Ruth had two more daughters – Susan and Lori. Lori was just a few months older than our oldest son, Jeff. Looking at pictures from the past, I can see that Ruth always dressed me well, curled my hair in pipe-curls, and then she always tied a pretty ribbon in my hair.

Ruth was always known as the family story-teller. Many times she told me of the time she took me to see the movie, "Lassie Come Home" when I was little. She said she had to take me out of the theatre because I was feeling so sad and crying so loudly. I guess it was evident from little on that I had a sympathetic heart.

Ruth also told me this story. She had dressed me up and curled my hair to take me somewhere special. I decided to go outside while she got herself ready. Our next-door neighbor girl, Susan, who was my age, was sitting on our front lawn. A while later, Ruth heard

Susan crying. She went to check on what was happening and found out that I was gone. Susan told my sister that I had kicked her in the head, and then I ran away. Susan pointed in the direction that I had gone. Ruth headed off to try to find me, but was not successful. After some time, she called our mother, who was working at Hill's Department Store. My mother came home, and the police were contacted. For over two hours the search was on. Then, Ruth told me that all of a sudden, I came walking into the living room. My dress was all wrinkled and my hair was a mess. She asked me where I had been, and I wouldn't tell her. After a while, she asked me where the pretty ribbon was that she had put in my hair. I walked into my bedroom and opened the closet door. There on a basket of wrinkled clothes laid my hair bow.

They figured out that after I kicked Susan and she started crying, I got scared. So I ran to the corner and turned right until I got to the alley. I walked to the middle of the block and then I turned down another alley that was adjacent to our house. I went in the back kitchen door, walked through the bathroom and into our bedroom and laid down in the basket of clothes that was in the closet. This was my hiding place. While I was taking a nice nap for over two hours probably having sweet dreams, the police and my family were having nightmares wondering where I had gone.

I'm really not sure why I kicked Susan. Most generally, Susan was being mean to me. I have many horror stories that I remember about her. But this time, I guess I was being the bad girl.

Ruth had a love for little children. Along with raising three of her own children, and taking care of my sister and me, she often took in foster children as babies. She certainly was always kind and good to me, and I felt her love. I knew I was extra special to Ruth when she invited my husband and me to stay at their home in Arizona and even allowed us to use their master bedroom. My siblings all told me that when they visited Ruth and Les, they needed to stay in motels or at other people's homes. Ruth was a good cook and loved hand-craft projects. I still enjoy some of the treasures she made for me. I miss the long conversations we would have on the phone after she moved to Arizona, as they were always special. Ruth passed away on October 28, 2008.

My sister, **LOIS,** was born on February 9, 1930, and married Carl Te Winkel in 1948. I did a lot of babysitting for their two children, Nancy and David. Their daughter, Amy was born to them when they were older. Amy was just a few months older than our first son, Jeff, so then Lois and I often did childcare for each other.

Lois had a job at the Hill's Department Store, where my mother worked, as an Elevator Operator. In the 40's, someone needed to manually operate elevators. She had to use levers to properly land the elevator on the correct floor. There were two doors that had to be opened manually as well. The elevator floor had to be lined up perfectly with the floor outside the door. Sometimes this took a little maneuvering to get it right.

Lois was quite ill when Nancy and David were small. I remember taking the kids to Cole Park and letting them play so Lois could rest. Lois would give me a dime, so after our fun at the park, we headed to Fessler's Drug Store to buy two coolers. The cost of a cooler (popsicle), was just a nickel. There were two sticks of popsicles in each package. The popsicle could be broken in two, so the three of us had plenty to share. Nancy and I sometimes argued who would get to wash the dishes. She usually won as she loved to play in the water. David loved to dump his chicken noodle soup over the top of his head when he was still a baby. He kept me hopping with all his energy.

I loved it when I had the chance to stay overnight at Lois' house when I was going to Sheboygan Christian School, especially when I was in 6th, 7th, and 8th grade. Lois lived close enough to the school so I could walk along with my friends and not have to travel all the way home to the Southside alone on the bus. Lois was an excellent cook, baker, seamstress, and she enjoyed crafts. She baked wedding cakes and special birthday and anniversary cakes for many years. After Ernie and I were married, Lois, my mother, and I baked Christmas cookies together. She loved to sing in her church choir, was fun and loving and always seemed to have a sweet smile on her face. A special remembrance was when she planned a party at their home for my classmates and me when I was in my teens. I will always remember the surprise visit my now husband, Ernie, made to Lois and Carl's apartment the day after I first met him. This entire story is told in how I met my husband under "Celebrating our 40th Anniversary". Our Christmas tree holds many of the beautiful, hand-made ornaments that Lois made for me. My memories of my sister Lois, will always be special. She was a sweetheart. Lois passed away on her 81st birthday, February 9, 2011.

ROBERT, Bob was born on January 13, 1928. Bob was the first of my older siblings that I remembered living with at home. I loved it when he bought a record player as our whole family loved music. We didn't have a T.V. at that time, only a radio, so playing music on the record player was exciting.

Bob served in the U.S. Naval Reserves after he graduated from High School.

Bob had a great sense of humor, a gentle spirit, and a winning smile. He was quite handsome and was loved by many. He had a great love for children and enjoyed spending time with all the nieces and nephews. For a time, Bob was a bus driver in Sheboygan. I was always excited when I had him for my bus driver, and I had the opportunity to sit right up in the front seats of the bus and talk with him.

He married Bernadine Federer and had three children – David, Sharon, and Ricky. I did babysit for their children when they were little until they moved to Menominee Falls, Wisconsin. Bob loved mission work and was active serving in his church.

Bob was my only sibling to get a divorce from his wife. After the divorce, he moved to Texas and Florida, and then to Arizona. When he was in Arizona, he met Mary. Shortly after Bob and Mary's wedding, Bob was in a car accident.

Sadly, Bob was killed in that tragic accident which involved a drunk driver. On May 7, 1981, at the age of 53, Bob was the first of my siblings to pass on. My mother already had her plane ticket purchased to Arizona that was scheduled for the day after Bob's accident. It was so good that she was able to be with her son for several days before he passed on in the hospital. My sisters, Rachel and Diane, flew to Arizona for a couple days and then returned home. My three brothers, Carl, Gerald, and Donnie, and my husband, Ernie and I flew to Arizona later for the funeral. Our flight from the Milwaukee Airport went out on Mother's Day, 1981. I remember seeing Wisconsin Senator Bill Proxmire who was traveling that day. As we passed in the airport, he wished me a Happy Mother's Day. I thought that was pretty cool. Bob's passing was a difficult loss for all of us. His friendly, fun-loving character, his love of serving the Lord, and his smiling face will be remembered.

My brother, **GERALD,** was born on March 11, 1932. After High School, Gerald, served in the U.S. Army. He was already a musician, so he was able to continue playing the Trombone in the Army Band. He soon found out that marching for hours in very long parades in the heat of the South was not an easy task. After his service, he enrolled in college and received his Bachelor's degree in music from U.W. Milwaukee. Later he went on to get his Master's Degree at VanderCook College of Music in Chicago, Illinois. He married Audrey Kranendonk in 1957. They had five children - Jerry, Tori, Sarah, Sally, and Brian. The foreign exchange student they hosted from Russia, Kostya, became a special member of their family.

Gerald was my first sibling to attend college. He was fortunate to receive financial assistance from the government because of his service in the Army. This was extremely helpful because my parents were not able to provide financial support. Life was interesting at our house when Gerald brought all the instruments home to practice on the weekends. We listened to a lot of squeaks and squawks until he mastered each instrument.

Music was always Gerald's passion, and the Trombone was his instrument of first choice. Besides teaching music in the Sheboygan Elementary Schools, Gerald was active in roles of leadership and teaching at his church. He had very good skills in home repairs and offered his expertise to many of us – (family, friends, and even strangers). Gerald and Audrey always had a love for gardening and graciously shared their bounty with others. Gerald also loved working outdoors helping others with landscaping. He removed five trees from our property. Cooking and baking are also enjoyed by Gerald. Once when he was probably in his teens, he made some donuts. Something was not quite right, and the donuts turned out rubbery. We had fun bouncing the donuts, and kidded him about making us "tires" to eat. Gerald was always a hard worker, blessed with many talents.

Our family was especially proud to see Gerald graduate from college. This was a great accomplishment that took a lot of work and determination.

My brother **DONALD,** Donnie, was born on February 20, 1934. He was not able to serve in the military due to health reasons. After high school, he went to work and also went to college. He attended U.W. Milwaukee, Lakeland College - Sheboygan, and later received his Master's Degree at VanderCook College of Music in Chicago, Illinois. His main instrument was the Baritone, but his degree brought him to the knowledge of playing all band and orchestra instruments. At times he worked full time at Armour Leather Company and also attended classes at Lakeland College. This took a lot of hard work and determination on his part. Our family was very proud of his efforts and accomplishments. He continued his education and received his Master's Degree in Music. He taught in the Sheboygan Falls Schools for many years until his retirement.

When I was quite young, I remember Donnie would offer me 25 cents to walk over to the drug store to buy him items like razor blades, shaving cream, etc. I loved the chance to earn money, so I gratefully took him up on the offer. Glander Drug Store was just a short block away from our house, so this was an easy way for me to make money..

Donnie married Mary Ann Pietenpol in 1957. They had four children - Pam, Penny, Danny, and Lisa. Viera, their foreign exchange student from Chile, became a special part of their family.

Donnie's passion for music carried over into his service in his church where he directed the choir and played in the Praise Band. He also directed the Pine Haven Men's Choir for over 20 years. Donnie and Mary Ann became snow-birds and loved to spend winters in Florida at their trailer home. Their daughter Penny, lived in Florida so their families were able to enjoy special time together during the winter months for many years.

Keeping active and enjoying times with family and friends were important to Donnie. When Donnie was in Sheboygan, he generally organized the monthly get-together for our siblings and spouses. This was usually lunch or breakfast at a restaurant. He enjoyed bringing in a special treat for all of us which generally was his homemade candies that came in personalized computer-made paper boxes. Many times he brought floral plants for all of us. Donnie had a heart for giving, and his gentle nature and kindness have been an attraction and a blessing to many. Donnie passed away on August 15, 2017, at the age of 83.

My sister, **RACHEL,** was a Valentine's Day baby as she was born on February 14, 1936. There are many special memories of times together with my sister, Rachel. For years while we were growing up, we had to share a bed. Even when we moved to a bigger house, and we had our own bedrooms, I sometimes snuck into bed with her. If I was having a bad dream and was feeling scared, she was always kind enough to provide me with a sense of protection.

After she married Verne Rademaker in 1954, she moved to Oostburg. They had three daughters – Debbie, Vicky, and Jill.

Rachel was our family's most accomplished piano player. She played a lot for family gatherings, at her church, and for other special events. Rachel was the pianist for the Pine Haven Choir during the time that my brother, Donnie, was the director. She also played the flute in the Central High School Band and in our church band.

A couple times my husband, Ernie, and I were invited to stay with Rachel and Verne at their condo in Orlando, Florida. We always had great times together. We especially enjoyed the good food and our evening Canasta games. Verne and Ernie usually were the winners, but one night Rachel and I told the guys we were going to continue to play until we won. It got pretty late that night, but we finally did win.

Rachel seemed to always be the one to be there for me as I was growing up and that role continued even after I was married. She traveled to Stevens Point with me when I was invited to speak at a United Church of Christ Convention. I was asked to share my knowledge on grief education from my work as Executive Director of Rainbow Kids, Inc. Rachel and I had made arrangements to stay overnight at a motel. After attending an event the evening before, we found ourselves stranded. My car would not start, and it was too late to get anyone to look at the car that night. We were not far from the motel so we were able to walk back. It was a bit difficult sleeping that night not knowing whether someone could fix the car. We were a long way from home. I consoled myself knowing that there were many Pastors from Sheboygan at the convention. First thing in the morning, I contacted a AAA service station. The serviceman told me they would pick up the car and work on fixing the problem. After my presentation that afternoon, I connected with the mechanic and found out the car was repaired. I found a Pastor from one of the Sheboygan U.C.C. churches who could drive us to the service garage. I was grateful to God that our trip home went well.

In 2009, Rachel and I made a trip to Froedert Hospital in Milwaukee, WI, to visit my husband after he had his second Bone Marrow Transplant. On the way, a woman in a pick-up truck to the left of us hit a patch of ice, and her truck went sailing across the road right in front of Rachel's car, circled all the way around to the back of us – hitting the passenger's side back fender, and then traveled around behind us before her truck came to a stop in the median. No one was hurt, thank the Lord, but a call to the police needed to be made. We were close to Port Washington at that time. After the police report was completed, we continued on to the hospital without any more problems.

Another time Rachel's car was side-swiped by a hit and run driver in front of our house on 13th Street and Main Avenue. Rachel had come to help us move into our new home. For some reason, she and I seemed to have a lot of crazy experiences involving our cars. We began to feel jinxed.

The amazing thing was, that both of us were always able to remain calm. I believe this was key to our support for each other. We trusted that everything would work out all right, and felt blessed that we were always safe. We were good at supporting each other through difficult circumstances. Yes, Rachel was the sister/friend who always tried to be there for me when I needed someone to lean on. Although, to date, her health has made life more difficult for her since she had a stroke, we still always enjoy our times together. Our sister-love has been and always will be very special.

My sister, **DIANE,** was born on December 27, 1938. She is just 2 ½ years older than me. She married Carl Joosse in 1957. They had four children – Randy, Steve, Wendy, and their wonderful, special, chosen daughter, Jody. Diane worked with foster care for many years taking children into their home.

Being the closest to me in age, we spent a lot of time together growing up. When we moved to the south side, we spent a lot of travel time on the bus going across town to the north side to Sheboygan Christian School.

We both loved to dance. On Friday nights, the Sheboygan YMCA had a dance for teens. The Jitterbug was popular when we were growing up in the 50's, so Diane and her friend taught my friend and me how to Jitterbug.

Diane was always a speedy worker. She seems to have endless pep and energy and loves to be busy. She has gifts of hospitality and service, and is the only one in the family who can play the piano by ear. She used this special gift often at her church, at family gatherings, at nursing homes, and at many other functions. When I needed a piano player for a retreat that I led, Diane was there with her keyboard for our time of worship and singing. She sang in the choir at Central High and also at church.

Diane's love and passion is to share God's Word with others, and this led her to working with women's groups through the jail ministry for many years. She also taught both adults and kids at her church and volunteered for many charity organizations. She is an in-charge person and enjoys taking over organizing many of our family affairs. She is the only sibling that has all four of her children and their families living nearby. I always felt that was a real blessing for her.

Did I always get along with all of my siblings? **No.** Did we sometimes have disagreements? **Yes.** Were there ever times that we were upset with one another? **Yes, there were.**

The bottom line is, that no matter what we had to deal with, we never stopped caring about one another. At times we needed to forgive one another, and just go on. Sometimes hurts happen in life, and mistakes are made. Sometimes siblings are not always as kind and thoughtful as they should be. There are times in life when we have to make a choice – do we want to remain bitter, or do we want to work to make things better?

My siblings and I were truly blessed to have been raised by Christian parents. We were taught Christian values at home, at school, and at church that we never forgot.

I chose to share some of my favorite memories of my siblings, as I believe in forgiving and forgetting the wrongs of the past. I am grateful that Jesus has forgiven the wrongs of my past. His example of love has taught me the joy of peace and contentment. Coming from a large family of five sisters and four brothers can be a real blessing. I thank God for blessing me with a loving family that provided so many special memories.

Childhood Memories

Growing up in a family with ten siblings was never boring. There was always a lot of activity and conversation in our home.

I have special memories of times spent playing and having fun together. I grew up at a time when we felt safe and secure in our environment. We were allowed to play outdoors until after the street lights came on. Our home was on an alley, so this is where many games with other children in the neighborhood were played. Some of our favorites were: Kick The Can, Tag – You're It, Red Light - Green Light, Captain May I, Red Rover, Jump Rope, Jacks, and Marbles. Favorite indoor games were Checkers, Snap, Old Maid, and Dominoes. Sometimes we would just spin around until we were so dizzy, we would fall down laughing. We selected the person we wanted to either be our partner or to be the person who would be eliminated by pointing to each person saying the words, "Eeny, Meany, Miney, Mo".

We spent a lot of time at the North Side Beach by Lake Michigan. We would listen to the radio to find out what the air temperature and water temperature was for that day. The radio announcer also informed us if there was a "water undertow" that we needed to be aware of. There was always a lifeguard on duty sitting on a very high chair overlooking the water. Their job was to watch carefully that everyone was safe. A rowboat was at the edge of the water to be used to rescue anyone who was out in the water needing help. The beach house had stalls where we could change into our bathing suits. We were given a wire basket in which our clothing was stored safely for us until we were ready to leave, and it came with a number on a pin that we attached to our swimsuit that identified which basket was ours. There was no charge for this service. Sometimes my brothers, Gerald and Donnie, gave my sister, Diane and me a ride to the lake on their bikes. We sat on the crossbar side-saddle and held on to the bike handlebars. This was not legal nor safe even back then, but this was what we did. My brothers usually took the alley route to the lake so they didn't get caught.

We loved to pack a sandwich, Koolaid to drink, chips, and cookies, and then go to Vollrath Bowl Park. We visited the animals at the zoo and played on the outdoor equipment. Swings, slides, teeter-totters, merry-go-rounds, monkey bars, sliding poles, and sandboxes were all there for us to enjoy. Sadie the lion's roar could be heard for miles around. The bears had a pretty big area to live in. The open pond area was a pretty place to explore the fish, ducks, and birds. The monkeys were always entertaining. We loved it when the peacock spread its feathers, and we could enjoy seeing all the beautiful colors.

After many of my childhood years of enjoyment, the zoo had to be shut down because of vandalism. The easy, free access to the zoo became a threat to the safety of the animals. For so many of us, this was a big loss. I was sad.

When the weather was bad, my sisters and I would play with our dolls. Often times we played with our paper dolls, sometimes called cut-outs. The dolls were made of thin cardboard. We could change the paper clothes on these dolls and often designed and cut out our own paper clothes to add to the doll's wardrobes.

Sometimes we would pretend we were putting on a show, and we would sing and dance. At times we just read books from the Mead Public Library. All the things we enjoyed doing were free, but that didn't matter as we always knew how to have a lot of fun.

These were some of the memories I had from before I entered 3rd grade and before I had my seventh birthday which would have been 1948.

The home my parents were renting at 1416 North 7th Street in Sheboygan was put up for sale. Our family – my parents, five of my siblings and myself, were split up for three months. We all moved into the various homes of our four married siblings. My parents and I lived with my oldest sister Florence, and her family. After three months, my parents found a large home that they rented on the South side of Sheboygan. That September, I was enrolled in 3rd grade at Franklin Elementary School which was located on 14th Street and Broadway Avenue just a few blocks from our new location. This school is no longer in existence.

After just one quarter of the school year, my parents were encouraged by Elders of our church to send my sister and me back to Sheboygan Christian School. My dad had always been active in the church, and the church leaders felt we should continue to receive Christian education. I know my parents could not afford the tuition, but assistance was always made available to them. We had to travel on the bus to get to the North Side in order to go to the Christian school. We lived on a corner and the bus stopped there to pick up passengers. We were pretty lucky because we could see the bus coming down the road from our kitchen window, then we would run through our house and out the front door, and were able to be on the corner before the bus got there. That was pretty convenient especially when the weather was bad. Coming home from Christian school, we were able to board the bus on the corner of 5th street and Geele Avenue, which was just ½ block away from the school. Waiting for the bus out in the rain or cold was not much fun. I remember a couple times when the bus driver didn't see me waiting on the corner, and he drove right past without picking me up. Having to wait a long time for the next bus to come was upsetting. Missing the bus was one of my worst nightmares.

When I was a little older, there were times my nieces, Sandy and Donna, and I rode our bikes to school. We didn't do this too often, as this was a very long ride, we never could be sure about the weather, and the hills were very challenging with our heavy, fat ballooned tire bikes.

Once we moved to the South side, my summer trips to the beach were to the South side beach. A new best friend, Janice, lived just one house away. Now I had good friends on both sides of the city.

Ice skating was a favorite thing to do in the winter. I would take the bus across town to skate at the Grant School ice skating rink, or sometimes I walked with my neighborhood friend to Roosevelt skating rink. There were a lot of ice skating rinks to choose from. There was always a building that we called a "shack" at the skating rink. We could go inside where there were benches to sit and put your skates on. We stored our shoes and boots on shelves in the shack. A man who we called, "Shacky", attended the shack. He kept a wood burning fire going in a big pot-belly stove so there was a place we could go to warm up. Vollrath Bowl was our favorite place to go sledding. When the weather was nice, we played tennis at the Vollrath tennis courts. If we wanted to play tennis after it was dark, we needed to put a dime in a box for the lights to go on.

On Saturdays I often went roller skating at the Ruma Roller Skating Rink with my school friends. Sometimes we went bowling at North Bowl Lanes or Playdium Lanes.

Our South side home was very close to the 1500 block of South 12th Street. This was an exciting place to live. We were just a short distance from Glander Drug Store, and about a block away was

Radke's Restaurant. Hertel's Grocery Store and Brockmann's Grocery Stores were only a block away. A furniture store, electrical store, jewelry store, movie theater, bowling alley, bank, 5 and 10 cents store, a bakery, and others were all a block or less distance away from our home. St. Peter Claver Catholic and Bethlehem Lutheran Schools were just two blocks away so there were always a lot of kids walking through our neighborhood. Once a year the street was blocked off and a dance and brat fry was held in the street right in front of our house. This was hosted by the Liar's Club. It was a fun place to be.

Glander's Drug Store and Radkes's Restaurant both had soda fountains. You could sit on a stool at a counter and have a soft drink, ice cream treat, or snack with your friends. Radke's also had some booths and sold lunches and dinners. A Coke - soda, or a bag of chips or peanuts were just 5 cents. Hamburgers were a quarter. You could buy a large variety of candy for a penny. Some candy was two for a penny. There were candy cigarettes, little wax shaped bottles with a small amount of flavored juice in them, Dots – very small pieces of sweet candy attached to a long narrow strip of paper. Chocolate malts made with real malt, ice cream sundaes, ice cream sodas, banana splits, and ice cream cones were always favorites. Ice Cream Sundaes were served in tall, fancy, glass dishes topped with whipped cream and garnished with nuts and a cherry on top. Jukebox players were available to play our favorite popular songs for the cost of three songs for a quarter or one song for a dime. My favorite song was "True Love" written by Cole Porter and sung by Bing Crosby.

Growing up in the 40's and 50's was a time when we felt safe in our city of Sheboygan. Our parents didn't worry if we were out after dark. I was comfortable taking the bus across town to the North side and waiting on the corner alone for the bus to come for my ride back home to the South side. When I think about this now, I can't believe I did this, as times have certainly changed.

When I entered 9th grade, I was enrolled at Southside Junior High. Since I was the only person coming in from Sheboygan Christian School, this was a bit scary and somewhat exciting. All my Christian School classmates lived on the North side, and they would be going to North High School. For the most part, I would only be seeing these friends at church activities. Living on the South side meant that after just one year at Southside Junior High, I then would be transferring again to attend 10th, 11th, and 12th grade at Central High. In 1959, I did graduate from Central.

I took clarinet lessons and was in the junior high, high school, and our church bands. I sang in our church choir throughout my high school years. I also took piano lessons for several years, but didn't get too far. I quit when I was in 5th or 6th grade. My short stubby fingers made it difficult for me to ever get as good as I would have liked to.

I always loved sports and enjoyed getting involved in intermural after-school sports. Basketball, volleyball, and baseball were my favorites. I also loved swimming. Girls were not involved in competitive sports as they are now, but we did have some opportunities to get involved in after-school programs with our classmates. I was selected to be on the all-star basketball team by my gym classmates. I was a pretty good athlete. For my efforts, I did receive special recognition for my sports involvement from the G.A.A. – Girl's Athletic Association.

Growing up, my only source of income was from babysitting for my nieces and nephews. I usually earned 25 cents an hour. I was thrilled if I could get in four hours and would earn a dollar. With that, I could purchase three yards of material, a zipper, and some thread to make myself a new skirt. I still remember some of the pretty plaid skirts I made. Sheboygan Christian School girls were given the privilege of walking over to Grant Public School for sewing and cooking classes. The first thing we learned how to sew was an apron. While the girls were learning to cook and sew, the boys went to woodworking and shop classes. We all walked the short distance together once a week for a couple years.

When I became a senior in high school, I was employed by Lloyd Bergset, a Certified Public Accountant. This was my first place of employment, and my starting rate of pay was $1.00 an hour. I typed many tax forms and some letters. I was proficient at taking Shorthand, so the information for the letters was dictated to me.

Memories of my teen years were good. I enjoyed life and the things I was involved in. My favorite book subject in school was English. Coming from a musical family, I always enjoyed being in the Band. Traveling by school buses to music festivals in different Wisconsin cities and earning special ribbons for performances brings back fun memories. If we received first place (blue ribbon) recognition for our solo, duet, or ensemble performances, we went on to perform at the state festival which was always held in Madison. This was a great honor that I truly enjoyed. I also enjoyed marching in parades playing my clarinet. Physical Education or Gym class was also a favorite of mine. I enjoyed basketball, volleyball, and swimming the most. I did quite well in my Shorthand and Typing classes. I proficiently took Shorthand at 90 words a minute. At times, I got to 120 words a minute. That was tops. My grades were above average. Some A's, some B's, and occasionally a C. Life was good, and I was happy.

My family was part of the founders of Calvin Christian Reformed Church. There were 25 families that branched off from First Christian Reformed Church and started Calvin CRC. I was in my teens at this time. We attended two services every Sunday – one in the morning and one in the evening. I attended our church youth group and was a member of the choir. I was always grateful for the time I had with my Christian friends and will forever be thankful for the knowledge that I gained. God was incredibly good to me, and I felt blessed.

"Praise the Lord, O my soul; all my inmost being, praise his holy name. Praise the Lord, O my soul, and forget not all his benefits – who forgives all your sins and heals all your diseases, who redeems your life from the pit and crowns you with love and compassion, who satisfies your desires with good things so that your youth is renewed like the eagle's." (NIV) Psalm 103:1-5

Have All The Fun You Want, But.....

When Ernie and I first met in January 1957, he was a senior at North High School, and I was a sophomore at Central High. (Our story of how we met will be told in another chapter.)

During basketball season, we sat on opposite sides of the Sheboygan Armory cheering for our own school teams. Being in the Central High Band, I had to play my clarinet at all the home basketball games. Ernie always sat with his friends on the North side of the Armory. The North-Central games were always big rivalries. At those games, both bands were up on the stage playing together. Ernie's brother Bill was in the band from North playing the drums. After the game, Ernie and I usually did meet for a date. I tried not to brag too much if our school team won. They usually did.

Ernie did not own a car when we first met, so our first dates were always with friends. We didn't go out every week. Ernie was working a couple part-time jobs at that time at Homer's Drive-In and The Milwaukee Journal. Later he worked for the Milwaukee Sentinel.

After Ernie and I had been dating only a short time, Central High, the school I attended, was having a Saturday night dance. Our friends, Ron and Janice, set it up that we would all go to this dance together. Ron would be driving. I was pretty excited as this would be my first dance date with a guy. I still remember the pretty navy blue dress with a white collar that I got for this special occasion.

Shortly before the dance, I was told by Ron that Ernie was not going to be able to make it. He told me that Ernie's Uncle had died, and he had to go to the funeral. I was very disappointed, but felt I needed to be understanding. Ron and Janice wanted me to still go to the dance with them. So I did go, but it was rather boring for me, even though I did get to do a little dancing.

It was not until a long time later that I found out the real truth about that night. First of all, I learned that Ernie's father and mother were the only children from their families that came to the United States. So that meant that all of Ernie's uncles and other relatives were still living in Switzerland. Ah Ha! So, the real truth was that Ernie absolutely, positively, did not go to Switzerland to his uncle's funeral that night. Instead, a friend of his talked him into double dating with another girl. Oh yes, Ernie did get caught on this one. That never did happen again. I found out later that at that time, Ernie really didn't like to dance, so he probably found it pretty easy to stand me up that night. As it turned out, he wasn't too happy with the date he got talked into going with. I guess I found some consolation in hearing that.

In all honesty, I did pretty much the same thing. I accepted a set-up double date with a guy I didn't know. That also was a "one and done" date. I was happy to date Ernie again.

When Ernie graduated that year, he started working at Jungs Shoe Factory. That is when he bought his first car – a green 1947 Plymouth Deluxe. After that, we usually went to a movie on Saturday nights. While we were in high school, we received a discounted rate for movies by showing our ID cards. There were quite a few movie theaters to choose from –the Rex, Sheboygan, State, Wisconsin, Majestic, Strand, and the Stardust Outdoor Theater. Ernie always picked the movie we would see. If he wasn't happy with his choice, we didn't leave the theater but instead of watching the movie, his interest turned towards me. Yes, up in the balconies of some of these movie theaters, hugging and kissing was quite common. I do remember there were times that I liked the movie, even if he didn't. I would try to keep watching and sneak peeks as often as I could, but I never won this battle. After a while, I guess I just gave up.

After the movie, we would always stop to get something to eat. Herzigers, Schultzs, Terry's, and Homer's Drive-In were our most popular spots. At Homer's, carhops came to your car to take your order. When the order was ready, they carried it back to the car on a tray that was propped up on the opened car window. Hamburgers and hot dogs, sodas, malts, french fries, chips and sometimes frozen custard or ice cream cones or sundaes were the usual choices.

After we were dating awhile, the first McDonald's opened up at the North side location a very short distance from Homer's. McDonald's was very small, with no indoor seating. You had to walk up to a window to order what you wanted. Sometimes we went there for their cheap 15 cent hamburgers. Hamburgers were a quarter at most of the other places, and a soda was a nickel.

At some of the restaurants there were Jukeboxes that had a huge selection of all the songs that were popular. For a quarter you could select three of your favorite songs to listen to. For a dime, you could play one song. I enjoyed so many of the songs, but "Love Me Tender" and "True Love", were definitely favorites. Sounds like I was a teenager in love.

The 50's and 60's were great years for fun music. Of course, Elvis Presley, the Beatles, Nat King Cole, and the Everly Brothers were favorites at that time, but there were so many others that recorded very good hits. I loved to go to the YMCA every Friday night to dance. A DJ played records of our favorite songs, and we had a blast dancing to the Jitterbug, to the Mashed Potato, to the Stroll, to the

Twist and many more. This was the Rock and Roll and Be Bop era, and we loved it. There were also many, many awesome love songs. This was a great time to be a teenager especially if you loved music and dancing. Dick Clark, the host of the popular TV show, American Bandstand, kept us informed as to the top hits on the chart each week. When I was off dancing with my girlfriends, Ernie generally spent Friday nights playing Canasta with his mother and his friend, Marvin. After we had been dating pretty long, he generally picked me up at the YMCA after the dance.

Many high school seniors looked forward to the day when they became 18 years of age. That meant they would be allowed to go to the teenage bars where beer was served. Because I was born in July, I did not turn 18 until after I graduated. I had been dating Ernie for a couple years by then, and he had made it clear to me that he would never take me to a teenage bar. He did not like what he saw there. The kids would get so drunk and beer was being spilled all over everyone. Ernie had made up his mind that this was not a place that he would ever take his girl – ME. This was not a problem with me as I never did like the taste of beer.

Living in Sheboygan, Wisconsin, we were pretty fortunate to have Lake Michigan so close by. North Point was a pretty popular place to take your girlfriend. Ernie and I spent many, many hours there. At that time, there was a very large area of dirt right along the water's edge where cars could park. (This is no longer in existence; now you can only find a small paved parking area facing the water)

There was nothing more romantic than a beautiful, summer, starry night down by the lake. The big moon would shine brightly across the rippling water, and with your car windows rolled down, you could hear the sound of the rolling waves gently splashing up onto the shore. What an awesome setting to fall in love. This was our favorite place to park.

But then, it didn't take us too long to realize that this was also the place where, at any moment, the bright, shining spotlight of a Sheboygan Police Officer could be glaring through your car window, blinding your eyes and scaring the tar out of you. I really don't remember the officers ever saying much of anything to us other than asking if we were okay. They never told us we had to leave. (I sometimes wonder what it would have been like to have a job like that.)

After those scary interruptions, I think we generally made the choice to just leave. I guess the beautiful moonlight glimmering across the water lost its romantic glow. Fortunately for us, these unwelcomed interruptions happened only a couple times while we were dating.

I would guess that most everyone dating in the 50's living in this area had special romantic memories parking down by the lake. It truly was a beautiful place to be.

Ernie and I dated for two and a half years before we were engaged, and then another year after I graduated from high school before we were married. The year before we were married, we purchased furniture for our living room, kitchen, bedroom, and a washer, dryer, range, and refrigerator. We made monthly payments on them and had them paid before our wedding date.

Our courtship was both fun and memorable. I will always be thankful for the respect that Ernie had for me. His dad was a strong influence on him in this respect. Ernie would tell me that his dad always said, "Have all the fun you want, but don't get gay." It's hard to believe that we could get through all those years of waiting, but somehow we did, and so our wedding day, July 9, 1960, had very special meaning as we said our marriage vows, and we became one. Our honeymoon destination was Chicago, Illinois.

Genesis 2:24 (NIV) "For this reason a man will leave his father and mother and be united to his wife, and they will become one flesh."

(More details on how we first met are included in "Celebrating Our 40th Anniversary.")

Marching Into Adulthood

When did I become an adult? That's a good question. Was it when I turned 18? 21? When I was first employed? When I got married and became a wife? Was it when I had our first child, or was it when my parents passed away, and I needed to carry on? Really, when did I become an adult?

For some of my classmates, turning 18 meant they now had the privilege of going to the teenage bars. They thought that was "big stuff". Probably made them feel pretty grown up.

Ernie and I were engaged at the time of my high school graduation. Ernie was now working full-time in the factory at Armour Leather (later named Armira). He worked in the Beam House where the wet cow hides had to be flung up onto a machine that removed the hair from the skin. This was a tough, smelly job, but he was very happy that he was earning good money, and was receiving good benefits.

It was decided that I would work a year after graduation before we got married. Our wedding date was set for my 19th birthday – July 9, 1960.

I was first employed during my senior year, and I continued to work a short time after graduation for C.P.A. Lloyd Bergset; but after a while I decided to look for something that paid more money and provided some benefits. I had only been working two weeks at the Vollrath Company as a stenographer when I was offered a job at Armour Leather. Because I really didn't like what I was doing at

Vollrath, I put in my two weeks' notice and took an office job at Armour Leather. Most of the time I worked either in the billing or payroll departments, but at times when needed, I also operated the switchboard, worked in purchasing, and sometimes I helped out in the Executive's office area where I took dictation and typed letters. I loved having the chance to help out in many different areas. I know I was appreciated as there were times that the department heads would argue as to who would get me to work with them for the day. The office manager had to step in and settle the arguments.

As planned, Ernie and I were married in 1960. Our first apartment was a two-story condo located on the corner of 12th Street and Bell Avenue. Besides going to work 40 hours a week, I began my duties as a wife and homemaker. This was a huge adjustment for me. Along with my added responsibilities, I became pregnant immediately after we were married. Morning sickness became a part of my life, and often the sickness continued into the later part of the day. After some time, the doctor suggested it would be best for me to quit working.

By 1960, our government had already authorized military service for all men. This was called a draft. Names were put on a list according to your birthdate, and when your name came up, you received a letter telling you that you needed to report for duty in the United States military. Ernie received his letter shortly after we were married, but because I was pregnant, he was exempt from having to serve. We were very happy about that until about three or four months later when I had a miscarriage. That changed everything. I went out to find another job and started working at Citizen's Bank in their bookkeeping department. Ernie had to notify the government that our status had changed as I was no longer pregnant. Not long after that, Ernie enlisted in the Army National Guard. This meant he would have to serve six months active duty. Then for the next several years, additional service would be required of him by going to weekly Monday night meetings. In the summer, Ernie would have to go to camp for two weeks and, occasionally he would have to serve on weekends. This would continue for two years. Then he was put on stand-by until his duty was completed in 1966.

We were both grateful that he chose the Army Reserves six month program, as just before Ernie left on the train for basic training in Fort Leonard Wood, Missouri, I became pregnant again. Before he left for duty, we had decided that we would move all our furniture into the upstairs of my parent's home, and I would live there until Ernie completed his military service. By the time his active duty was completed, I was seven months pregnant. Just before Ernie returned, I decided to surprise him, and find an apartment. My family helped me move in so when Ernie returned, he and I were set to continue our married life together. I quit my job at Citizen's Bank, and Ernie returned to his job at Armour Leather. A couple months later, we became the proud parents of our first son, Jeff, born in February 1962. Caring for a baby was our next adjustment. I had done a lot of babysitting for my nieces and nephews, so I did well with becoming a mom. We moved two more times before Jeff was one and a half years old, and during this time, I also had a second miscarriage.

When Jeff was two, I started working at St. Nicholas Hospital in the Accounting Department. I worked full-time from 3:30 pm until midnight. Ernie was home from work before I had to leave, so he was able to take care of Jeff. We lived close to the hospital so I was able to come home to eat dinner with my family. Having only one half hour, wasn't much time, but I could do it. Not long after we were in this routine, Ernie bought me a dishwasher – or was it really for him? I think it was.

When our second son, Tim, was born in April 1965, I started working part-time at the hospital, so I was home by 9:30 pm. In

February 1969, our third son, Todd was born, and at that time, I became a stay-at-home mom.

I truly enjoyed these years as it meant so much to me that I was able to be there in our children's lives. I became active in Washington Elementary School's P.T.A. I served on the P.T.A. board for many years eventually taking on the role as President. Later I was elected to be the Vice-President and then President of the Sheboygan City P.T.A. For my service, I was awarded an Honorary Lifetime Membership in the State P.T.A. I'm not sure, but I think the P.T.A. probably died out before I did.

Teaching Vacation Bible School at our church in the summer was always a great joy. Because of my great love of baseball, I became the coach for our oldest son, Jeff's, little league baseball team. I also volunteered as a Cub Scout Den Mother for our kids and their friends for many years. My life was quite busy, but these were years I will always cherish.

For the next eight years, I enjoyed my time being at home caring for our family. In 1974, Ernie started working in supervision at Armira Leather (Armour Leather's new name). In 1978, he became a superintendent on second shift. We decided that I would look for a part-time morning job as Ernie would be home to care for the kids at that time. My next place of employment was at Security First National Bank in the Accounting Department. After working here for several years, we had one more surprise. Our fourth son, Scott, was born in November 1981. Yes, he was a surprise, (a good one). I was 40 and Ernie was 43 at the time of his birth. After a couple months on maternity leave, I continued to work part-time at Security First National Bank. Then in 1983, we were faced with another huge decision in our lives.

Armira in Sheboygan was most likely going to be closing. Ernie was asked the big question – Would we be willing to re-locate to Tennessee? After a lot of tears and much discussion, we made the choice to go along with the transfer of Ernie's employment to Armira's plant in Bolivar, Tennessee. The secret of Armira's closing had to be kept between Ernie and me until the announcement would be made publicly.

Both of our dads had already passed on. In 1982, about a year after my mother had a stroke, she became ill again and wound up in the hospital. After the stroke, it had been decided that I would be given power of attorney rights to help out with her financial affairs. She had been doing well for a while, but now she was back in the hospital.

Shortly after she was there, she told me that our Pastor had gone to visit with her. While he was there, he read from the Bible. She told me what passage he had read, and I felt inclined to look up the scripture verses. When I read the words, I had a strong feeling that God was telling me that my mother was going to die soon. She would not be leaving the hospital alive. I remember telling some of my siblings this story. I'm not sure that they believed my words. It's never easy to face the loss of a loved one.

I felt the desire to visit my mother in the hospital as much as possible. Scott was only 19 months old at that time. I was still working part time at Security First National Bank. I found myself trying to balance my time with work, taking care of my family of four sons and my husband, and making visits to the hospital to see my mother. I wanted to be there with her as often as I could as I believed these were going to be her last days. I wondered whether she would ever have to know that I would be leaving Sheboygan. I believe I was hoping that I would never have to tell her this, as I knew she would have been heart-broken.

My 42nd birthday was coming up soon. My best friend and co-worker, Janel, was going to be on vacation the day I would have ordinarily brought in my birthday treats. I didn't want Janel to miss my celebration day, so I decided to bring my treats to work a week early so Janel could be there. It was very good that I made that choice.

On July 7th, 1983, I made my usual trip to the hospital to see my mother. When I got there, she told me that the doctors said she could go home the next day. By home, they meant – Sunny Ridge Nursing Home. My mother had tears when she told me this. She was 82 years old and was truly hoping that her life would soon be over and that she would be going to heaven. She was so ready to pass on. I tried to console her and told her, "There must be some reason that God still wants you to be here. We may not know what it is right now, but we'll just have to trust that God knows what is best for you and your life."

I remember feeling a bit confused, as I had felt so sure that God had been telling me that she would not be getting better again. The scripture I had been led to read truly had me believing that this hospital stay would be her final days here on earth. Despite my confusion, I found myself trying to console and encourage my mother.

Our conversation turned to my telling my mother how pretty she looked. My mother had a beautiful glow on her face that night. She looked like an angel to me. I talked with her about it, and she told me that several of the doctors who had come in that day had also commented on how pretty her face was glowing. It was so outstanding that I got a mirror to show her how beautiful she looked. She pulled out an Avon bottle and told me she had put some Oil of Olay in that bottle. She said that she had put some of that lotion on her face that day.

We continued to have a nice visit, and she seemed to be in better spirits before I left.

When I went home that night, I felt sad for her. She was tired, and so ready to go to her home in heaven. When I went to bed, I prayed to God and talked with Him about my confusion with thinking that my mother would not be leaving the hospital alive. I apologized to God that my thoughts had been misdirected and that I was so wrong in my thinking. I told God that I trusted Him completely with my mother's care; I knew He was in control and that all would work out for the best.

On Friday, July 8, 1983, the very next morning, I was getting ready for work when I received the call from my sister, Florence, telling me to come to the hospital, our mother had taken a turn for the worst. Wow! All I could think about was that maybe she truly was going home. Maybe God was taking her to her home in heaven where she truly longed to be. My emotions were mixed, but for the most part, I felt so happy for her. It sounded like her wish was coming true.

I called my boss to tell him I would not be coming in to work. I realized now how good it was that God had directed me to bring in my birthday treats a week early. He knew very well I wouldn't be going to work that Friday before my actual birthday.

Most of my siblings and their spouses were able to be at the hospital with our mother. My sister Lois, and brother Gerald, were out of town.

I felt so blessed that I was able to be at my mother's side holding her hand until she breathed her last breath. I could tell her I loved her and that it was okay for her to go to her home in heaven. I felt confident that I would be okay.

That morning, my mother went home to be with our Lord and Savior, Jesus Christ. In the back of my mind, I was grateful that my mother would never have to know I would be leaving her and would be moving to Tennessee. I still could not talk about this move to anybody except Ernie.

My siblings and I made the funeral arrangements, and the following Monday, our mother's funeral took place at Calvin Christian Reformed Church. It was a beautiful service. Pastor Bert De Jong entitled her funeral message, "Wealth and Riches are in her House", from Psalm 112:3. He emphasized the fact that – "She was not wealthy by the standards of the world, and yet, she was a rich lady, one of the wealthiest in the City of Sheboygan." He spoke of her wealth being in the riches of a long life. He talked about her family being her wealth. Her wealth was not in property, or money. Her happiness was in her children, grandchildren, and great-grandchildren. She prayed every day for all of us and remembered all the dates of our celebrations. He reminded us that she loved us more than anyone else on this earth loved us. All those who knew her, loved her. She was a saint. This was his message.

My boss, Hugh Dales, from Security First National Bank, attended the funeral and commented later on what a beautiful service it was. I was so proud of my mother and I was so happy to tell everyone that my mother had gone home. She was in heaven, exactly where she wanted to be.

On Tuesday, Ernie and I had to return back to our jobs. Before I left home, Ernie called me from work to let me know that he had just been told that it would be on the news that day that Armira in Sheboygan was closing. This was incredible. We had just experienced the emotional time of my mother's passing and funeral, and now, the day after her burial, we were facing another huge emotional time. We both knew this would be tough news for so many people. Over 300 people, including some relatives and good friends would be losing their jobs with the Armira plant closing. This would be a huge loss. Ernie and I were about to face another big challenge in our lives.

Ernie told me he was coming home from work. We needed to hold each other. We needed to have some tears. Then we felt the need to go and speak with our Pastor. After that, we both went to work. The first thing I needed to do was tell my boss the news. It was hard for him to hear that I would be leaving. Another huge change in our lives was just ahead of us.

The word was out, and by August Ernie and I were flying to Jackson, Tennessee to find a new home. Our move-in day was set for October 31, 1983. Ernie, Todd, Scott and I would be moving in. Tim would join us a couple months later as he needed to complete his first semester of college in Sheboygan. Jeff would remain in Wisconsin and complete his senior year at Whitewater University. Both Tim and Jeff stayed with their Grandma Meise temporarily after we left Sheboygan.

When did I become an adult? That's a good question. Life is full of so many changes. One by one, we do what it takes to adapt. Being responsible and adjusting to the challenges that life brings can be a continual process. Life is an adventure. We continue to grow, and to learn, and we mature, and somewhere along the way, we become adults.

NOTE: I would like to share something that was revealed to me from the Scriptures years after my mother passed away.

Remember when I mentioned that I had noticed my mother's face was glowing, and she looked so beautiful the night before she passed on. Several of the doctors had also seen that special glow on her face that day and had commented to her on this.

Years later, when I was studying the book of Acts, I came to the story of Stephen. In Acts, Chapter Six, we read that Stephen was full of God's grace and power and did great wonders and miracles. This brought opposition from members of the Synagogue. Stephen was seized and brought before the Sanhedrin (the Jewish governing body) for questioning. Acts 6:15 says, "All who were sitting in the Sanhedrin looked intently at Stephen, and they saw that Stephen's face was like the face of an angel." He was filled with the Holy Spirit. (NIV)

Right after Stephen made his incredible speech recorded in Acts 7, he was stoned to death. The radiance of his face reminded me of the glow that was evident on my mother's face shortly before she passed on.

Since this was revealed to me, I've heard other people's stories concerning the time just before their loved one had passed on. They had also seen that special glow on their loved one's face, and not long after, God took their loved one to their heavenly home.

I believe this was just an extra special blessing that God allowed me to witness with my mother's passing. Yes, she was a saint. I thank God for all the wonderful memories I have of a Godly Mother.

Leaving Home

When did you leave home? That's a good question.

For some people the answer would be - they left home when they went to college. For others, it may be when they got married, or maybe when they got a job.

I guess I'd have to say I first left home when I got married. It was my 19th birthday, July 9, 1960.

Shortly after Ernie and I were married, I became pregnant. Not long after that Ernie received his Draft notice and was called to enlist for military service. Because we were expecting a baby, he did not have to report for military duty. Several months later, I had a miscarriage. That changed Ernie's military status. He made the decision to sign up to serve in the Army National Guard.

I thought I had left the home I grew up in for good in 1960 when we were married. I was wrong. Less than a year later, I was moving back to live with my parents. I really couldn't have afforded to live on my own with the wages I was making working at Citizen's Bank in the Bookkeeping Department. So all of our furniture and belongings were moved into my parent's home. We were fortunate that my parents lived in a two-story home. We were able to set up our own living room and bedroom on the second floor.

Six months later, shortly before Ernie returned from active duty, I left my parent's home again, and this time I felt quite certain it would be for good.

Ernie and I rented an apartment in Sheboygan at 417A Ontario Avenue where our oldest son Jeff, was born, February 8, 1962. This apartment was one block away from the lake and not far from Sheboygan's downtown. We stayed here less than a year. Jeff's first Christmas and birthday were celebrated in our next apartment at 2005 North 13th Street. We were here only three months when the landlord decided to move into this apartment himself. I had a second miscarriage in the short time we lived at this location. We moved to our next apartment at 1722A North 11th Street in 1963. This is where Tim was born a couple years later on April 22, 1965. In 1967, we moved again when we purchased our first home at 1416 Logan Avenue. Jeff was starting kindergarten at Washington Elementary School just a short block away from our home. Both Todd and Scott were born at this location. Todd was born on February 12, 1969, and eleven and a half years later, Scott was born on November 12, 1981.

In 1983, Armira Leather Corporation – the place where Ernie was employed, closed down. I guess I would have to say, "We- (Ernie, Todd, Scott, and I) left home again." We were transferred along with 25 other families from Armira in Sheboygan, Wisconsin. Armira paid for all our expenses with this transfer including the purchase of our home in Sheboygan. We were moved to Jackson, Tennessee, where we bought our second home at 112 Skyview Drive. We left behind our oldest son Jeff, who was a senior at Whitewater University along with many of our extended family - including Ernie's mother, Emma Meise. She was our only parent living.

A little over four years later, in 1987, Armira closed its plant in Bolivar, Tennessee. Fortunately, Ernie was able to obtain employment with Tecumseh in Sheboygan Falls, Wisconsin. Tecumseh agreed to pay our expenses for the move back to Sheboygan, Wisconsin. So once again, we – (Ernie, Scott, and I) left home. This time we left our second and third oldest sons Tim and Todd, behind. Tim had finished college, graduating from Union College with a B.A. in Accounting. He obtained a good accounting job in Jackson, Tennessee, and Todd had just started his college years at Jackson State Community College.

Todd often tells this story: "Generally, when kids grow up and go to college, they (the kids) leave home. Well, when I, (Todd), grew up and went to college in Jackson, Tennessee, it was my parents that left home."

Jeff told us that when we left Sheboygan in 1983, and he was still in college, he often would drive to the home that we left on Logan Avenue. He wished so badly that he would have been able to go back in and find his parents and three brothers there. When he had college breaks, Jeff was able to stay with his Grandma Meise in Sheboygan. This became his temporary home. Jeff graduated from U. W. Whitewater University with a B.A. in Marketing in 1984. That summer Jeff married his wife, Debbie, and they continued their married life in Sheboygan.

It was pretty traumatic for both Jeff and Todd when their parents were the ones who left home when they were in college. Leaving home can sometimes bring feelings of loss and sadness.

It took several months for us to find a home in Sheboygan after we left Tennessee. We lived with our son Jeff, daughter-in-law Debbie, and grandson Ryne, who was one and a half years old at that time. Ernie had been promised a job at Tecumseh in Sheboygan Falls before we left Tennessee. Scott was enrolled in kindergarten at Washington Elementary School, and I spent much of my time searching for a home to buy.

We were all thankful when we could leave our son and daughter-in-law's home and move into our two-story home at 2611 N. 13th

Street. This was the third home we purchased. The location of this home was ideal for Scott to attend Washington Elementary, Urban Middle, and North High schools.

After a terrible bout with pneumonia, and a scary situation where firemen had to carry Ernie down the stairs from our upstairs bedroom, Ernie decided he wanted to live in a Ranch style home. In 1997, we left our home on 13th Street and purchased our 4th home at 2712 N. 31st Street in Sheboygan. Scott was 15 years old at the time. This was a very difficult move for Scott. He did not want to leave the nice location where he had easy access to North High School.

None of us knew how important it was going to be for us to be in a Ranch Style home. Only God knew.

A couple months after our move, Ernie was diagnosed with Multiple Myeloma – Bone Marrow Cancer. Many times his illness brought him to where he would not have been able to walk staircases. It was truly a blessing that God encouraged us to leave our two-story home and settle into our Ranch style home. At the time of this writing (2017), we have been in this home for twenty years, and Ernie is having his third bout with battling his cancer. Chemo treatments were started up again in July 2016.

Guess I'd have to say that I "left home" quite a few times in my life - all for good reasons. This adventure of life continues on. I may not be done with having to "leave home", but I do have the assurance, that someday, I will be settled into my final, eternal home located in heaven, where I will live in glory forever – never again to have to **"leave home"**.

"And The Band Played On"

My interest in politics more than likely would have never happened had it not been for my incredible brother, Carl Otte. He was 18 years older than me. Carl was the second child born in our family of ten children, and I was the youngest. When I was very young, he served our country during World War II, in the US Army in the European Theatre.

Carl had been working at Armour Leather Company in the Beam House Department. My husband, Ernie, and brother-in-law, Don Jensema worked there as well. Slinging wet, heavy, slippery cow hides up into a machine that took the hair off the hides, dressed with big knee-high rubber boots, large rubber aprons wrapped around their bodies in front and in back, plastic wrapped around their arms, and plastic gloves on their hands, in a hot, smelly factory was **not** a job for wimps. The guys used to say, "It smelled good on payday." This was their consolation as they did earn good money. Carl did this work for almost 20 years.

In 1967, a vacancy opened up for a First District Assemblyman. A special election would be held to fill the vacancy for this position. Carl and Ernie talked, and it was decided Carl would run for the Assemblyman position, and Ernie would be his Campaign Chairman. Ernie often kidded later that he felt if he could get Carl out of his Beam House job, Ernie could get Carl's job and that meant Ernie could make more money.

Prior to this time, Carl had served on the Sheboygan County Board. He was an active member of the Union at Armour, serving in leadership positions including that of Union President.

So the race began. There were 11 candidates who decided to run for the Assemblyman position. Debates were held at the Sheboygan Armory. Carl was up against some highly educated men. The final two elected to be on the ballot were Carl and Arvin Christianson.

Some may think I am prejudiced, but I do have to say, my husband Ernie was a fantastic campaign chairman. Organizing a great campaign was his expertise. It really helped that we had a huge family. Block captains were assigned areas they needed to cover so we could canvass the entire city with Carl's brochures. Our committee worked on newspaper and radio ads. Many friends came out to campaign for Carl.

We planned a victory party that was to be held at Standard Hall. While we were waiting for the election results, my siblings and I came up with new words to the tune of "On Wisconsin". After the results came in and it was announced that Carl had won, (it was by a little less than 300 votes), our family got up on the stage, and we sang our song called, "On to Madison." We were so proud. Our brother was heading to Madison as the newly elected Assemblyman.

Because this was a special election, Carl had to run again the following year – 1968. This time the margin of victory for Carl against opponent Karl Keil was 62.8%. After winning these two elections, Carl continued to be elected to serve as our Assemblyman until 1982. In 1982, he ran for the position of State Senator and was successful again. He served as our Senator for the next four years.

As the years of campaigning went on, our committee got better and better. We had a lot of fun doing this. Carl was a long-time tuba player. He was a member of the American Federation of Musicians Union for over 60 years. He played tuba with the Wuerl Band, Sheboygan Civic Orchestra, and the Sheboygan Municipal Band. He marched in parades with the Sheboygan Pops until he was in his 70's. Because music was a big part of his life, we decided to use his tuba for campaign ads. The song that became his "token" song was "Born Free". At times, the entire ad was just Carl playing 'Born Free' on his tuba. At the end of the song, the only words spoken were – *This ad was authorized and paid for by the Otte For Assembly Committee, Ernie Meise, Chairman.* The minute you heard the tuba music playing "Born Free", your thoughts immediately went to Carl Otte. Another year, we also used the "Dueling Banjos" song. We had Carl on his tuba and a friend, Jeff Schneider, on the banjo dueling out this song. Can you imagine that? It was awesome. After the election was over, our thank you ad in the press was characterized with Carl and other winning Democrats on a band wagon surrounded by music notes. Our son Jeff was very good at cartoon character drawings so we had Jeff draw these ads. The caption read: "And The Band Played On."

At times, Carl's opponents would come up with nasty ads. Carl and the committee never resorted to this type of campaign. Carl always maintained his integrity. His faith was strong. He was known to be an advocate for the "Neediest of the needy". He was a champion for those who were often unheard or ignored – the poor, the elderly, and the mentally ill. People described him as compassionate, humble, friendly, nice, and caring. He always was interested in what others had to say. He gained the respect of his colleagues and was appointed to the prestigious position of serving on the Joint Finance Committee while serving in the Senate.

One year, in 1978, eleven years after Carl's first election, he was unopposed. That didn't mean the campaign committee took a break. An article in the Sheboygan Press written by Dawn Jax

Belleau, a press staff writer, was entitled, "No Beer And Beans This Time For Otte (No Opponent Either)."

In past elections, our fundraising events and victory parties were usually held at Standard Hall or Emil Mazey Hall where colored checkered table cloths were used. For one of our spaghetti suppers at Standard Hall, we sold 500 tickets. Their seating capacity was 250. Extra tables were set up in the coat room, hallways, and bar area. You would think the owner would have been upset with us for over-selling tickets. Instead, he loved it as he made huge profits that night.

For the 1978 event when Carl was unopposed, the committee decided to host a cocktail party fund-raiser with white linen table clothes. This event was billed as, "An Evening With Carl Otte", and was held at Executive Inn. Ticket cost was $20.00, and 300 tickets were sold.

Dawn's press article referred to this event as being "ironic". This was not our usual chicken, or spaghetti dinner, or soup supper with ticket cost ranging from $2.75 to $5.00. Guests in attendance were Armira (formerly Armour Leather) Tannery workers who had previously worked with Carl, many city and county labor leaders, fellow legislators, family, and many friends. Along with these guests, Dawn was shocked to see several Sheboygan County Republican Party Chairmen and a host of business and professional people who were not known to show up at Democratic Party "bean feeds". Dawn stated, "The odd mix was enough to cause several arrivals to quickly check their invitations just to make sure they were at the right party. For Carl Otte, who had represented Sheboygan in the Wisconsin Assembly since 1967, it was exactly the right party."

Dawn wrote that the evening's brightest moment came when a parade of 11 tuba players marched through the cocktail crowd, playing "On Wisconsin," and the Otte theme song from previous elections, "Born Free". Ernie had connected with the North High School Band Director, Rod Gibson, to set up this surprise for Carl. Carl loved it.

Armira's Vice President, Francis Dunn presented Carl with a leather briefcase saying that he hoped it would remind Carl of the people he had once worked with.

Carl stated, "I've never forgotten where I came from. I appreciate where I came from." We had placed a photo of Carl on a memorabilia table that had been taken years before where Carl was standing at the machine he ran that removed hair from cowhides. Armira Leather sometimes used this picture that they had taken of Carl and used the caption – The Making of a Politician.

The Chairman of the local Republican Party, James Horstmann, told Dawn it wasn't surprising to him that so many non-Democrats had come to the gathering for Carl. He said Carl was a sincere and dedicated representative, a receptive listener who was aware of the concerns of business and professional people. Other State Representatives traveled from across the state to be at this event honoring Carl. They stated their respect for Carl's honesty and integrity.

Some extra special memories of politics were having the opportunity to meet many political leaders, attending Governor Patrick Lucey's Inaugural Ball, and attending dinners for Presidential hopefuls with Carl, his wife Ethel, and my husband Ernie. Probably the Kennedy Dinner at the Pfister Hotel in Milwaukee was the most memorable. Cost to attend this dinner was $100.00 a plate. Carl was kind enough to take care of this for Ernie and me.

An added remembrance of my political experiences came when Hubert Humphrey was campaigning in Sheboygan for the position of United States President in 1968. I had the privilege of accompanying our son, Tim's Cub Scout Troup on the piano, as they sang a patriotic song at a political rally held in support of Candidate Humphrey.

I truly believe the example set by my brother Carl, was instrumental in who I became in my life. People would have described me as being a quiet, shy person. I believe working with my brother and seeing him achieve great things in his lifetime encouraged me to find confidence in myself. Serving those who were hurting and helping those with special needs became my life's passion. Carl and I came from humble beginnings. With God's guidance, we chose to devote our lives to serve those who were less fortunate. With sincere compassion, Carl acknowledged over and over again that he felt so blessed. His gratitude was always first of all to God.

It is 2016. In November a new President will be elected.

In March, we took a trip to Lebanon, Tennessee to visit our sons, Tim and Todd, and their families. Our granddaughters, eight year old Kaitlyn, and six year old Maddie were enjoying time with me in the motel pool. Kaitlyn, a second grader, is very intelligent and is mature beyond her years. She said to me, "My Daddy said I should ask you what you think about Donald Trump. Do you think he's a Christian?" I responded to her questions. Then Kaitlyn said, "My Daddy said he doesn't think he's going to vote because he doesn't really like any of the candidates. Grandma, do you think it's a good idea not to vote?" My response was, "No, I don't think it's a good idea to not vote. Someone needs to be our President. We need to listen to all the candidates when they are speaking for themselves, and decide which one is the most knowledgeable and would serve our country the best." I have to stress that we listen to the words when the candidate is speaking for themselves. It is so sad how the media and others love to take the persons words and twist the meaning of what they actually said to bring out uncertainty and deception.

My dad John Otte, always taught us this - "Voting is not only a right and a privilege, it is also our Christian Duty." Ernie and I agree with my dad, and we always vote.

What we are witnessing this election year, words cannot describe. I can only wish campaigns were like what we once experienced with my brother. My prayer is that God will bless America and our leaders, and that we will truly be "One Nation Under God".

After my brother Carl passed on, I felt inclined to write the following tribute. Carl's family had asked me to do a eulogy at the funeral service, but the Pastor did not allow eulogies unless the speaker was from the same church denomination. I didn't qualify. In light of this, I decided I could still share these words with Carl's immediate family as well as our extended family with this tribute.

A Tribute To My Brother, Carl Otte

As most of you know, I had the privilege of spending a lot of time with Carl, not only through many years of political campaigns and many years of retirement, but also during his last days on this earth in the hospital. I am so blessed to have many wonderful memories of an awesome brother. In the last couple weeks, many people have written articles that were published in our local newspaper. Carl was described as humble, servant, compassionate, advocate, caring, kind, etc. All of these words accurately describe Carl.

Coming from a family of ten children and going through the depression years put our family in the classification of being poor. Working in what was called the "Beam House" at Armira Leather Corporation for 20 years helped to teach Carl what the term "hard work" really meant.

When Carl first talked with my husband, Ernie, about running for a seat as a State Assemblyman, Ernie did not hesitate to encourage Carl to run for this position. Ernie agreed to be his campaign chairman. I was asked to be his campaign secretary. Carl won that first election in 1967 and so many more. Carl was off to Madison, and those of us who loved him and supported him watched a man who was born to be humble, soar to great heights as he worked diligently to serve the people of our city, county, and state.

How proud he made us feel. He was a man with strong Christian values. The Christian education he received every day in his home, in Sheboygan Christian Elementary School, and in his church helped him to stand strong for what was right and good. Carl loved the Lord, and he knew Jesus Christ as his Savior.

One of the things we heard him say so often was, "I will never forget where I came from." He never did. He fought hard to help the poor and the needy. He lived his life with so much gratitude. Over and over again, we would hear the words from his lips saying, "I am so blessed."

January 1, 2011, shortly after 12:30 p.m., I made my annual call to my brother, Carl, to wish him a Happy New Year. He returned the wish to me. When I asked him how he was doing, he said he felt miserable. I said, "Oh no, I hope you didn't get the flu." He said that it was just a cold, and he didn't think he would get the flu because he had received the flu shot. We talked about watching the Rose Bowl Parade and found out that both he and Ernie had dozed off in their recliners for about three quarters of the parade while his wife, Ethel, and I had enjoyed the entire parade. He did tell me that he was awake to see the U. W. Madison band play and was grateful he could enjoy that.

As always, he shared with me how blessed he was. He reminded me that our dad had died when he was only 75 years old, and our mother was 82 when she passed on. Here he was already 87 and a half years old, and he was again counting his years as such a great blessing.

We chatted a bit about the Badger football game that was coming up later in the day. I told him that when I talked with our son, Tim, he had said that the people in Tennessee where Tim lived, were referring to the Wisconsin Badger vs. Texas Christian game as the "David and Goliath" game. I found this comparison very interesting. As most of you may know, Texas Christian is a very small college compared to U. W. Madison. Carl and I shared our excitement about watching the game later that evening.

If you watched the game, you know, Texas Christian (the little "David" university team) won over the Badgers in a very close, hard fought game.

The next time I saw my brother was the very next day, Sunday, January 2nd, in the hospital emergency room. He was in a coma, not responding.

In trying to put together Carl's situation, it seemed pretty clear that he became very sick later Saturday night, as there were signs that he did not have the ability to completely get undressed that night and never went to bed. He was still partially clothed and found non-responsive the next morning by his wife Ethel, still in his chair.

At the same time that Lynn, Carl's youngest daughter, and her husband John, (an EMT by profession), were calling 911 for help, I was in church at Bethany hearing a message about our First Responder. Pastor Ted shared an enlightening message that reminded us that Jesus is our First Responder. He is always with us, caring for us, taking care of all our needs. We may never know exactly what all transpired with Carl that evening, but one thing we can be assured of is that his First Responder, Jesus, was there with him every moment.

I don't know how many of you were able to see that Badger football game. I also don't know how many of you hung around to see the interviews and celebration that took place after the game. If you did hang around, as I did, you would have seen the interview that was done with the Texas Christian University quarterback. The reporter asked him how it felt to have won this game knowing that they were the small university coming up against Madison's Big Ten Team. The quarterback answered, "I really didn't think about it. I just came into this game with the words in my heart from

I Peter 5:6 that say, "Humble yourselves, therefore, under God's mighty hand, that he may lift you up in due time." (NIV)

In the middle of a restless, tear-filled night, after spending that first day with Carl and his family at the hospital – (first in E.R. and then in I.C.U.), I was reminded of the words of this interview. I truly believe that these words of scripture were the last that were brought to Carl just before he began his final days of being lifted up to heaven. What beautiful words for him to hear. At times, during my visits to the hospital, I had the privilege to tell Carl that I truly believed that Jesus was waiting for him and that he would definitely be greeted with the words, "Well done, my good and faithful servant." If anyone was a great role model in humility and dedicated service, it was Carl.

The words of Carl's favorite hymn, "When I Survey The Wondrous Cross", say so much about Carl's humility and his great love of our Lord. He knew the amazing love and sacrifice made for him on the cross of Calvary by our Prince of Glory, Jesus. He did not boast of his accomplishments in this life. With gratitude always in his heart, he continually told everyone, "I am so blessed". That's all that mattered. The grace he received because of the great sacrifice of Jesus Christ, our Lord and Savior on that cross, was all that mattered.

It's never easy saying "Good-bye" to someone you love so much. To my special brother and loved one, Carl, I would like to say, "Till we meet again."

Thanks for so many precious moments. They will forever be cherished in my heart.

Your loving sister,

Judie

This Can't Be True

In 1997, my husband, Ernie, was having stiffness and pain in his neck that he attributed to his stressful job situation. He was 59 years old at that time and was working as a plant production superintendent at Amcast Industrial Corporation in Cedarburg. After the pain had been there for over two weeks, I encouraged him to go see the doctor. I reminded Ernie that in 1984, when he had surgery for deterioration of a vertebrae when we were living in Tennessee, the surgeon had told him that he may need more surgery in the future. I was concerned he had more deterioration on his spine. Ernie thought it was just stress as there were many stressful things going on at work.

I made an appointment for him to see the doctor. Dr. Schleevogt ordered some tests to be run. A few days later, Ernie was asked to come in for another blood test. Not long after that, we were called in to get the results of the testing.

On September 3, 1997, the doctor informed us that the test results showed that Ernie had cancer – Multiple Myeloma – Bone Marrow Cancer. We certainly did not expect to hear the dreaded big "C" word. I was in total shock. I felt like I couldn't even move. I felt numb. Ernie asked the doctor if this was a "death sentence." The doctor said there were treatment options, and he was sending us to see an Oncologist – Dr. H. Marshall Matthews. We left the doctor's office, and when we got home, we just held each other and cried. After we could pull ourselves together, we took on the tough task of calling our family and friends to tell them the bad news.

We met with Dr. Matthews, and he informed us that if Ernie went through chemotherapy and had a stem cell transplant, he could probably live for another five years. He also told us that if we didn't have a religion or faith, we needed to get one, as this would help us through dealing with the cancer.

I remember thinking that this couldn't be true. I thought that when they did further tests, they would find out they were wrong. I was in denial for a long time. It was just too hard to believe or to accept that Ernie, my husband, had cancer.

When I saw other couples arguing and treating each other badly, I wondered why this cancer was happening to us. We loved each other. Some couples didn't really seem to even love each other. I was asking God, "Why us?" When I saw people laughing and feeling happy, I wondered how anyone could be feeling so happy. The sadness I was feeling was so deep, I couldn't see past it. My emotions were all over the place and were very tough to deal with.

Dr. Matthews referred Ernie to Dr. Vesole, who was an expert in the field of Multiple Myeloma Cancer and transplants at Froedert Hospital in Milwaukee. Ernie's transplant would take place in Milwaukee.

Ernie went through chemo treatments for four months to kill off the bad cancer cells in order to get him to the point of remission. He lost his facial hair and didn't have to shave. His eyebrows were gone, but he didn't lose much of the hair on his head. He really wasn't concerned about losing his hair. He had already made up his mind that when he became bald, he would get himself a sucker, and then he could act like and look like Kojac. Food didn't taste very good because of the effects of chemo, so he lost a little weight, but not much. For a while, he thought I had forgotten how to cook.

Everything seemed to taste like "metal" to him. Despite his loss of appetite, he always remained over-weight.

After his chemo treatment was completed, we went back to see Dr. Vesole in Milwaukee. The first thing he said to Ernie was, "What are you doing with all that hair on your head? It doesn't look to me like you lost much weight neither."

Then he looked at me and said, "But I'll bet there were times when he was pretty ornery and crabby."

I said, "Yes, he was, but that's normal too."

Dr. Vesole looked at Ernie and said, "She's tough, isn't she?"

Ernie replied, "Now you know what I have to put up with."

We all had a good laugh. When you are dealing with cancer, it's so good if you can just find some times to laugh and have some fun. We found out that each day was another day to enjoy, and that "Life is precious." Dr. Vesole was very impressed with how Dr. Matthews had gotten Ernie to the point of having his transplant.

The testing showed Ernie was in remission, so the next step was to collect his good stem cells to be used for his transplant. Ernie was able to be his own donor because the cancer was not in his lymph nodes.

We made two trips to Froedtert Hospital for the stem cell collection. The bags of good stem cells were collected, saved, and stored at the hospital. We found out later that they had collected enough stem cells for two transplants. The second dose would be saved at Froedtert through a special freezing process and would be ready for use if Ernie would ever need them at a later date. At that time, they felt they could preserve his stem cells for five years.

The first day Ernie was admitted to Froedtert, they inserted a PICC line in his chest to be used for all the IV medications he would be needing to get him through the transplant. That same day the huge dose of chemo was injected into Ernie, (more chemo than he had for the prior four months of treatments). The following day, Ernie's collected good stem cells were injected into his body. Ernie had been told the average stay at the hospital after a stem cell transplant was about 23 days, so that's how long we expected him to have to stay. The day after the transplant, Ernie was feeling so good, he asked if he had to stay in bed. He was told he could get up and get dressed and go to the patient lounge. He did have to stay in the Bone Marrow Transplant Unit, as special care was taken to keep the air and all the surroundings germ free. The transplant unit was located on the eighth – top floor of children's hospital.

The next day Ernie got up, got dressed, and went to the patient lounge to watch a movie. The doctors came in, and one of them said, "Let me begin by telling you that it's not often that I come to see a patient, and the patient looks better than the doctor!" The doctors decided to send him home just three days after the transplant. Ernie set a record…no one had ever done that at Froedtert before. We couldn't believe it, but we were so grateful he could come home so quickly.

We were told that Ernie had to see Dr. Matthews in Sheboygan one day and the next he had to see Dr. Vesole in Milwaukee and continue this routine every day. He could be at home, but every day we saw one or the other doctor. The trips to Milwaukee were always tougher on him as this was an hour drive – one way. To Dr. Matthews' office we traveled only two minutes one way. As the days went on, Ernie became sicker and sicker. Finally, on his eighth day after the transplant, when we were to see Dr. Matthews in Sheboygan, he was so sick that the doctor said he had to be admitted to the hospital. It is typical that around the sixth to eighth day, the patient will start getting very sick as their immune system goes down to nothing. The huge dose of chemo starts taking effect. Then the battle begins. The hope is that his collection of good stem cells that were injected into him would start to multiply, and the immune system would start to come back again. Dr. Matthews gave us the choice of going back to be admitted at Froedtert in Milwaukee, or he said Ernie could stay in Sheboygan for the completion of his care. Dr. Matthews said they would be able to care for him in Sheboygan, so we decided that it would be a lot easier for us to be close to home. Scott, who was a sophomore at North High, was still living at home. It was definitely easier for me to be staying in Sheboygan where I could be there for both Ernie and Scott. We thought it was extremely special that Dr. Matthews brought Ernie up into the hospital in a wheelchair himself and had him admitted into Neutropenic Care.

Ernie was the first patient that had a bone marrow transplant being cared for under those circumstances at St. Nicholas Hospital. We found out in a hurry that this may not have been the best choice. Some of the nursing staff did not know how to care for stem cell transplant patients. One nurse was banned from ever caring for Dr. Matthew's cancer patients after she broke one of his picc-lines that had two lines for IV's to be administered. Next she put an IV drug (potassium) into his arm vein that caused severe pain. This all happened in one day. One of the aides came to Ernie's rescue after the nurse started up the IV pump a second time running the potassium through his arm again causing the extreme pain for the second time. The aide probably wasn't supposed to turn off the IV machine, but she reacted to stop Ernie's pain and did it to help him. We were extremely grateful that she did what she did. Of course, there were a whole lot of meetings taking place after all this happened. Dr. Matthews was not too happy. The beautiful thing is that the aide– Stacy became a life-long friend to Ernie and me. After going through this experience with us, she decided to become an oncology nurse. We were invited to her graduation and then to her wedding. She worked at John Hopkin's Hospital for a while after she graduated from college, and then she worked at Sheboygan Memorial Hospital for a while. Next, Stacy came back where we got to see her occasionally when she joined the St. Nicholas Hospital staff. Most recently, she has become an Oncology Nurse Practitioner working with Dr. Bettag, who is in partnership with Dr. Matthews. Every year, we have kept in touch with her as we exchange Christmas cards – (Stacy sends family pictures to us.) Stacy and her husband have caught up with Ernie and me now. They just had their fourth baby boy in January, 2014. We are so happy that she has become a special part of our lives.

Ernie was in the hospital 18 days after that. It was rough. He didn't have an appetite. For days he went from his body shaking profusely with the chills to then burning up with fever. Back and forth he went – from chills to sweats. Tina, another special aide, gave Ernie extra special care and also became a life-long friend. Ernie really didn't remember a lot of what happened those days. I can tell you, it was terrible to watch. I visited a lot, but encouraged others not to come. With his immune system down to nothing, he was at great risk of getting sick if he picked up anything contagious. We couldn't take that risk. The hospital staff tried so hard to get him to eat something and even told him that they would bring whatever he wanted. He ordered a steak and baked potato – his favorite. He took one bite, but couldn't eat that either. Finally he was well enough to come home. Dr. Matthews watched him very closely, so we were going to the clinic often. They took a lot of tests and sometimes called us and said to bring him in right away as he needed treatment. There were times he needed a shot every day. We went to the clinic during the week and the hospital on weekends for these. He had a lot of X-rays, scans, blood and urine tests, and he went in every month for an IV treatment to help strengthen his bones.

Ernie did go back to work at his job in Cedarburg working part time after a while. In 1999, he decided it was time to retire early, and he went on disability. The doctor told him to get his affairs in order, and to do and enjoy all the things he wanted to do, as his days would be numbered.

You'll Have To Talk To
The Man Upstairs

"For I know the plans I have for you," says the Lord, "plans to prosper you, and not to harm you, plans to give you hope and a future." (NIV) Jeremiah 29:11

In the year 2002, I had decided I should have my hysterectomy. My doctor had told me it was time for me to do this, so I called and set up the surgery for February 25th.

I called our son, Todd, who was living in Jackson, Tennessee, and told him of the plan for my surgery. Todd responded with the words, "Oh, good, Mom!" "I was going to tell you that you needed to do this now."

I was totally puzzled by Todd's response. I didn't remember even telling him that I would probably need to have this surgery at some time. Todd really didn't want to talk about it when I asked him why he responded as he did. He said he would maybe tell me someday.

I had the surgery and recovered well. Ernie was at home and was a big help to me with taking care of some of the household chores. In April, when Scott had Spring Break, Ernie and I had decided to take a trip to Tennessee to visit Todd. I was planning to teach Vacation Bible School in June, so I brought my materials along to work on in the car. I always loved teaching Vacation Bible School. By the time we got to Todd's house, I was all excited about the materials and the lessons I had been studying. I was sharing my excitement with Todd. Then Todd asked me, "When are you going to teach this?" I told him it would be in June. Then he said, "Oh, that's why." I asked him what he was talking about. Then he told me this story.

On the night of the New Year, 2002, God spoke to Todd and told him that he needed to tell me that I should be having my hysterectomy as soon as possible. Todd said that he was told that there was some urgency that I needed to be ready for. Something would be happening in June.

We both were amazed at the encounter that God had with Todd and for the vision for my future that was foretold. We were in awe that God had chosen to connect with Todd in this way.

Well, June came, and I had a wonderful week teaching Vacation Bible School. I always looked forward to this opportunity. I really believe I loved Vacation Bible School as much as the kids did. Sharing the love of our Lord and Savior with over 100 children every summer was definitely one of my greatest joys in life. I loved it so much that even after our children and grandchildren were too old to attend the classes, I got them to be my helpers so they could continue to be a blessing to other children, and they could also be blessed in the process. These years, (more than 25), gave me some of my most precious memories in life, and I thank God for the awesome experiences of Vacation Bible School.

The week after Vacation Bible School was done, while we were still in the month of June, Ernie started having extreme pain that ran down from his lower back down into his leg. The pain was so intense, the doctor had to put him on Valium and other very strong narcotics. He had Morphine, OxyContin, Hydrocodone and others to try to combat the extreme pain. He could not drive, as he felt like he was floating being on these narcotics. X-rays showed some spot on the bottom of his spine. The doctors couldn't figure out what it was. There were times the pain was so bad, I had to call 911, and he had to be taken to the hospital to be put on IV pain medication as the pills were not enough. Once this happened when Scott was still home from college for the summer. Scott was concerned about his Dad and wanted to go along to the ER. While we were there waiting together, Scott asked, "Mom, I'm going to be going back to college soon, what are you going to do when I'm gone?" I told him that I didn't want him to worry. I would be alright. I told him I know how to call 911, and would get the help his dad would be needing. I knew this was tough on our kids to see their dad have to deal with so much pain. The next day when Scott went to work, he was making so many mistakes, his boss had to take him off the job he was doing. The following day his dad was doing better, and Scott was able to concentrate on his work again. Cancer definitely affects everyone in the family. It was even hard on our kids who were living far away.

The doctors continued to be puzzled by the spot on Ernie's spine. In July, a Neurologist was called in, and he suggested that Ernie have an Epidural. Ernie was admitted to the hospital August 1, 2002, and continued to be kept under a lot of pain meds. He was medicated so strongly, that when he was sleeping, he snored so loudly that you could hear him way down at the end of the hall. Finally, the day came when he was taken down for the Epidural. When the surgeon saw he was still on a blood thinner, he sent him back to his hospital room. Ernie needed to be off the blood thinner before they could do the Epidural. On August 5th, his blood was ready so the Epidural could be administered. Ernie was in the hospital two more days, and then came home. The pain had subsided. Praise the Lord!

The next morning, Ernie had breakfast and shortly after that, while he was resting in his recliner, he started shaking profusely and having terrible chills. I called the Neurologist's office to report what was happening. They asked what his temperature was. Ernie had already gone back to bed to get under the covers to try to warm up. I went to take his temperature and discovered that it was 102.4. With Ernie's Multiple Myeloma Cancer, Dr. Matthews had told me if his temp gets to 101, I needed to take him to the E.R. immediately. I called the doctor back and told him that I would have to bring Ernie back to the hospital as his temperature was up. The doctor called the hospital so they were ready to admit him when we got there.

The nurse caring for Ernie took his temperature and said it was only 99 degrees. I did not believe her as he was burning up with fever and kept falling asleep. When he did wake up, he would ask for water and would be saying things that didn't make sense. Like – "We should have taken the bus." We never took the bus anywhere. The nurse said he couldn't have water, but he could have ice chips, so I fed him ice chips every time he came to, and put cool cloths on this head and body to try to bring down the fever.

It seemed like forever before his doctors got to the hospital. When they came, I watched them all test certain movements with his body. I told the doctor that the nurse said his temperature was only 99 degrees and that I didn't believe that was right. When the nurse came in, the doctor told her to take his temperature again. He said, "He's burning up with fever." The doctors went out to confer, and determined that he had Spinal Meningitis. In the meantime, the nurse came to take Ernie's temperature again and found that it was 105 degrees. She said, "Oh, I need to go tell the doctors." Really!!!

The person who did the Epidural told Ernie later that only one in a million would ever get Spinal Meningitis from an Epidural. Ernie was that "one in a million". I told the Neurologist and our Family Doctor that I wanted them to call Dr. Matthews in on this. They did call him. An MRI was ordered and when Ernie came back to his room, Dr. Matthews was there. When the attendants were struggling to get Ernie back on his bed, Dr. Matthews said, "Let me do that." I watched as Dr. Matthews, himself, picked Ernie up into his strong, loving arms and got him back into the hospital bed. Then he ordered a very strong antibiotic IV for him. Ernie was not coherent for a very long time. When he would come to, he would be saying silly things, the fever had gone up so high. He was very sick. I decided I was going to stay the night with him as I knew he wasn't even able to call for help if he needed it.

Late that evening, Pastor Ted and his wife, Betty, came to the hospital. We talked awhile, and then we all held hands and prayed over Ernie. Our daughter-in-law, Debbie, was there with us. This was after 10:00 p.m. Shortly after they all left, Ernie's fever broke. He started sweating profusely, and he came out of the bad danger that he was heading for. Ernie has no recollection of this day until after the fever broke. We were so grateful to the Lord that he did not suffer any bad effects from having Spinal Meningitis. Once again, we saw the healing hand of our Lord keeping him from serious danger. On August 10th, he returned home. This scare happened on August 1 when he was admitted to the hospital. By the end of August, we were seeing our lawyer to set up our will.

Ernie was hospitalized again with extreme pain from September 13 – September 20 that year.

In November, I was calling 911 again, and Ernie was taken back to the hospital. The paramedics had a terrible time trying to transport him as he was in so much pain. He had just taken a morphine pill. They had to give him more morphine in order to even transport him. By this time, I was feeling that I may have been selfish in not wanting to lose my husband. I remember crying and telling God that if it was His will, that it was alright with me for Him to take Ernie to heaven. I could not stand to see him suffer any longer. This time it was for 18 days that he had to be on IV pain medication in the hospital. They tried several times to get him back on to the pain pills so he could go back home, but it took them 18 days to do this. He continued to have to take strong medication through December.

After we got into the New Year, 2003, all of a sudden, the pain was gone. The mysterious spot on Ernie's spine was also gone. I asked our family doctor what the doctors had done now to get rid of that terrible pain.

He replied, "If you really want to know the answer to that question, you'll have to talk to the man upstairs, because we didn't do anything. We really didn't know what to do."

Then I said to him, "Thank you for telling me where all the credit is due, because we have been talking with the man upstairs, and we will give him all the glory for healing Ernie."

Thank you, God, for your healing mercies!

That truly was the end of the eight to nine months of this terrible pain. Ernie was weaned off the narcotic drugs by March 18, 2003.

Now, remember how God had spoken to Todd at the beginning of that year, 2002, and how he said something would be happening in June, and Todd needed to tell me that I needed to have my hysterectomy early that year so that I would be ready for something big that was going to be happening. At first we thought that the reason was so I could be healed and ready to teach Vacation Bible School. That may have been part of it, but in all honesty, we realized later that God had a far bigger reason for me to be healed. I needed to be ready to care for Ernie through this very difficult nine months of time that he was dealing with extreme pain. God knows all things. He is in control and sometimes cares for us in mysterious ways. He has always been faithful to us and has always provided for all our needs. All He asks is that we trust in Him. We certainly can do that.

Years later, I realized, - 2002 was actually Ernie's fifth year since he had been diagnosed with cancer. (To be truthful, I did not want to know when our five years was going to be up, so I never allowed myself to figure this out or even think about it.) Instead, I found myself just wanting to focus in on every day and enjoy each day as best we could, even though I had been told that Ernie was only given five years to live with the kind of cancer he had.

Yes, 2002, was an interesting year. A year of much testing for Ernie and me, but God carried us through it all, and showed us His plan for our future was far from over.

PRAYER

Thank you, God, for your great love and healing! Your incredible kindness and compassion are beyond our comprehension. Help us to remember, You know the plan You have for our lives, a plan that will prosper us, not harm us, a plan that will give us hope and a future. Thank You for your indescribable love for us. Amen

There were so many things that we were able to enjoy in those first five years. Scott graduated from North High School with honors. We were ecstatic when he received a $10,000.00 Minnie Reiss Detling Scholarship. Scott went to U. W. Madison where he graduated with a double major receiving a degree in both Risk Management Insurance; and Finance, Banking and Investments in just four years.

We also had a very big party for our 40th anniversary in the year, 2000. Our children did a fantastic job making this celebration delightfully special. Our oldest son Jeff, took care of offering the prayer and reading scripture. Tim put together a game he called,

"Who wants to be a Meisenairre?", using some of our guests as the contestants. Answers to the questions were multiple choices of information about Ernie or my life. Todd designed the invitations and had us view a video of highlights of our married life that he put together. He also read the stories he had Ernie & me write of our interpretation of "How We Met". Scott put together his speech on special attributes of both Ernie & me, which earned him a standing ovation from the 150 guests at the dinner party at Klemme's Wagon Wheel. Debbie & Lisa worked on music for Ernie & me to dance to. They chose Nat King Cole's – "Unforgettable" and "L.O.V.E." Guests were invited to share experiences or memories of Ernie and me on note cards which they sent back with their dinner reservations. Pictures were taken of all the guests and a book was put together of all the special memories. It was an incredible celebration. Our kids did an awesome job making this so special. Some of our guests asked if they could have our children. They were so impressed with the time and love put into this special celebration. This was all done with the thoughts that this would be our last chance to celebrate a special anniversary. At that time, Ernie was expected to be gone in just two more years.

Ernie had good days and bad days, but the cancer stayed in remission. We knew the cancer cells would always be there, but they were staying quiet. We made a trip to Mayo Clinic in 2006 as a recommendation by Dr. Matthews, but were told not to change anything Dr. Matthews was doing, as the cancer cells were staying quiet.

God continued to bless us with so many wonderful trips to Tennessee, Florida, Arizona, and Missouri and with so many great times of celebrations.

At the time of this writing, we will have celebrated our 57th wedding anniversary, and Ernie is a 20 year cancer survivor. Praise God from whom all blessings flow!

A Divine Intervention –
An Amazing Miracle

It wasn't until 11 years after the first transplant that Ernie's counts were getting to where another transplant needed to be considered. This was amazing, as Ernie already had been given more than twice the amount of time he was expected to live. When he was first diagnosed, he was given only five years.

Here I was again, just filled with denial. Getting through that first transplant was so rough on Ernie, I just couldn't get myself to even believe he'd be going through this again. It was amazing. He was being so brave. He went through all the chemo treatments to get him into remission so he would be ready for the transplant. At the same time, I was just going through all the motions, thinking this really would never, ever have to happen again. Denial, denial.

The months went by, and we were visiting Froedtert Hospital to talk with Dr. Hari. There was a new Bone Marrow Transplant Unit built there now. I was very impressed when I saw the awesome set up of this twelve patient room unit. The date for Ernie's transplant was set for May 26, 2009. The extra stem cells that were collected in 1998, at the time of his first transplant were amazingly still there and preserved well. We were told that a new method of storing stem cells made it possible for that collection to still be good. The medical technology used for helping Multiple Myeloma Cancer patients is so incredible.

On May 7th, we spent the day at the hospital where they did extensive testing to make sure Ernie would be strong enough to go through a transplant.

At our final visit before the transplant, we were told Ernie did well with all the testing, and they were ready to proceed with the transplant. I asked Dr. Hari if he would be using less of a dose of chemo for Ernie because he was older now (71 years). Dr. Hari said, "No, he would be getting the same amount as was normally given." We were told Ernie would have to stay in the hospital at least three to three and a half weeks, and then we needed to stay in the area for another two weeks so he could be watched closely and could get to the clinic or hospital quickly if he needed care. I, so tactfully, came out with, "I'm not going to take him to some dirty motel." They gave us some information on Kathy's House where patients were able to stay and said I should check this out online. I did check Kathy's House out after we got home and decided I would talk them into letting me take Ernie home when the time was right. I did not like the setup of this house as we would be sharing the kitchen and other areas with a lot of other people. I was very concerned about Ernie being exposed to something contagious, and didn't want him to be put in this situation.

About a week before the transplant was to happen, I received a call from a nurse from Dr. Hari's office who gave me instructions on the plans for the transplant date. Just a day or two before this call, I had heard on the news on TV that the Swine Flu (H1N1) had hit a Milwaukee hospital and that several people had died from it. They didn't say which hospital it was, but, of course, I was very concerned for Ernie's condition. I was hoping the flu was not at Froedtert. I asked the nurse, "Are you still going to be doing this transplant with the H1N1 flu being in Milwaukee?" She answered, "Oh, yes, we'll be just fine."

May 26th came, and we were actually heading to Milwaukee where Ernie would have his second bone marrow transplant. Again, he had the PICC line put into his chest. Then he went to the Bone Marrow Transplant Unit where he was put in room #10. At 5:00 p.m., the nurse came in and gave him the huge injection of chemo that took about 20 minutes, but before she did that, a doctor had come in to tell us that they were going to give Ernie 10% less chemo than they normally do. Hmmmmmm. What a surprise that was for me. I guess I thought, maybe they actually liked my idea of giving Ernie less chemo because he was a lot older now.

Ernie had to eat ice chips for 20 minutes before the injection of chemo and continue to eat ice chips for a total of one hour. This is to help the patient from having problems with mouth sores. Ernie did an excellent job with this. The nurse complimented him. When she was finished with this procedure, she asked him if there was anything else she could get him. Ernie responded, "I could use some de-icer." She laughed and said that was the first time she had ever heard that request.

The plan was for me to leave and drive back to Sheboygan at 7:00 p.m. We figured by then the traffic from people going to the Brewers game would be settled down. I got in the car and was just making the turn around the Marquette inter-change when this whole thing hit me. I started crying (this was really not a good place to be crying on this busy freeway.) The reality of the transplant hit me hard, and I was sobbing. I cried out to God saying, "It's too hard. It's too hard. It's just too hard, God." I knew there was no turning back now, as the dose of chemo was already injected into his body. My days of living with denial that Ernie would never have to go through another transplant were done, and I had to face reality. Then my prayers turned to pleading for God's help, begging Him with all my heart – "Please help him through this. Please, please help him, God." I knew God heard my prayer as immediately, I felt a peace come over me. I sensed God's presence and my eyes were dried. I got home safely feeling assured that God was going to get Ernie through the tough battle ahead. He would be there for us and everything would be alright. I went home and slept peacefully. In fact, I slept peacefully every night, feeling confident that God would see us through.

Our son Tim, flew in from Tennessee that first Friday with plans to stay until Monday. I picked him up at the Milwaukee airport, and we checked into a motel near to the hospital. Scott joined us for one night. Ernie was still doing very well and loved walking around in the unit which was set up so he could walk in a big circle around the large unit. We all walked with him and Scott decided the four of us should have our own Milwaukee Brewers' Sausage Race. Scott assigned each of us to be one of the sausages. Ernie and Tim were leading the way while Scott and I trailed behind. When we got to the last lap, I quickly snuck ahead of everyone so I could be declared the winner. Scott said, "Oh Mom, did you have to act like a hot dog?" He had told me earlier that I had to be the Chorizo. Oh yes, there were many times when we just took time to have a little fun. This was so important to keep our spirits up.

After our walk, we all went into the lounge and played some Cribbage, our favorite family game. One day that weekend, we asked if Ernie could go outside. There was a beautiful, sunny area with a pretty, stone water fountain, benches to sit on, and paths to walk on that we could see looking down from the window in Ernie's room. Ernie was told he could do this if he wore a mask. The next day we wanted to do the same thing, but were told that he wasn't supposed to be going outside. The staff working that day was quite surprised that Ernie had been given permission to do this the day before. The rule was that he was not allowed to leave the Bone Marrow Transplant unit.

We had a very nice family weekend together. We were also aware that sometime during the next week would be when Ernie's immune system counts would be down to nothing, and that's when the real battle for him would start. We had been told approximately which day that would begin – somewhere between the 6th through the 10th day after the transplant. Again, I really didn't want to focus in on this. I went to visit him almost every day. Family and friends offered to drive me, so this was very helpful. Day after day, I would get to the hospital and Ernie was up and dressed and looked pretty good. We always enjoyed our time together.

On the 8th day, visitors had to wear a mask in Ernie's room. That night he started to get diarrhea and said he was now quarantined. The next day he had a little trouble with diarrhea after eating his meals, but that was the only problem he encountered. He told me that they tested him for the next three days to make sure he was alright. Ernie did complain that the toilet paper was too rough and not friendly for people dealing with diarrhea.

The next time I visited, there was a cart with yellow gowns, blue rubber gloves, and pink masks in front of Ernie's door. Before I entered, I asked why it was there. I was told that anyone entering the room had to put on a clean set of each of the items. When we left the room, the complete set had to be discarded in Ernie's trash in his room. The carts were in front of all the patient's rooms now. The patients were at the point where every precaution needed to be taken to protect them from any germs, as they did not have an immune system to fight off anything. The large dose of chemo kills off all the stem cells. Then the good stem cells that were injected into Ernie needed to start to do their work. The hope is that they would continue to multiply to build up a fresh start of good stem cells. This process is slow and takes a long time to get the patient where it is safe for them to be functioning again outside of this hospital unit.

On day ten, I got to the hospital and found Ernie up and dressed – as usual. He was looking very good. He was still eating (not as much, but he was getting good nutrition). He had great color, didn't lose any hair, didn't get mouth sores, nausea, fever, or chills, or any of the normal symptoms of a Bone Marrow Transplant patient. The doctors and nurses were in total amazement. Everyone else was sick, but Ernie was doing so well. God was caring for him in a very special way.

The following weekend Jeff & Debbie and Scott and Debbi came for a visit. We were all dressed in the yellow, blue, and pink – gown, gloves, and mask. When Scott entered the room, he said, "Quack, Quack." Debbie decided to take a picture of the rest of us. Because the masks looked like a duck's bill, we all decided to say, "Quack, Quack, Quack, Quack", instead of "Cheese". I know, we are pretty silly once in a while. Again, we found time to find some humor in what was a pretty stressful time in our lives.

The doctors checked Ernie's mouth often to see if he had any mouth sores, and they always seemed shocked that he didn't get any. Ernie just told the doctor, "Of course I don't have any mouth sores, I ate all my ice." He was pretty proud of himself that he could do that as eating ice for one hour was not an easy task. He was told that doing this would help with mouth sores, but never did they say, or even believe that eating that ice would totally prevent him from getting any mouth sores.

I don't believe they ever had a Bone Marrow Transplant patient that got up every day, took a shower and got dressed, ate every meal, took walks around the unit, and sat up in a chair until bedtime. What they are used to seeing is very sick patients who don't have the strength to get out of bed and have to be fed I.V.'s for nourishment. They get so sick they can't keep any food down. We know the story, because this all happened to Ernie with his first transplant 11 years before. We all were expecting these things to happen again, but they never did.

Ernie was allowed to order his choice of foods for each meal from a menu he had been given. He was told to call the kitchen with his order a half hour before he wanted to be served. He never complained about the food until the second week he was there. He couldn't figure out why his food came later than usual. The hot foods were already cold, and the cold foods were warm. The usual person from the kitchen didn't deliver the food into his room anymore. Now the nurses and the doctors brought his food tray in. He asked one of the nurses if the other people were complaining about the food. She said, "No, they aren't complaining about the food, but that's probably because none of the other patients are eating." Then he knew, they must all be too sick to even eat. That was quite amazing. He was the only one of the 12 who was still eating. He found out later that the person from the kitchen wasn't allowed to come into his room, so the food just sat outside his door till one of the staff brought it in to him. At this same time, he was told that it would be best if he just stayed in his room and walked in there. Ernie wasn't very happy with this new rule, but he did what he was told.

On day 17, Ernie called me in the morning to tell me that he was told he could go home that day. Wow! We were quite shocked and very excited. He said we needed to meet with the nurse that afternoon for instructions before he was discharged.

This was awesome news as it was only 17 days. We had been told earlier that he had to be there at least three to three and a half weeks. Coming home? We had also been told he had to stay somewhere in the area for another two weeks after he was dismissed. I was elated that I wouldn't even have to try to convince them that I wanted him to come home instead of having to stay at Kathy's House. We had a hard time believing this was really happening. Thank You, Lord!

That afternoon, Ernie and I met with the nurse for instructions. While she was talking, I noticed a few small red spots on Ernie's arm. I asked what that was, and the nurse said it was just a little rash. She said she would put some Sarna lotion on it and give him some Benedryl before we left. She also said I should buy some Benedryl tablets when I got his other prescriptions, and he could take them as needed.

We got him packed up and headed back to Sheboygan. Home, Sweet Home! We were just thrilled how well he had gotten through what could have been a very tough battle. This second transplant was so much easier for him to get through. There just was no comparison to what he dealt with the first time around. God did help Ernie through this transplant. So many members of our family and so many friends were praying for Ernie, and we know he heard our prayers. When I was in doubt, He saw my tears and gave me peace that He would care for my husband. I was so grateful and thanked God for His incredible loving care.

**Only, at this point,
we did not know the rest of the story.**

After I settled Ernie in his comfortable recliner, I headed to the store to pick up his prescriptions. By the time I got back home, Ernie was telling me he needed some more Benedryl, as the rash seemed to be getting worse, and his skin was itching a lot. So I gave him the Benedryl.

It was time for supper, so I called him to come to eat. He said he wasn't hungry yet, so I sat down to eat alone.

Not long after, he said the itching was getting really bad. I told him he probably needed to call the doctors at Froedtert to see what we should do. They had sent a phone number for us to call if we had any questions. Ernie did call, and the doctor told him that he had to come right back to the hospital. We couldn't believe it. That was the last thing we wanted to do. I called our kids, Jeff and Debbie, and it was decided that Debbie would drive us back. By now, Ernie's skin looked terrible. It was very red with what looked like little pin pricks all over it. Ernie said the itching and burning of this strange looking rash was unbearable.

I didn't even have Ernie's suitcase unpacked, so I just put it back in the van, and we were on our way back to the hospital. The hour's drive back to Milwaukee was very tense. Later, Debbie had said she was praying that nothing would happen to Ernie while we were still traveling.

Ernie's Room #10 was still ready and open for him to go back into. This time, the room was not looking warm and inviting. His balloons, cards, and other decorations that had made the room look more cheerful were back at home. The room looked so bare and unwelcoming. The doctors came in to check out the rash and were puzzled by this. They really didn't know where it came from, and they also didn't know how to treat it. Debbie and I had to stay in the lounge just outside the unit. When it got pretty late, we needed to head back to Sheboygan as Debbie had to work the next day. Before we left, we poked our heads in Ernie's room to say "Good-bye". He looked so sad, and all he said was, "I feel so miserable."

That night, I could not control my tears. This was a real set-back. I spent my sleepless night praying and crying.

I was awakened the next morning by the phone ringing. It was Ernie. He told me to bring some more pajamas. He also told me he was waiting for the head dermatologist to come to check out his rash. He told me that his skin looked like a red alligator and that the rash covered his entire body. His skin burned and itched so badly, he said he couldn't stand it. He was told not to take a shower, so he was still in his pajamas. It was summer so his pajama was short-sleeved with short pants. The rash was clearly visible to him.

After his call, I went straight to my computer to put out a prayer request telling all our friends and relatives what had happened. I asked them all to pray for Ernie. I had been emailing Ernie's progress throughout his transplant experience. Everyone was keeping him in their prayers, and he had been doing exceptionally well.

About an hour later, the phone rang again. It was Ernie. This time he said, "You'll never believe what just happened. I was just sitting here in my room waiting for the doctors to decide what they were going to do about the rash, when all of a sudden, I had this warm feeling come through my body. It was a warm, flushing feeling that started at the top of my head and just continued on down through my whole body. I looked at my skin, and you won't believe this, the rash is completely gone."

Wow! Praise God! This was truly a miracle! Ernie told me he put his call light on. The nurse came to his room, and she was totally shocked. She said she was going to get the doctors. The doctors came in, and the doctor who had worked with Ernie throughout the night looked at him, let out a loud yell, and almost fell over backwards. He said to Ernie, "I want to see your whole body." He checked his body all over, and was totally amazed. His skin was beautiful and totally clear again. There was no sign of the strange rash. He asked Ernie what had happened and Ernie told him, "It must have been divine intervention." Yes, we know, that is exactly what it was. God had performed a miracle for all of them to witness. None of the medical staff could explain what had happened, but we can know. God totally healed Ernie and used this experience to let us all know that God is in control. God is real. God is all-powerful. God performs miracles. We all need to believe. Our God is an awesome God!

The doctors decided they wanted to keep Ernie another night just to make sure all was well. The next day he came home - (Day 19), and this time he was home for good. Some of the nurses were glad Ernie had come back because he had left the first time without them being able to give him a "good-bye hug". They also said they decided to give him, "The Best Trouper Ever Award". Every time he has been in the care of nurses and doctors, it seems like they all fall in love with him. He has a way of leaving his mark. He is "Unforgettable". My "One in a Million" man.

A week later, we had an appointment in Milwaukee with Dr. Hari. They took a lot of tests and everything looked good. The doctor started weaning Ernie off the meds he was still on. He was told to stay away from crowds and avoid getting a cold or flu.

The following week we had another appointment. The testing continued to look very good so more of his meds were taken away. Dr. Hari was so pleased with Ernie's progress. We were told he didn't have to come back for a month.

When we returned on July 23rd, Dr. Hari was full of smiles as he talked about Ernie's amazing transplant experience. Then he told us this story. The reason that they wanted to get Ernie out of the hospital early was because Ernie was the only patient that did not get the H1N1 (Swine) flu. All the other eleven transplant patients in that unit were extremely sick with that flu, and at that time, three of them had already died. He told us that it is pretty much impossible for Bone Marrow Transplant patients to live if they get the flu as their immune system is not functioning.

WOW, WOW, WOW, WOW, WOW, WOW!!! Ernie & I were totally shocked with this news. How great is our God! Believe me, when we walked out of that clinic, I think we were so in shock. I felt like a zombie. I felt like I was floating and my feet weren't even touching the ground. To think that God showed His amazing love and healing to Ernie, and allowed him to even go back into that hospital to perform still another miracle, and once again, let him come out of this hospital situation unscathed, this was just incredible. Ernie was the oldest patient in that crew of 12. Eleven of them were battling this deadly flu, and all twelve of their immune systems were totally wiped out from the chemo they all received. Three of the twelve had already died. This news was so shocking – to say the least!

How can we thank our gracious God? What words can describe His incredible love for us?

We will most likely never know if the other eight people made it. God knows. The staff at Froedtert knows. We prayed for them. My thoughts have wondered whether giving Ernie the 10% less chemo helped him. Was that why he didn't get as sick as the others did? One thing we do know is that God has blessed us with many prayer warriors. We have felt and have seen the power of prayer time and time again. We also know that God works in such mysterious ways, His wonders to proclaim. One thing is sure, we have felt His indescribable love for us in so many ways, and will be eternally grateful for His faithfulness to us.

It is now 2017, and this will be Ernie's 20th year since he was first diagnosed with cancer. Fifteen years more than the five years Dr. Matthews thought he would have. Dr. Hari told us he gives his first transplant patients only three years to live and second time transplants only half that time. Do the math.

God has been so good. The honor and the glory are to Him alone.

So often in my life I am reminded of the words of inspiration in the beautiful song entitled, 'God Will Take Care of You'. No matter what is going on in our lives, we have the assurance that God will take care of us. We may be tested, become dismayed, tired and weary, but we can find comfort and peace beneath His wings. I love to sing this song over and over again when I'm needing help. He will take care of you. Thank you, God, for your incredible love and care provided for us every day.

Dear Lord, Help us to put our trust in you always. Amen

"It Will Be An Adventure"

"It will be an adventure," she said. My sister Rachel, and I were having a farewell luncheon at City Streets Restaurant enjoying the beautiful view overlooking the city of Sheboygan and Lake Michigan. City Streets was located on the top floor of Sheboygan's tallest building which was called Security First National Bank at that time. In just a few days, my husband Ernie, our two youngest sons Todd and Scott, and I would be heading off to the new adventure. We were moving from Sheboygan, Wisconsin, to Jackson, Tennessee. Our son Tim, would be joining us in December after he completed his first semester of college at the U. W. Sheboygan Extension. Our son Jeff would be staying in Wisconsin to complete his senior year at U. W. Whitewater.

In July, 1983, Armira Leather Corporation announced that they would be closing their plant in Sheboygan. Ernie had been asked if he would be willing to transfer his employment to Armira's leather plant in Bolivar, Tennessee. We, along with 25 other Sheboygan families, had decided to make this move.

In August, Ernie and I had been flown to Jackson, Tennessee, to look for a new house. We were successful in finding a beautiful, brick-ranch, four-bedroom, three baths, living room, kitchen, dining room, family room, deck, two-car garage home. This would be our biggest and best home. It was awesome. We were so excited. The cost of homes in Tennessee were low compared to Sheboygan.

Armira took care of hiring movers, selling our old home, and all costs involved with making the move. We didn't have to do anything other than select and purchase our home in Tennessee.

Move in date was set for October 31, 1983. We stayed in a motel our last night in Sheboygan to make sure the movers had everything packed and were ready to roll. After they were out, we could clean up and lock the doors for the final time. The next morning Ernie, Todd, Scott, and I were headed to Tennessee for our new adventure.

We stayed one night at a motel in Jackson, and the next day we were ready to settle into our new home. The boxes were piled up high in all the rooms ready for us to start unpacking. Along with all this, we made sure we were ready. Yes, we knew that on our move-in day, the doorbell would be ringing a lot. It was "trick or treat" time. Even our adult neighbors were having a Halloween party. They all came over to say "trick or treat", and introduce themselves to us.

Scott was just under two weeks away from being two years old. All this confusion was a bit too much for him. A couple times he came to me crying. He told me he wanted to go home. I picked him up and held him and tried to explain that this was our new home now.

He said, "No, this is 'house', I want to go home by Jeff and Debbie and Grandma and Tim."

He came to me several times repeating these same words. After a while I realized that when we had come in August to purchase this house, I had taken pictures of all the rooms. When we saw our family and friends, I would always ask them if they wanted to see our house. From the pictures he had been looking at, Scott was identifying this place as "house".

Todd, who was fourteen at that time, was a big help with the move. We decided we should try to get Scott's bedroom set up as soon as possible so he would feel more at home.

Todd really accepted our move to Tennessee very well. He seemed to be ready for this adventure. It probably helped that he had an awesome bedroom waiting for him with his own beautiful private bathroom facility. It was so nice, (Todd's room became the guest bedroom whenever we had visitors).

The next Sunday, we visited the Presbyterian Church that had been recommended to us by our Sheboygan Pastor. We liked it. It was the type of worship we were used to in Sheboygan so we felt at home at this church.

I took Todd to Tigrett Junior High School the next Monday to get him enrolled and set up his class schedule. Everything went well except our disagreement as to whether he should take Band for one of his classes. He had been discouraged with Band in Sheboygan and didn't think he wanted to continue playing his trombone. I didn't give in. I told Todd he could always quit later if he really didn't like it, but I wanted him to at least try the Band here. He reluctantly agreed to do this.

We were not in Jackson, TN. very long when a woman from First Presbyterian Church came to visit me at our home. She introduced herself as Mary Catherine and gifted me with a home baked sweet bread. I had been up on a tall ladder with a mop trying to clean off the cathedral ceiling and paneled walls in our family room. Of course, I was excited about our beautiful new home, so I gave her a tour. We had a nice visit. It was easy to warm up to this sweet, motherly person, and I truly appreciated having a visitor from the church that we were planning to join.

Another surprise visitor came to our door from Jackson's Welcome Wagon. She brought a big basket full of gifts and certificates from many of the businesses in Jackson. This was awesome. After we were settled in, Scott and I got in the car, and we searched out these places to receive our free gifts. That was a good way to get me acclimated with the city. It also got me connected to Jackson's Newcomers Group.

Becky Chaplain, who became a best friend, lived in our sub-division. She heard I was interested in Newcomers, so she stopped by to encourage me to attend the next meeting with her. Becky had a son who was just a few months older than Scott. Soon after we met, we started baby-sitting for each other and often went on outings together.

There were other people coming to our door to welcome us as well. It didn't take me long to realize, we were living in the 'Bible Belt'. I had never, in my whole life, been asked so many times what church I attended. This was an important question. People living in Jackson wanted to know that you were connected to a church. My oldest sister Florence, had encouraged me to find a church as soon as possible when we got to Tennessee, so our church membership papers could be transferred from Sheboygan. This was a priority for me.

Tim flew to Jackson in December 1983, after he completed his first semester at the U. W. Sheboygan Extension. He lived with Grandma Meise for a couple months after we had moved. In Tennessee, he continued his schooling at Jackson State Community College.

We were only in Jackson a few months when Ernie started having problems with pain in his arm. He was so busy adjusting to his new place of employment that he just kept going. Eventually, the pain got so bad, he had to take the time to see a doctor. Our family doctor did some testing and then sent him to see an orthopedic surgeon. He was diagnosed with deterioration of a disc. The disc was fractured. He had to have surgery on his spine. We were told this was very serious, and he could wind up being paralyzed. This was pretty scary.

There was no family support for us here, - so I thought. As it turned out, Mary Catherine, the kind woman from our church, told me that she was going to come and sit with me through the surgery. She invited another lady from our church to join us. While we were waiting together, Mary Catherine told me that the other woman's husband was the anesthesiologist that was attending to Ernie, and the surgeon was also from our church. I was so grateful for their company and support. The surgery took more than two hours, but the results were very good. We were so grateful that Ernie had an excellent surgeon for this surgery. God was looking after us and provided for all our needs.

Ernie had to be off work for six weeks and was told to take it very easy at home.

It had already been planned that my good friend, Janel, and her husband, Barry, would be coming from Sheboygan to our house for a week. I knew Ernie would be returning home the day after they arrived, so I didn't tell them about the surgery. I didn't want them to worry. I thought this would actually be nice for Ernie to have company around to spend time with. Janel and Barry were loading up their car bringing lots of goodies that we had ordered. They had lots of special treats from Sheboygan that we were not able to purchase in Jackson. As it turned out, another friend Ann, from Sheboygan heard that Ernie had surgery. When Ann told Janel about this, she and Barry were concerned, but they also felt confident that I would have told them if they should not be coming. So they headed to our home, not certain about what they would find with Ernie's situation. As it turned out, it was so nice to have them with us. Barry and Ernie played cards and sat out on our deck to pass the time. We all had a wonderful, relaxing time, and we were so grateful for their visit. In fact, we had such a great time, they continued to come every year to stay with us for a week. It was always great fun for all of us.

Life in Tennessee was definitely different. Wherever we went, the minute we spoke, people knew we were not from the South. Many times I was asked where I was from. One time I asked the person asking where they thought I was from. She guessed, "Sweden". Yes, we definitely sounded like foreigners. Todd picked up a Southern accent pretty quickly. Being in school helped, I'm sure.

I found it interesting to compare the different terms we used. For instance – we got in a carpool with some of the neighbors where we took turns taking the kids to school. When one of the Mom's called me, she would say, "Would you like me to carry Todd to school today?" That sounded funny to me, but then I thought about what I would have said – "Would you like me to pick up Mike today?" When I thought about it, my words must have sounded just as funny to her.

In Tennessee, people would say, "Mike has to throw papers after school." We would have said, "Mike has to deliver papers after school." In our Tennessee neighborhood, parents drove their kids in the car and the papers were actually thrown out the car window onto the people's driveway.

Once I went to a luncheon for our Newcomers Group. We all had to bring a dessert or salad to pass. When I got to the event, a woman asked me what I had brought. I told her I brought bars.

She shouted, "WHAT?"

Becky, my friend smiled and told her, "She brought cookie bars".

I'm not sure what kind of a bar the woman thought I had in that pan. All I know is she was totally shocked when I said "Bars".

Ernie went to the Barber. He had asked the previous owner of our home for a recommendation for a good Barber in Jackson. While he was getting his hair cut, the Barber asked him how things were going with the move. Ernie told him that he was busy straightening up the garage. The Barber seemed shocked. He said, "Sir? I know that Mr. _____ was a very particular man. It's hard for me to believe that his garage was crooked or falling down." Ernie was just trying to tell him he had been putting things in place in the garage.

We had a lot to learn. At times we just had to chuckle.

Ernie and I received an invitation to a Christmas party at the home of Mary Catherine and her husband. They lived a short distance outside of the city. When we found their home, I was amazed at the large amount of property they had. Later, we realized that some of the buildings housed their hired servants. This was a new experience for us. There were many elite guests at the party. Mary Catherine, as always, was very kind and gracious to us. After being entertained and served by their hired staff, I did realize that I probably shouldn't have asked her earlier for her recipe of the good bread that she had brought to our house as a welcoming gift. Now I understood why she never gave me the recipe. We were in a different place, on an adventure, and I had a lot to learn. I felt so grateful that Mary Catherine was always kind and receptive to who I was.

The very first summer we were in Tennessee, I signed up to teach Vacation Bible School. Our church ran V.B.S. eight days straight. That was not an easy task, but we did it. I continued to teach V.B.S.

every summer we were in Tennessee. This was something I always loved doing in Sheboygan, and I loved that I could do this in Jackson as well. Scott was able to attend the classes, and Todd volunteered to be a helper.

I also got involved with a Women's Bible Study group at our church shortly after we got to Tennessee. After a while, I took on the leadership position as the Treasurer of this group.

After our first summer in Jackson, I enrolled in a ceramics class through the Recreation Department. I loved this class. We purchased our own slip, poured this into the molds and went through the whole process of making the ceramic piece. My favorite project was making my Nativity Set. As I painted each piece, I felt so inspired. I sometimes stayed up very late at night, and didn't want to stop painting. As I completed each piece, I set it on the mantle above our fireplace. Later, Ernie made me a wooden stable. To this day, I love bringing this all out at Christmas time. My family has a hard time believing that I made this. I do know where the inspiration came from. It was so special.

The Newcomers Group in Jackson was very active. I enjoyed this group. I met a lot of women who were in the same situation as I was. My life became filled with many opportunities of good things to do. I remember the first Christmas party we had together. We were singing some Christmas songs. I couldn't believe it, that when we sang the song, "I'll be home for Christmas", there were so many women in this group crying. I felt grateful that all of my children, our future daughter-in-law Debbie, and Ernie's mother would be with us in Jackson for Christmas.

I was glad Scott was still at home with me when we moved to Tennessee. We could go just about everywhere together, and we certainly were enjoying our adventure. Ernie had to travel 30 minutes to Bolivar to work each day and generally he wasn't home until suppertime. He really never got to know the city of Jackson very well, but I did.

Our church started a women's volleyball team which I joined. We competed in a league with other churches and had our own gym in one of our three church buildings. I'll never forget one game where I was serving and the other team could not return the ball. I kept on and kept on serving until I was almost feeling guilty. We were playing against the St. Mary's Catholic Church team, and two of my friends from Sheboygan were on that team. When it got to where we needed one more point to win that game, I messed up. Of course, with only one more point needed, we still did go on to win that game. We actually took first place in the league a couple years, and second place another year. I really enjoyed having this opportunity.

The most difficult thing for me living in Tennessee was the heat and humidity that we had to deal with for at least three to four months in the summer. Spring and Fall were absolutely beautiful. Red Bud trees, Magnolia trees, huge Azalea bushes, and so many more beautiful plants and trees were things I hadn't seen the beauty of in Wisconsin. To me, it just seemed like God took His paint brush and painted a beautiful masterpiece in that city. I was totally in awe at the beauty of God's creation in Jackson, Tennessee. I felt like I was in a spectacular, miraculous wonderland. I talked with excitement about it so much that Ernie would continually remind me that I had better be keeping my eyes on the road when I was driving. I did need to hear that warning. The huge pine cones on our Southern Pine trees in our backyard were awesome to decorate with. To this day, I am enjoying centerpieces I put together when we lived in Jackson.

Scott went to a morning pre-school at a Lutheran church when he was four. He was so ready for school. Todd was a great mentor for Scott, and was sitting Scott on his lap teaching him on his computer when Scott was only three years old. He taught him Math while sitting at the kitchen table by using wrapped candy. I took Scott to the library and read to him every night. He was reading books before he went to kindergarten. It was amazing how quickly he learned everything he was taught.

While Todd was helping Scott with academics, Tim was helping Scott with sports. They played a lot of whiffle ball baseball in our family room. When the weather was nice, they played baseball in our backyard. When Scott was four, he joined a pee-wee league baseball team. It was so hot in Jackson, the little kids played in shorts, tee shirts, and baseball hats. Scott knew very well which direction to run after he hit the ball. Some of his team mates ran in the direction of third base instead. They apparently did not have a big brother teaching them the game at home. It didn't take Scott very long to see our Jackson house as his home.

As I said, we did have a lot to learn. We came from Sheboygan, Wisconsin where the population was about 50,000 people when we left. When we moved to Jackson, Tennessee, their population was a bit less. While we lived in Jackson we saw this city grow. Many transplants settled there. Sheboygan had very few black families when we left in 1983. There were a good number of Hispanic and Hmong families in Sheboygan.

When we moved to Jackson, this was quite different. At Tigrett Junior High School, where Todd was first enrolled, the ratio was 60% White and 40% Black. When he went to Jackson Central Merry High School, the ratio was 70% Black and 30% White. Before the end of the year, this ratio changed somewhat due to the high rate of mostly Black dropouts. Many White families had moved to the North end of the city so their children could go to Jackson's North High School, which was predominantly White. Other families enrolled their kids in a parochial high school that was quite expensive to attend and all students there were White. We read in the Jackson Newspaper about the "White Flight". This was all new to us.

I met a beautiful black woman who became a very good friend of mine through the Newcomers Group. Ella truly was beautiful, both inside and out. She told me that her dad was a Baptist Minister, and her mom was a school teacher. Her parents lived in another state. Ella was in Jackson with her husband David, and their two boys. We connected right from the start.

Ella started attending First Presbyterian Church where we were members. After a while, she started to sing in the choir. She had a beautiful voice and she told me she really loved the music at our church. She was also very gifted in playing the piano. She had been coming to our church for some time. One day I asked her why she didn't join the church. I encouraged her to do this. Shortly after that, she did become a member.

There was only one big problem. Up until then, I believe, there had never been any black families belonging to this church. I'm sad to say that for some of the church members, this seemed to be a big problem that Ella's black family had been allowed to become members. I truly had no idea this would be a problem with some people, but to be honest with you, I really didn't care.

At one of our women's meetings, one of the women very sarcastically said to me, "Your friend is here, why don't you go over and talk with her?"

My immediate response was to be excited and happy. I said, "Oh Ella's here, good." I did go right over to spend time with her.

Ella was also in my Women's Bible Study at church. I believe the great majority of the families from our church were extremely wealthy. When I went to their homes, they had very big, beautiful homes and many of them had hired black servants. This was all new to me, but I wasn't a part of this group or a part of the church to be looking at our differences. To me, we were all equal in God's sight, and I felt content that God had sent me there to be a part of a different culture for a reason.

Ella, and her friendship, will always be treasured in my heart. At one of our women's Bible study meetings, just when the hostess had started her closing prayer, I felt the top of my wedding ring and realized my diamond was missing. After the prayer, I immediately told Ella. She jumped up and said she would go out and search the car while I back-tracked where I had walked in that home. While I was searching, I mentioned to several of the women that I had lost my diamond. Several of them told me of their same experience. They also shared that all of their diamonds had been found.

Ella came back inside after searching the car. When she walked into the living room, she spotted something sparkling on the carpet under a chair near to where we had been sitting. It was my diamond. She found it. What a blessing! The diamond that I wear has some extra special meaning now, because of my treasured friend, Ella. She is truly a gem.

Until recently, I had never thought about something that happened between Ella and myself, because it really didn't mean anything to me at the time. When I took my turn to host the Women's Bible Study Group at our home, Ella asked if she could help me. I said, "Sure that would be great." Ella stepped right up to my pretty, silver coffee and tea service that I had just received from my siblings at our 25th anniversary party. Ella chose to serve the coffee and tea to all of us. When I think of it now, I think – How Humbling!

I am so grateful for the Christian education that my family provided for me at home, at Sheboygan Christian School, and at church. I was grateful that as a child, I learned this song: "Jesus Loves the Little Children, ALL the children of the world, Red and Yellow, Black and White – They are PRECIOUS in HIS sight. Jesus Loves the little children of the world." Jesus loves us all. We are all precious to Him. He has commanded us to love one another, just as He has loved us. God had prepared my heart and had given me knowledge that I needed to live out no matter where He sent me. I'm so grateful that I had the opportunity to choose to do this.

We made many trips back to Sheboygan. One year we traveled back five times. It was a long 12 hour trip, but it was always wonderful going back to see family and friends. There were no seatbelt laws at that time, so Scott had the entire back seat to play with his toys, stand up, sit down, or when he was tired, he could lie down to take a nap. He was a great little traveler. He even put up with his dad's CD's playing polka music for all those hours.

Special events that we traveled back for were Jeff's graduation from U.W. Whitewater. He received a B.A. degree in Marketing in 1984. Jeff and Debbie were married in August 1984. They planned a wonderful 25th Anniversary celebration for us in Sheboygan inviting many friends and relatives in 1985. They even hired a band so we could dance. This was really special as we didn't even have a band for our wedding. Also, Jeff and Debbie's first child, our first grandson Ryne was born in 1986.

Ryne's expected birthdate was overdue, and on June 6, he was finally born. We already knew that we had to go back to Sheboygan in two weeks after Ryne's birth. When we got the call that Ryne had arrived, we decided we would just wait to see him when we went back to Sheboygan in two weeks. We hung up the phone after we received the good news of his birth. I went back to my work at the kitchen sink and started having tears, and Ernie was sitting in the family room in tears. All of a sudden, he said, "Let's go." He didn't have to tell me that twice. We immediately started packing our bags, and early the next morning we headed off to see our first grandson. We couldn't wait to hold him.

The trip to Sheboygan was challenging. After only two hours of driving, Ernie told me he felt sick and wondered if we should just get a motel and maybe go back home the next day. With all my heart, I didn't want to do this. I told him I could drive awhile, and he could go in the back seat and rest. This was interesting because I had never driven even one block on any of our trips to Sheboygan. I was determined, I could do this. After Ernie slept a couple hours, he thought he could drive some more. That didn't last long. I got back in the driver's seat. By the time we got to Milwaukee, I was getting extremely tired. I was really fighting to keep my eyes open. Generally, I am the car sleeper. At that point, Ernie was able to drive the last hour. I immediately went to the hospital when we got to Sheboygan, and Ernie went right to bed. We had made plans to stay with his mother on this visit. After another day, Ernie was feeling better, so he did get to see Ryne at the hospital. This was so special. It was official. We were now Grandpa and Grandma Meise. We were so proud.

We were only in Tennessee for a little over four years. Armira Leather in Bolivar, Tennessee, where Ernie was employed had been taken over by another person. Ernie, and some of his co-workers in management were asked to invest in the company. We had to come up with $4,000.00. Not long after, the Union went on strike and the new person in charge made the decision to shut down the plant. Ernie did get his investment money back, but he no longer was employed. Most of the employees in supervision were given a pay-out. Ernie was told he would get the same. After a short time, he was informed that he was one of a few that would receive a pension. We have been very fortunate to receive this.

Ernie looked for employment in the Jackson area, but nothing was coming up. Fortunately, he was offered a job at Tecumseh in Sheboygan Falls, Wisconsin, just before Armira had closed. The plant in Tennessee would be closing in November. He would start at Tecumseh in February.

At the time we realized the plant in Bolivar was closing, I was still the Treasurer of our church women's group. I had to turn over the books to have them audited by a man from our congregation. I received word later complimenting me for the neat, accurate job I had done with the books. Along with this came a special "Thank You" for my service.

I was also on a committee at church working to select members to become Elders and Deacons. The committee had voted for me to become a Deacon, even though I told them, I most likely would have to move because Ernie was losing his job. I guess they had high hopes that I could stay.

At our last women's meeting at church, Mary Catherine sought me out. She expressed how sorry she was that I had to be leaving. We had a very good relationship right from the start, and I was so grateful that she had been there for me. My mother had died just a few months before we left for Tennessee. She was like a mother to me, and she always accepted me for who I was. I truly felt her love.

Mary Catherine said to me, "You have certainly left your mark on this church."

This was a very special compliment coming from her. Most of all, I was grateful that God did use me, my life, and my service to bless others while I was 650 miles away from what had been home. I was different. God blessed me with an open mind that was willing to learn and be accepting of any differences. He also gave me a dedicated, determined heart that was destined to be teaching no matter where He sent me.

I went back to that church when we visited our kids Tim and Todd, a couple years after we had moved. We knew a new Pastor was just coming in at the time we left Jackson, so we hadn't met. After the service, we shook hands, and I told the new Pastor that I was visiting, but that we had been members of that church. He asked me my name, and when I told him, he said, "Oh, I'm so happy to meet you. I've heard a lot about you." I guess I did leave my mark on that church. Thanks be to God!!

I had also taken on the position of Secretary at my friend, Becky's church in August shortly before we had to leave. Her husband Carl, was the Pastor at Grace Presbyterian Church. It was very hard for them to let me go. They kept hoping Ernie would find employment in the area so we could stay. We had become very good friends. Besides being their church secretary, I also took care of their three children a lot. Scott and Ellis became pretty good friends. We knew we would be leaving special friends behind.

Before we left Tennessee, we decided to take Scott to Disney World in Florida. Scott was now six years old and in kindergarten. He was doing so well in school and was given special privileges because of his reading and math skills. His teacher was sad to see him go.

Tim had completed his first two years of college education at Jackson State Community College, and then he transferred to Union University. Union was located in Jackson, so Tim could continue to live at home. This was beneficial for him. He was our one and only son who graduated from college debt free. With free lodging, meals, scholarships, and a part-time job, this worked out well for him. Tim graduated with honors with a B.A. in Accounting. He had obtained a good accounting job in Jackson just before he graduated, so Tim was doing well and wanted to stay in Tennessee when we moved back to Wisconsin.

How was Todd's experience in Tennessee?

One of the best things that ever happened to Todd was that he did give in to my persuasion for him to take the Band class at Tigrett Junior High. Tigrett's Band took top honors in the state that year. The Band was so good that they cut a record. The Band Director won Best Director Honors in their competition in Nashville. It was an incredible experience for Todd. He loved it.

After Todd completed a good year at Tigrett Junior High, we needed to check out where he would be attending high school. Todd's high school years at Jackson Central Merry were quite interesting. Just 12 years before we moved to Tennessee, Jackson Central High School – for white students, and Merry High School – for black students, had been court ordered to be integrated. The two high schools were on opposite sides of a road – both were set back quite a distance from the roadway. A very long walkway was constructed up above the road for the students to cross over to get from one school to the other. The West Campus - Jackson Central H.S. had air conditioning. The East Campus - Merry H.S. did not. On the very hot, humid school days, only floor fans were available at the East Campus that had originally been called Merry H.S. It was very hard to stay awake under these conditions. Certain subjects were taught at the West Campus, and others were taught at the East Campus, so all students had to attend classes that would take them to both buildings. I remember attending an open house and was quite amazed at all the dreary green painted rooms with nothing colorful at all on any of the walls at the older Merry High School building. It was quite depressing. What a contrast to what we had experienced in Sheboygan.

Another huge difference for us was the Physical Education program. The high school program did very little in this area. Todd did things like play ping-pong. The students never exercised to the point where they got heated up and sweaty. That was probably a very good thing, as there were **no** showers.

Todd did continue on with awesome music experiences in the band at Jackson Central Merry High School. In high school the band competed in three different areas – Concerts, Parade Marching, and Football Field performances. They had awesome looking band uniforms, and they did a phenomenal job. Music in Tennessee was more than we could have ever expected. This was truly a blessing for Todd. At times, Todd was asked to play in churches with a brass quartet. We were all pretty surprised that the kids were compensated for doing this.

The year we left Jackson, Todd had just started his Freshman year at Jackson State Community College. Neither Todd nor Tim wanted to leave Jackson, so they decided to stay together when we had to return to Wisconsin. They stayed in our home for several months until it was sold, and then they moved to an apartment.

After Todd went to Jackson State Community College, he went to Union University to get his Bachelors of Social Work Degree graduating with honors. (He also played his trombone in Union's

Band.) From there he went to The University of Memphis to get his Master's Degree in Counseling.

For Ernie, Scott, and me, our adventure in Tennessee was over. God was taking us back to Sheboygan to continue on with the rest of the story, called life. After living with Jeff, Debbie, and Ryne for ten weeks, we found our next home to settle into at 2611 N. 13th Street in Sheboygan.

Celebrating our 40th Anniversary

July 9, 2000

Because Ernie had been diagnosed with Multiple Myeloma Bone Marrow Cancer in 1997, and had been given just five years to live, we decided to have a big celebration for our 40th Wedding Anniversary. Our four sons and two daughter's in law worked hard to put on an awesome event.

Our son, Todd, and daughter-in-law, Debbie, put together a video highlighting our dating years and the 40 years that followed. One of the things Todd asked both Ernie and me to do was to write our stories of how we met.

Ernie was a senior at Sheboygan North High School when we met and was 18 years old. This was his story.

HOW WE MET

High school basketball was into full swing in late 1956. North played a game that I attended with two friends, Ron and Bill. After the game, it was "business as usual", which meant "cruising" 8th Street looking for girls.

On this night, Ron was driving and spotted three girls walking near the 8th Street bridge. As was the custom, we asked if they wanted a ride. They continued to walk, and Ron continued to drive along side of them for at least 50 feet.

Next thing, the three girls piled into the back seat.

The following night, we three guys tracked down the whereabouts of the "pickups" with the help of what Bill called, "his girl".

Judie was baby-sitting at a home on Huron Avenue in an upstairs unit. Her girlfriends and we three guys went to visit. We were not there very long, and the home owners came home. As we exited the stairs going down, we explained our visit as various home maintenance personnel.

The next weekend, again with the help of Bill's girl, we "just happened" to meet again at the YMCA dance. Our relationship continued on from here.

My friends Ron & Bill dated the other girls for a while, but soon after they were back to "cruising", looking for another pickup.

I, (Judie) was a sophomore at Central High School, and I was 15 years old. This was my story.

HOW WE MET

It was a Friday night, and I was walking home from a dance at the YMCA with two of my girlfriends.

I lived on the South side, so we were walking down 8th Street and were near the bridge when a car with three guys in it pulled up and asked us if we wanted a ride. One of my friends immediately said, "Sure". My other friend was a bit more hesitant, and I said, "No, I'm not getting into that car." After a lot of persuasion, I reluctantly made the choice to ride along (my other option would have been to walk home alone).

After getting into the car, the guys told us they were from Milwaukee. I immediately made up excuses why I needed to get home right away. I even lied and told them I would go with them the next night, (I knew I had to baby-sit, and they would never be able to find me again). I was so scared that I told them to drop me off at a place that was a block away from my house so they wouldn't know where I lived.

The next night, Saturday, I did go to baby-sit for my niece and nephew, Nancy & David Te Winkel. The doorbell rang, and in walked my two girlfriends along with the three guys. The guys had it all figured out that Ernie was the one who would get me. I told them they needed to leave. After they were there just a short time, my niece, Nancy, called out that their mom & dad were home. The guys and my girlfriends left quickly, and as they passed my sister and brother-in-law Lois and Carl on the way out, Ernie introduced himself as the plumber, and one of the other guys said he was the electrician.

The next week, on Friday, I made my weekly trip to the YMCA for the dance. While dancing with my girlfriend to Jitterbug music, I was tapped on the shoulder. I turned around and saw Ernie. I was so frightened, I took off as fast as I could across the dance floor pulling my friend along with me. I was scared stiff of this guy, who I still thought was from Milwaukee.

That evening, I found out who he really was. Ernie was a senior at Sheboygan North High. I was also told that he was an "all right" guy. I felt a lot better about this, and when he asked if I wanted a ride home that night, I did accept the offer. In 1957, we began to date regularly. In 1959, we became engaged, and in 1960, we were married.

Todd read our stories to our guests who were invited to Klemme's Wagon Wheel for our special celebration and dinner.

Jeff offered the opening prayer and read scripture from I Corinthians 13.

Debbie and Lisa, our daughters-in-law, arranged for us to dance to Nat King Cole's song – Unforgettable.

Tim put together a game entitled, "Who Wants to be a Meisenaire". Tim's wife, Lisa, assisted him with this. Guests were chosen to be the contestants. The contestants were asked questions that helped everyone learn more about Ernie and me. The money they won by answering the questions right was donated to Ernie and me. It amounted to a little over ten dollars. Everyone had a lot of fun with this game.

Scott put together a presentation – "Defining Ernie & Judie Meise" – aka Mom & Dad. Scott's presentation included words that all four of our sons came up with that defined Ernie and me. This is what Scott presented:

Who is Judith Meise aka Mom?

She is caring.

Whenever we need a shoulder to lean on, Mom is there. She always has the doors of communication open. She is available to listen to our problems, offer us simple, but valuable insight when it is so desperately needed, (and) she did other special things such as reading us bedtime stories. She has a genuine care for our problems which leads to her next trait.

She is compassionate.

Mom is the one who always has the time to help someone in need. She has given much of her life to helping others. She is truly concerned about the well-being of others. (She is) A true humanitarian. She has peace in her heart, and it is obvious that she has been trying to make others have peace in their hearts as well.

She is supportive.

If you don't believe in yourself, she will believe for you. (She is) Always an optimist. She won't point out a person's faults and make unfair judgments. She'll search for your positive side, and make you feel good about what you have accomplished. In her soft, but effective voice, she commands encouragement.

She is thoughtful.

Mom is the one who will remember to send out those cards and gifts to others at special times. She'll be more than happy to go out of her way to make sure your life is more enjoyable.

She is a servant.

Mom never had a cushy desk job or any steady career. It is obvious that she has a lot of time on her hands, right? Wrong! She cooks, cleans everything in sight, washes clothes, irons clothes, takes care of her children, grandchildren, and husband, and she also finds time to volunteer. We should have bought a cape for you that says "supermom" on it. Jeff put it nicely by saying, "Mom did many different things for many different people throughout her life. She has been involved in so many things that I can't even begin to mention them all. The bottom line is she's been very busy." Right now, Mom works with Rainbow Kids, leads a women's Bible study, and helps out with a co-dependency group. Even though she isn't technically employed by some business, she has managed to work many hours for the Lord as well as for the family. Keep up the good work (Mom). No complaints here!

Also, Mom is beautiful.

One night when I was younger, I had just finished watching the conclusion of the Miss America pageant, and I was disappointed with the winner. I went to express my concern to my mom, while she was engaging in one of her favorite past times – ironing, of course. I told her that she should have been Miss America. It didn't matter that she was 40 plus years old. It truly is hard to miss my mom's vibrancy. I will always remember my mother smiling. Her heart and soul are truly beautiful. In my opinion, Mom, Miss America has got nothing on you.

Finally, she is gracious.

My Mom doesn't complain about her state in life. She doesn't envy other people's possessions. To her, the rusty, blue Pontiac that she drives is a Mercedes. Today she sits here after 40 years – content.

Mom, you're number one – you always will be! Congratulations! I hope to have my picture next to yours one day by some of the words that define who you are to us. Oh, I forgot to mention..... my khaki pants never have any wrinkles. In conclusion, you're awesome, Mom.

Scott's presentation continued on with words that our four sons came up with that defined their dad.

Where does Ernie Meise's aka Dad's picture belong in the dictionary?

He is loyal.

Obviously, he is here today after 40 years, but he also stuck with polka music. As you may or may not know, polka music is not cool, but my dad has never been a conformist. He also has always been a Chicago Cubs baseball fan. For those who know baseball or sports in general, the Chicago Cubs are bound to set a new record of futility. It has been over a century since the Cubs have won a championship. This is the longest drought in any professional sport, nevertheless, he remains loyal. Also, it is obvious who my dad will vote for on election day, because he always stands by those democrats. Scandals or no scandals!

He is the chef.

You may think that you had a great Fourth of July meal, but it was nothing compared to the BBQ ribs I got. My dad said to me, "There will come a time when you wish that you would've known how to make meat like this, but I'll be dead and buried before that time." For those who have dined at the Meise household, you know that my dad takes supper time seriously as evidenced by his "fry out" skills. Dad, your children's stomachs thank you for all those great meals.

Being the chef and supplying great meals without an outrageous restaurant bill implies that my dad is generous.

His kids may confuse him for a bank at times, but he is there whenever one of us kids comes across a time of financial burden. He is willing to give when there is a need. He has made many donations of food, clothing, and money. I probably never mentioned to him that his contribution of pennies this past Christmas helped our class in homeroom win the penny war for charity. We got pizza – so thanks, Dad!

Next, he is the super superintendent.

He is a leader – with his exact and effective speeches. He is confident when given control. He didn't need a degree from a prestigious university in political science or business administration. His understanding of people qualified him to lead. He knew what people expected from government, therefore, he was able to manage successful campaigns. He knew how to do things right, consequently, he went through a series of promotions. Aside from work and politics, he has kept four sons in line. Let me tell you Dad, that you have done a super job overseeing our lives.

Dad didn't become a leader overnight. He had to work for it. Which leads to his next trait.

He is a hard worker.

He preaches the value of hard work and practices it as well. Dad follows the philosophy that a little hard work hasn't killed anybody and there are no handouts in life. He has not been afraid to spend a little extra time to make sure that the job was done correctly. In order to advance in life, he chose the path that involved a strong work ethic. Success did not come to Ernie Meise, but the other way around. He is, as he says, a graduate from the school of hard knocks. His devotion to his family and work has convinced his children that he should be the employee of the month, every month. Dad, your children are trying to adopt your anti-laziness lifestyle, but it will be difficult to top the teacher.

If I didn't mention the next characteristic, I wouldn't be talking about Ernie Meise.

He is the king of thrift.

Master of budgeting. Mister Practical. Ernie Meise is a notorious coupon shopper. He has left his legacy of always trying to get the most out of a dollar. "I won't buy it unless I have a coupon," he'll often say to us. If any of you have visited our basement, you may have thought that we were preparing for Y2K. If there was an apocalypse, our basement would be the hot spot in town. His ideology about saving money may have led to some radical practices such as, making his sons all go through the checkout at the supermarket on "limit one per customer coupon days," however, he has taught us all how to spend money wisely.

Finally, Dad is assertive.

For those of us who have dined with Ernie at a restaurant, you know that the service and food better be good, or else. Dad is not afraid to "kindly" tell someone that he has received "second place" service and food, but in all honesty, he is just trying to get what he wants, and there is nothing wrong with that. It is evident today, after 40 years that Dad got what he wanted in his marriage. It is obvious to everyone that his wife did not take "second place". Thank God!

It just so happens that you, Dad, are also number one along with Mom. We, your kids, couldn't have asked for a better father, and by the way, we have forgiven you for having to listen to your polkas. In conclusion, I want you both, Mom and Dad, to enjoy life together as you have in the past. Congratulations!

Scott received a standing ovation for his presentation. He worked hard on this. When he was busy typing his speech, he told me I was not allowed to come into our office area. He didn't want me to see what he was preparing. He told me he wanted this to be an A+ paper, because I was an A+ Mom. What an awesome compliment.

Our four sons and two daughters-in-law put together an incredible 40th Anniversary Celebration for Ernie and me. At the end of the party, many of our friends and relatives complimented us on what a great job our kids had done to make this celebration so special. Some of them said they wanted our kids. I told them I would never trade our kids for anything in this world. Ernie and I are so proud of them all and love them very much. We have been blessed. God has been so good to our family.

For unto us a Child is born – unto us a Son is given.

Our Christmas Gift – Year 2000

(This Christmas letter was sent to our relatives and friends December 2000).

For over a year, I (Judie) had been thinking about buying a coffee table for our living room. Recently, my husband, Ernie joined me in the search. We always came home thinking that what we saw wasn't just right, or it cost too much. My favorite was an oval, cherry wood table that I had seen at the J.C. Penney's Store. It was now sold.

After getting my hair cut and a permanent at Penney's Salon this week Wednesday, I wandered into the furniture department. I thought maybe now that the store was closing, I could find a good table that we could afford. At the farthest end of the department, I spotted a tightly wrapped oval shaped package. I found a clerk to ask what was inside the package. She opened the package, and I was amazed to see that it looked like the table I had always wanted. The clerk told me they didn't have this ready for sale, and a price wasn't on it yet. She read the tag and went off to get a price for me. Her efforts were in vain, and I was told to come back later.

Another clerk, who was talking on the phone, held up a finger to signal me to wait for her. She told me she could help me. So, again, we went back to the wrapped table lying on the floor. I was given permission to take a better look at the table. The clerk was called away to help another customer. I opened the package and saw a flaw on the end of the table, but felt okay about this, as the store-closing discounted price still looked pretty good to me.

Then another clerk came to help me, and she told me that these items came from Milwaukee and were all badly damaged. She tried to warn me that this would not be a good sale, but my desire to get this table could not be swayed.

After an exchange of not-too-pleasant words between the two clerks, as to who was going to get my sale, I proceeded to pick up the table. The clerk offered to carry it for me several times, but I insisted that I was okay. I could carry it. So my heavy, but precious treasure was carried to the cash register and paid for.

I could hardly wait to get home to tell Ernie that I had found the table I wanted.

The two of us immediately put the legs on the table and set it upright. Then came the fun. After dusting off the table top, I proceeded to bring out the items that would decorate our new table.

Just the day before, I had received a big, scented, three-wick candle from a friend, Mary. This was a gift from her for my being her Bible study leader at church. Next, out came a box that had been in my closet for the last six months. It held a beautiful crystal bowl on a pedestal, a 40th anniversary gift from our friends, Janel & Barry. The candle fit perfectly in the bowl with room around the edges for the Christmastime decorative potpourri that I had purchased in Jackson, Tennessee that fall. A white doily that had been packed away in a drawer was set under the bowl, and it all looked so beautiful, just perfect. I placed two tall candles alongside of the arrangement, and I felt so pleased.

After I finished, I sat down to admire the beautiful addition to our home. The light from the bay window in our living room reflected on the top of the table, and many scar marks were exposed. I was quite amazed that I had not seen them before. It was obvious that this table had not been taken care of. I thought about people in my life who would have taken that table right back to the store and demanded a refund. This was far from perfect.

Then I was reminded of the words Ernie had read on the bill, "ALL SALES ARE FINAL." Still, I felt content. There was something special about that table.

Friday was cleaning day, and I brought out some special wood lotion that I hadn't used in years. I gently rubbed the lotion on the new table. It seemed to shine so beautifully, and I felt so happy.

Saturday morning, I sat down on the couch in the living room to relax and have a cup of coffee, and there it all was – OUR CHRISTMAS GIFT.

First, I saw the large candle. There were three wicks in that candle that reminded me of – God the Father, Jesus His Son, and the Holy Spirit. THREE IN ONE. The crystal bowl and white doily reminded me of His purity and holiness. In the potpourri, I saw our journey in life, with all the hills and valleys that we travel through. I looked at the table with all its scar marks and flaws, and this reminded me of us, His children, - FAR FROM PERFECT.

As I reflected on all that was before me, I was reminded of the true Gift of Christmas. I remembered that Jesus came to take me home. He carried me alone. I was not too heavy for Him. He paid the price for me. Now I belong to Him. He purchased me even though He knew I was not perfect. That didn't matter to Him. He knew I was scarred. He knew I had many blemishes. He could see them all. He knew that there were times that I had been wounded and even abused by others. I remembered that He promised that He will always care for me. He will take me in His hands and gently soothe my wounds with His anointing oil. He will cover me with His love.

In His eyes, I will always look beautiful. The two candles reminded me of myself and my friends. I was reminded that we need to stand tall, and be strong. In my heart, I felt the importance that we need to receive our light from God, and that we need to share the story of His gift of love with all those we know.

As the tears flowed from my eyes, I whispered, "THANK YOU, GOD, FOR YOUR INDESCRIBABLE GIFT OF CHRISTMAS."

Ernie, Scott, and I wish each of you, our special relatives and friends, a Blessed Christmas and a Happy, Healthy New Year!

II Corinthians 9:15 (NIV) "THANKS BE TO GOD FOR HIS INDESCRIBABLE GIFT!"

NOTE: When my friend Mary read my Christmas letter, she was amazed. The Christmas gift she had originally purchased for me was a darling wooden decoration with three angels. The morning of our Bible study Christmas party, Mary frantically searched her house to find this gift. Running out of time, she was led to the large candle with three wicks. She was disappointed she couldn't find the angel gift, but decided she needed to give me the candle instead. This is so amazing. I love how God works, so mysteriously - His wonders to perform. God did allow Mary to find the angels later. Mary presented me with this gift as well on Christmas Eve and told me her story.

Where Do You Work?

Part of the definition of the word "job" is – Tasks, Chores, & Duties. In my mind, this could include a variety of things.

Where do you work? I wonder how many times I've been asked that question. Now that I am retired, the question is – "Where did you work?"

I have met some people who were employed at the same place for 40 to 50 years. That was not the case in my life. The longest time I spent anywhere was with Rainbow Kids, Inc. where I took on the position of being the Director. I served with Rainbow Kids for almost 25 years before I retired. Many of my hours were volunteered.

At a pretty young age, I started babysitting for my nieces and nephews. Often times I just volunteered my time. Sometimes my compensation would be a candy bar or an ice cream or a Popsicle treat. When I started babysitting for compensation, I received 25 cents an hour. I loved it when I could get in four hours of babysitting. That would mean I had earned a dollar, and with that dollar I could buy three yards of material, a zipper, and some thread. One dollar was enough money for me to make myself a new skirt. I loved to sew. I still remember some of the pretty plaid skirts I made during my teen years.

When I was a High School Senior, I was hired by Certified Public Accountant, Lloyd Bergset. I started out working part-time hours after school and weekends. After graduation, I worked full-time doing secretarial work. I typed a whole lot of tax forms. Occasionally,

I took short-hand and typed letters for my boss. My rate of pay was $1.00 an hour. This was a pretty boring job where I had to type a whole lot of numbers which was not a favorite thing to do.

Less than a year later, I decided to find a job where I could receive benefits and better pay. The Vollrath Company hired me as a stenographer, and I made $1.10 an hour. Vacation and holiday pay were a part of my benefits. I thought this would be a step in the right direction, as Ernie and I had plans to marry the following year.

Ninety-nine percent of my working hours here were spent listening to recordings on a Dictaphone machine. Strict rules were abided by. At 8:00 am, when a loud horn sounded, you had to be at your desk working. The same horn blew at 12:00 noon and again at 12:30 p.m. indicating the start and finish of your lunch time. Break time and the end of the work day were also announced by the sounding of the loud horn. During lunch break, I didn't seem to have much in common with the other girls who were working here. Stories of their having fun stealing – siphoning gas from people's cars and other "risky" behavior did not make me comfortable. Throughout every day, it was very rare that a live person talked to me. The company executive's letters were typed by listening to the men's voices on the Dictaphone machine. In all honesty, this job really was not a good fit for me. I hated it so much that I sometimes cried at the end of the day.

At the time I had applied at the Vollrath Company, I had also applied for work at Armour Leather Company. After two weeks of the routine that I truly hated at Vollrath, I was offered employment at Armour Leather. I immediately gave my two-week notice to terminate my employment at Vollrath. This was in the year 1959.

At Armour Leather, I worked in many departments. Often times the department heads argued over who I would be helping. The

Office Manager had to step in and make the final decision as to who I would be working with each day. Billing, Payroll, Purchasing, Switchboard, and occasionally working as a stenographer in the executives' office were all a part of my job. I loved the knowledge I gained and the opportunity to work with so many people. My rate of pay was $1.25 an hour. Holiday and vacation pay were included.

During my time of employment at Armour Leather Company, I married my husband, Ernie. He also worked at Armour Leather at that time. Ernie worked in the factory in the Beam House.

Not long after we were married, a difficult pregnancy forced me to quit my job that I really liked at Armour Leather. Later, this pregnancy turned into a miscarriage. Ernie had to report for military duty. So in less than a year after we were married, I experienced the loss of a good job, the loss of a child, and the loss of my husband's companionship. At this time, I began my next job at Citizen's Bank of Sheboygan in the Bookkeeping Department.

Shortly after my husband had to get on the train for Basic Training in the Army Reserves, we found out that I was pregnant again. Despite a whole lot of morning sickness, I continued working while Ernie served his six months of active duty in 1961. When he returned, I quit my job at the bank and a couple months later, our first son, Jeff, was born – (1962).

The next two years, I remained at home enjoying my duties as a wife and mom. During this time, we moved three times, and another three-month miscarriage took place.

My next place of employment was St. Nicholas Hospital in the Accounting Department. I worked from 3:30 pm until midnight. This worked out nicely for our family as Ernie was home from work to care for Jeff, and we lived close enough to the hospital that I could go home to eat dinner with my family. I did a lot of work on the NCR Bookkeeping Machine including Payroll, Billing, Taxes, etc. at the hospital. Sister Luke was my boss. I was the only non-Catholic working for her. She always kidded me that she was going to have to convert me. As it turned out, we had a lot of respect for each other. It was pretty quiet at work as I was working alone for the majority of the evening. After our son, Tim, was born in 1965, I continued to work at the hospital part-time. About four years later – in 1969, our third son, Todd, was born, and I again took on the role of being an at-home wife and mom.

The next eight years of my life I enjoyed being a special part of my children's lives. I took on the duties of teaching Vacation Bible School every summer at our church. I also became a Cub Scout Den Mother for our boys and their friends, Little League Baseball Coach for Jeff's team, and a P.T.A. volunteer. I served on Washington Elementary School's P.T.A. as Vice President and President. During this time, I was also elected to be the Sheboygan County P.T.A.'s Vice President and then President. For my service, I received the P.T.A. Honorary Life Membership Award. I'm not sure, but I believe I may have outlived the life of the P.T.A., but that's okay, I truly enjoyed these duties

It was so much fun being able to be home with our boys enjoying all their activities and watching them grow. Many moms were working so, at times, I was the only mom that could attend special programs the kids put on in their classrooms. This was a real blessing for me.

My husband wound up on second shift for a couple years at Armira, and Jeff, Tim, and Todd were now in school. It was decided that I would look for part-time work once again. I accepted an offer to work at Security First National Bank in the Accounting Department as an Accounting Clerk. This position included the duties of the

Bank's Cost and Responsibility Accounting. My skills of accuracy and speed on the calculator were a great asset for this position. I worked from 8:30 am until 12:30 pm, so I was back home before Ernie had to leave for work. Several years after I started working at the bank, son #4, Scott, arrived - (1981). Our future daughter-in-law, Debbie, and a neighbor, Wendy, took care of Scott so I could continue my part-time work at the bank. This was another job that I truly enjoyed. At one point, my boss offered me an opportunity to become a Vice-President. He told me I would have to work full time. Again, please forgive me for the crazy things that quickly come into my head and pop right out of my mouth. The truth is that I responded to this offer saying, "Who will feed my vultures?" Yes, that was me speaking. I had five hungry guys at home that needed me to be there to keep them happy and fed. That was a priority in my life.

In 1983, Armira closed its plant in Sheboygan, and Ernie was transferred to their plant in Bolivar, Tennessee. Our family settled in Jackson, Tennessee, where I again took up the role of being an at-home wife and mom. When we left Wisconsin, our oldest son, Jeff, was a senior at U. W. Whitewater. Three of our sons moved with us to Tennessee. Tim was just starting college, Todd was in 9th grade, and Scott was just turning two. That next summer – 1984, I volunteered to be a Vacation Bible School Teacher at our Tennessee church – First Presbyterian. I also became Treasurer of our Women's Ministry Group, took a ceramics class, joined the Newcomer's Group, played on the church volleyball team, chauffeured my kids to school and work, and enjoyed my role as a wife and mom.

After Scott started kindergarten in Tennessee, in 1987, I was asked to become the church secretary at my friend Becky's church – Grace Presbyterian. Her husband Carl was the Pastor. Becky had decided it would be best to give up her position as the church secretary and decided it would be good if I would take over. My part-time hours worked out well with Scott being in school. Unfortunately, my time at this job was only for a few months.

Late 1987, Armira Leather in Bolivar, Tennessee, closed, so we had to say goodbye to our friends in Jackson after being there only four years. This time our sons, Tim and Todd, stayed behind. Tim had received his degree in Accounting at Union University and had a good job, and Todd had just started college in Jackson. Ernie, Scott, and I returned to Sheboygan, Wisconsin, where Ernie had found employment at Tecumseh in Sheboygan Falls.

My work would continue back in Sheboygan, Wisconsin

TODAY, You Need To Be The Pastor

Early January 1988, Ernie, Scott and I returned to Sheboygan, Wisconsin.

Ernie and I had decided I would not look for employment for at least a year. That was our plan, not God's. The Pastor at Hope Reformed Church called me shortly after we started attending this church. He encouraged me to apply for a position on staff that would involve children's and women's ministry. I was hesitant, not feeling confident that this was something I could do. I spoke with my sister-in-law, Audrey, and she reminded me of things I had done in the past. She felt confident that I would do well with this work. After a bit of soul-searching, I came to the place where I felt I needed to trust God with His will for my life. I applied, and found this was definitely God's plan for my future. Interaction with the congregation became very important. My expectations of working in a church were very high. This would be heavenly. Right? I quickly learned there would be challenges that I would not have expected. None-the-less, I loved the opportunity to serve God and His people. Teaching and studying scripture became a tremendous blessing, and I learned to love the work God called me to do.

Soon after I started this job, I did find out that the devil loves to attack and try to destroy the church. I had been hired only a short time when I was handed a letter that had gone out – anonymously, to all the members of the congregation. The letter stated accusations that the Pastor had hired me illegally. I have no idea what this person was trying to get at as the Consistory members (Elders and Deacons) were the people who interviewed me and had the right to hire me. The Pastor was not involved with this process. Not only was this accusation pretty shocking and hurtful, it was absolutely – NOT TRUE.

So the journey began. It was very important for me to learn to stand strong for the work that God had called me to do. In doing so, my faith and love for the Lord grew. My previous lack of confidence in my having the ability to teach Bible studies, turned into a strong fight for me to be allowed to lead a Women's Bible Study. At times I felt like I was Daniel in the Lion's Den as I was peppered with questions as to why the leaders of the church should allow me to lead this Bible study. As it turned out, God was on Pastor Gary's and my side, and after a difficult and sometimes depressing fight, I was allowed to start up the Women's Bible Study called "Coffee Break".

Serving God and His people became my passion. Pastor Gary was truly my mentor. I will be forever grateful for his counsel, wisdom, and encouragement that continued to guide my direction. Teaching Vacation Bible School for children for over 25 years has been a great blessing. Leading Women's Bible studies has also been a great joy. For more than 30 years, God has continued to allow me to serve in this area. I will forever be grateful that God sent me to Pastor Gary at Hope Reformed Church to find my direction and purpose in this life. At one point in time, Pastor Gary did tell me that he felt our move to Tennessee was crucial in my journey in life and that this experience prepared me for what God had planned for my future. I found this to be very true.

Less than two years after I took on the position as Church Life Coordinator at Hope Reformed Church, we had to say goodbye to our Pastor and his family, as he took a call to serve at a church in Florida. This was a huge loss for me. I was losing my spiritual mentor and very good friend. I truly didn't think I could continue my work at the church. After the third time of Pastor Gary telling me, "You can still do the work that you are doing here, even if I leave," I finally came to realize, I could no longer tell him, "No, if you leave, I am leaving too." So I told Pastor Gary that I would stay and try to do my best. Again, I knew I needed to trust God with His plan for my life.

Not long after Pastor Gary left, I was called to one of my greatest challenges in my life. It was Monday morning. I arrived at church and was getting ready for the Women's Bible study that I led – "Coffee Break". It was shortly after 9:00 am when the phone rang. I answered it, and the woman on the other end of the line asked to speak to the Pastor. I told her that we didn't have a Pastor there at that time. She asked me who I was. I gave her my name and told her that I was employed at the church as the Church Life Coordinator. She proceeded to tell me that there had been a tragic accident. There had been a fire and two children had died in the fire. She gave me the names of the two children. My response was, "Oh, NO". The oldest boy was our son, Scott's good friend from church. Scott had just received the invitation to Ty's 8th birthday party. We had just taken Ty along to his first Milwaukee Brewers Baseball game. Now I was being told that the lives of Scott's friend and his six year old brother were taken in this fire. I broke down and cried. I could not believe what I was hearing. The woman told me that I needed to get myself together right now and get to the hospital. She said that the mom and the four year old brother were at the hospital, and I needed to be there with them. I told the woman I was just getting ready to lead a Bible study and that I would be there as soon as I could. I hung up the phone and sobbed uncontrollably. I knew that I needed to cancel the Bible study and go to the hospital. I took care of canceling all my appointments for the day, got in the car, and made the 30 minute drive to the Plymouth hospital blinded by my tears. Over and over again I was saying, "I can't believe this is true".

The nurse at the hospital greeted me and immediately took me to the Mom's room. I was ushered through a large crowd of people to get to the bedside of the Mom. All the people in the room were strangers to me, except the mom and her surviving four year old son, Kyle. As I walked into this room, the nurse announced loudly, "The Pastor is here now." My thoughts went to "WHAT?" She should have known I wasn't a Pastor. Her statement was not true, but it didn't seem to be the right time for me to be correcting her. Later, this nurse called me the Pastor again. When I had a chance to talk to her, I said, "You know I'm really not a Pastor." Her emphatic response to me was, "Today, **you** need to be the Pastor". My thoughts were – Really? Me? Okay, then Lord, please help me.

When I arrived at the hospital, the dad/husband was not there. I had been told that he had remained at the property watching the fire consume their home, their place of business, and two of their children. The dad/husband arrived at the hospital that afternoon - hours later.

How do you console a mom who just escaped a raging fire by jumping out a small bathroom window three floors up? She had dropped her youngest son into the arms of a neighbor and state patrolman, and then she had to come up with the courage to jump herself, while hearing the screaming voices of her other two children whose lives were being consumed by that ravaging fire. Her only hope was that the firemen would get there soon and would rescue them. Truly, this was so devastating, there really were no words of consolation.

Although there did not seem to be any good words of consolation, I realized later that God had given me all that was important that day. God blessed me with two arms that were capable of holding and hugging the Mom's trembling body as she continually reached out to me to be hugged. God blessed me with two ears that were capable of listening to every outburst of hysteria that came from her lips. God blessed me with two eyes that were capable of crying, and my sympathetic tears flowed freely along with hers. God also blessed me with a heart capable of empathy, so I could feel with her - her pain. Sometimes, all that we can do is – **just be there**. I could do that. I could be there. We never know just how important our presence can be. The days, weeks, months, and years that followed continued to be a huge challenge, but I could be there.

The funeral for the two boys was very difficult to get through. Pastor Gary was asked to make the trip from Florida to perform the services. He honored the family request and flew back to Sheboygan. We were so grateful that he was willing to help us through this difficult time. I wasn't sure what my role would be in this. I found it difficult for me to now be temporarily working from the Pastor's office when with all my heart, I wished it was still Pastor Gary's office.

As it turned out, the Mom needed me to remain at her side through the entire service. I sat in the front row with her holding her hand. After the service, I held her up as she stumbled along down the aisle of the church trying to reach out and cling to the caskets of her two boys. She was crying hysterically.

The words of the soloist will stay with me forever – "Safe in the Arms of Jesus". These words remain so comforting and meaningful to me.

Because our son, Scott, was a good friend of the oldest boy whose life was taken, I received a phone call from the dad/husband's parole officer, requesting that I bring Scott in to be questioned. He said it was mandatory that I do this. Scott was not quite eight years old at that time.

The first question this officer asked Scott was, "Did your mom tell you what you should say when you came here?"

Scott said, "Yes".

Then the officer asked him, "What did she tell you to say?"

Scott said, "She told me to tell the truth".

The officer looked at me, smiled, nodded his head, and went on questioning Scott.

The result of this meeting resulted in immediate imprisonment of the dad, who had been on probation after serving a year in jail having been convicted of being a pedophile. Prior to this meeting, I did not have this knowledge, and I was shocked when I found this out. This imprisonment had occurred during the four years we were living in Tennessee. After hearing the probation officer question Scott, I felt confident that Scott was protected from any harm, even though he had been at this family's home without proper, required supervision. I was so thankful that God had protected our child.

Not long after this event, three men from the Federal Court System in Milwaukee came to our church seeking me out for questioning. One of the men was an Assistant U. S. District Attorney. The men had come looking for the "Pastor's wife". The church secretary insisted there was no Pastor's wife there at the church office. She told them the Pastor had left Sheboygan and was now in Florida. After talking with them a while, and dealing with their insistence that the person they were looking for had to be there, she realized they were really looking for me. She brought them in to my office, which was still temporarily in the Pastor's office. These three men spent a long time questioning me about the day of the fire.

Weeks later, I was asked to meet with them for more questioning at a Sheboygan Court House Building. Important information came out of that discussion. Not long after that, I received a subpoena to testify before a Grand Jury in Milwaukee. When that process was completed, I received a subpoena to testify at the Federal Court Building in Milwaukee. The United States Assistant District Attorney who was the prosecutor for this case questioned me several times because I had been at the hospital with the mom and surviving four year old son the day of the fire. I was also there when the dad arrived later, so I had spent time with him as well. At one point, everyone except the mom, husband, their son, and me were the only ones allowed to be together in the hospital room. The nurse had ordered everyone else to leave the room. Knowledge that I had gained from this experience was needed to be brought in as part of the testimony in the week-long trial.

The mom informed me later that she had told the dad that she had an appointment to meet with authorities. She said she intended to report that her husband was sexually abusing their boys. She told me she planned to leave him. Of course, this report of abuse would have put him back in jail. She told me that he had persuaded her to sleep at their home that night telling her the kids needed to be there because the school bus would be picking the boys up in the morning. They agreed that the dad would sleep at his parent's home that night.

The first scheduled trial ended as a mistrial at the time of opening statements. I truly was grateful that God had put me in the office of the U. S. Assistant D.A. that morning to encourage him. When the mistrial was announced, he was pretty shaken. I remember telling him that I felt strongly that God must have stopped this trial for good reason. I also told him that I knew that there were so many people praying about the trial. Then he told me that he and his mother had been on their knees praying during the night. In time, we learned that my thoughts on the importance of the trial being delayed turned out to be true. There were several more key witnesses that came forward with very important testimony that was brought out at the final trial.

Eventually, the dad was convicted of setting the arson fire that took the lives of the two boys. He was also convicted of attempting to take the lives of his wife and their four year old son. This whole process took over two years.

Much of my time was spent working with this family through this devastating ordeal.

The bonding between the mom, surviving son, and myself became very special. At this time, 2016, more than 25 years have passed. Attendance at graduation parties and close support through the dad's funeral have brought us together throughout the years. Kyle was only in his late teens when he was called on to plan his dad's funeral. His dad, who had now died of cancer, had been incarcerated most of Kyle's life. This was the dad who had been convicted of killing his two brothers and attempting to kill his mother and him as well. Now Kyle was the survivor who had to make the funeral plans. Kyle called and asked if I could be there for him. My support was definitely needed. As we sat together in the front row at the funeral service, Kyle was squeezing my hand tightly - continuously. It was difficult to listen to words that made his dad sound like a saint. Feelings of anger, hurt, and confusion had to be dealt with. I was grateful that I could be there. My love and concern for these friends will always be there.

A beautiful wooden angel that was received as a gift from this family and their friend, Colleen, remains in my home as a visual reminder of them. Along with this gift was a card that read:

"Do not forget to entertain strangers, for by so doing some people have entertained angels without knowing it." (NIV) Hebrews 13:2

"We decided you must be an angel. For always being there...We thank you!"

At times, our employment can take us on challenging journeys. At times, we may be called to "Go the extra mile". How many times are we called on to perform the tasks that fall under the blanket statement in our job description that reads – "Perform all other duties as requested". I do believe that with the strength and guidance that only God could provide, I was able to do far more than I would have ever imagined. There is a saying that goes – "If God calls you to it, He will help you through it". All He asks is that we are willing to respond to His call. Sometimes He asks us to "Just Be There". Our faith and our trust need to be in Him. Always!

Colossians 3:23 (NIV) "Whatever you do, work at it with all your heart, as working for the Lord, not for men."

Time To Move On

When you know you were called to the work you are doing, and you love what you are doing, it's not easy to say "Good-bye", and move on.

This was my experience in leaving my position at Sheboygan's Hope Reformed Church.

When I was first hired in 1988, it seemed so right for me to be there. Not only did I love Pastor Gary's preaching on God's Grace, I also loved the passion and mission that he had for helping people who were struggling with difficult situations in their lives. He set up support groups for people going through divorce, death, abuse, addictions, etc. He had professionals in place to lead these support groups. Just before he took the call to Pastor in Florida, he had the Rainbows For All God's Children program set up at the church. This was a peer support group program for children who were grieving a loss due to death, divorce, separation, or abandonment. The ministry that was at Hope fit perfectly with what was in my heart.

It was over two years before the next Pastor came to Hope. I continued to do the work I had been doing with the children's ministry and also with leading Women's Bible studies.

It wasn't long after the new Pastor arrived that most of the support groups were discontinued. Changes were made and some of the opportunities for help and growth were no longer a part of the church.

As time went on, I felt I was no longer the right fit for the job I had taken.

After a meeting with Vacation Bible School volunteers and the Pastor's wife, I got into my car heading for home, and I started to cry. I was so distraught at some of the words that were spoken at that meeting. I got home and continued to feel so sad. I went to bed and still had struggles with my emotions.

In the stillness of that night, God spoke clearly to me. I was told that I needed to get everything in order in my office. I needed to move on. Along with this knowledge, God also brought a feeling of peace to me that everything would be alright. I felt so content and rested in that assurance.

The next day, the Pastor realized that I had intentions of leaving. (I had typed an announcement for Vacation Bible School and omitted my name as a leader). The Pastor was very upset and came to talk with me to try to persuade me to stay. He felt it would not be good for the church. I knew in my heart, I could not disobey the command that God had so clearly given to me. I cried some more, and tried to convince him that everything would be alright. Needing some assurance and support, I consulted another Pastor, and told him my story. He assured me that I needed to listen to what God had told me and encouraged me to go to Bethany Reformed Church to help Pastor Al. I knew that I needed to leave the people and the church that I loved. It would not be easy.

I did make sure everything was in order in the office before I left. My friend came to help me move my personal belongings out of the office. This would be my last day working at the church that I had grown to love.

Ernie, Scott, and I left for a trip to Jackson, Tennessee, to visit our sons, Todd and Tim that weekend. Sunday morning we attended Todd's church. The service was touching. The message and the songs just seemed to touch deeply into my heart and soul. I remember the Pastor's daughter singing the song with these words – "Thank you for giving to the Lord. I am the life that was changed." The words of this song are so beautiful, and they really hit me. Then the Pastor had a prayer and an altar call inviting anyone who needed prayer to come up to the front of the church.

We were sitting on chairs in the last row. I was sitting between my sons, Todd and Scott. While we were standing and praying, my tears started to flow uncontrollably. The grieving of my job loss was hitting hard. I continued to cry in silence. Suddenly, I felt someone touching me. I opened my eyes and saw a woman standing beside me. She asked me to come to the front of the church with her. She said she wanted to pray for me.

I have to be honest, altar calls were not a part of my spiritual life, so I was not comfortable going to the front of church with her- especially not now when I was crying so hard.

Realizing my hesitancy in going to the front of church with her, the woman then asked if she could pray for me right there. I nodded my head – yes. I truly don't remember what she all said, but I do remember that every word that came from her heart and lips were exactly what God wanted me to hear. Words of comfort and assurance that God would be with me and help me through my loss.

Todd heard the words of this lady's prayer and later commented to me how special and so right this prayer was for my needs.

We all experience times of loss in our lives. We need to remember that with each loss, there will be the opportunity for a new beginning. I truly believe that all our experiences in life can help us to grow. When we experience a loss, we have a choice to make. Do we want to remain bitter, or do we want to become better?

One of my favorite scripture verses comes from Jeremiah 29:11 "For I know the plans I have for you, "declares the Lord, "plans to prosper you and not to harm you, plans to give you hope and a future." (NIV)

God is forever faithful to us. All He asks of us is to - trust Him, and believe in Him. He knows exactly what He is doing. Never forget- He is your Father in heaven, and He loves you more than you could ever imagine.

The next chapter – "Over to Rainbows" will reveal Gods plans for my future. Truly, our God is an awesome God!

Over To Rainbows

We had moved back to Wisconsin from Tennessee in 1988. That same year, I started working at Hope Reformed Church. That summer, I was walking across the playground at Washington Elementary School, when I spotted an old acquaintance, Sue Seymour. We were both going to get our little guys, my Scott, and her Paul. The boys were attending the summer school program for tykes. Sue was very excited when she told me that she was heading to Colorado for training to become a Director of the Rainbows For All God's Children program. She told me this peer support program was for kids who were grieving a loss due to death, divorce, separation, or abandonment in their families. She would be part of a group of Christian educators who were hoping to get this program going in Sheboygan.

Before Pastor Gary left Hope Church to Pastor a church in Florida, he went through the Facilitator Training for Rainbows For All God's Children that Sue was teaching. He told me the training was very good and that it would be beneficial for me to go through the training as well. He told me the knowledge would be helpful to me in working with people who were dealing with a loss situation.

One of the women involved with getting R.F.A.G.C. started in the churches in Sheboygan came to speak to members of Hope's governing board. It was decided that Hope would become a supporting, member congregation. Along with providing financial assistance, part of the church's commitment would be that they would take their turn hosting the 14-week program when needed.

Pastor Gary had told me that he had several people lined up to work with the program when Hope would be called on to host a session. He also told me that he didn't expect me to get involved with this program. He felt I already had enough to do with my other duties at the church. So that was the plan – so we thought!

After Pastor Gary had left for Florida, Sue called to see if Hope would be willing to take their turn hosting R.F.A.G.C. I told her we would like to take our turn. What I didn't realize was that two of the three people who had told Pastor Gary they would coordinate this program, now had to back out. So, in time, I realized that it would be necessary for me to step in and take over. Two women and I went through the Facilitator and Coordinator Training led by Sue. In 1990, we hosted this program at Hope, and that is when my Rainbows journey began. Our experience was so great, we were asked to host another 14-week session the following year. Again, it was a huge success.

Many churches throughout Sheboygan County expressed interest in becoming supporters of this program. In a very short time, Sheboygan's newly formed, ecumenical organization of R.F.A.G.C. became so large that it became necessary to become incorporated. In doing so, we needed to come up with our own name. In Sheboygan, we became known as Rainbow Kids, Inc.

After Sue directed Rainbow Kids for three years, she approached me with the big question – would I be willing to go to Illinois to be trained to become the next Rainbow Kids Certified Director. Sue told me she needed to step down from this position as she was too busy. Registration for this program was growing. It was discovered that the need for support for grieving children was great in our county.

My hours at Hope Reformed Church had become less due to budget cuts. I had been praying to God for direction as to what He would like me to do with my extra time. When Sue called me with the opportunity to become the Director of Rainbow Kids, God immediately reminded me that I had just been asking Him to guide me to additional work. I told Sue of my circumstance, and she encouraged me to put in my application. At the end of my interview with the Rainbow Kids Board of Directors, I was told by the President, Pastor Paul Baumann, that the Board had no intention of interviewing anyone else. It was decided that I would be sent for R.F.A.G.C. Certified Director training that summer, July 1992. The week-long training was done by the Founder, Suzy Yehl Marta, and her staff in Mundelein, Illinois.

This job started out as a volunteer position. After a while, it was determined I would receive $150.00 every three months as an "honorarium". I worked from my home using my own computer, printer, and all other office equipment needed. Rainbow Kids did have a part-time hired staff person. Anne Skowlund was in an office where administrative duties were performed and Board of Director meetings were held. A copy machine was there for my use. Anne and I connected by phone or computer a lot.

My duties were to perform trainings for the volunteers serving as facilitators and coordinators, oversee the programs being held at our church sites, nurture the volunteers and participants, represent Rainbow Kids in the community, and report to the Board of Directors once a month. Required reports were also sent to R.F.A.G.C. headquarters in Illinois.

The name of Suzy's program changed to RAINBOWS, and in 1995, my title was changed to RAINBOWS Registered Director. Suzy had good reason for changing the director's title. By this time, there were RAINBOWS sites in 48 states in the U.S. as well as in many foreign countries. We were told that in some foreign country the word "certified" meant "mentally unbalanced". So this became a very good reason for our title to be changed from "Certified" to "Registered Director".

Around 1998, the Board of Directors decided to give me hourly pay. This was truly a blessing, as Ernie, my husband, had recently been diagnosed with Multiple Myeloma – Bone Marrow Cancer. It wasn't long after that he needed to go on disability retirement.

In 1999, I organized a pilot program written by RAINBOWS Founder, Suzy, for the parents of our Rainbow Kids participants. Four adults were asked to be a part of the pilot program, called Prism. The bonding, healing, and support of the participants was incredible. There was no doubt in my mind, we needed to move forward with offering this program, and our Board of Directors agreed. In the year 2000, Prism was offered to all adults who were grieving a loss. Now families could come to our programs together and receive the support they needed to work through their loss. It was a blessing to see that families were healing together.

When Anne left her position in 2004, my duties increased. I had been attending week-long Enrichment Trainings every three years with Suzy and her staff at St. Malo Conference and Retreat Center in the beautiful, snow-capped mountains of Colorado. This was located high up in the mountains - a two hour drive from the Denver Airport. The view from my private outdoor patio was spectacular. It was here that I first saw a double rainbow after a storm. We were in class learning every day and usually in the evening as well. Suzy always gave us one evening off, so I usually chose to go shopping with a group to Estes Park. Once I had the opportunity to travel by car with three others to see the Rocky Mountains. That was amazing! I smile every time I remember this experience. One of the women making this trip up to the top of the

Rocky Mountains had begged me to come along on this venture. She kept saying she would feel so much safer if I went along. I'd like to believe that what she saw was my closeness to and faith in God. I am glad she insisted I come along, as being able to see God's amazing creation in the mountains was truly a blessing.

In 2004, a request came to me from Deb, a mom whose husband had just been deployed to Afghanistan. Deb told me that her children were needing help. Her teenage daughter was experiencing headaches and stomach aches and was missing a lot of school. Not only was she missing her dad and having concerns for his safety, she also had to deal with classmates who didn't support the war. Their discussions often became political debates that were very upsetting to her.

Fortunately, back in Illinois at RAINBOWS Headquarters, Laurie Olbrisch, RAINBOWS Vice President, had just put together the "Silver Linings" program. This material was designed to help children who were dealing with a crisis in their lives. Laurie told me that this program could work for children dealing with the deployment of a loved one. Working closely with Deb and Laurie, I was able to set up and offer Silver Linings for Military families in the Sheboygan area. This six-week program was a big success. Deb was so excited about this experience, she wanted other military families to be offered the support of Silver Linings as well.

When the war first began, the news media was right there filming the battle. Every day on the news, we saw the fighting and bombing right in our homes on our television sets. I couldn't believe this was televised. The military wives said they could not watch the news. This was just too hard for them to see this.

Deb had served in the military in the past. She now had a position of leadership where she was to keep the families back at home informed about any special information regarding the troop Deb's husband was in. She was the military's contact person.

Deb and I had just started working on our plans to bring other military wives, mothers, and children to Sheboygan for support, when Deb received the news that there had been a bombing in Mosul. This was the location of her husband's unit. Her fears began to rise. She told me later that she left her house and just wandered around for hours at the Mall. She was afraid to go home, as she feared that she would be receiving that dreaded knock on her door. After a long day of wandering, she got the courage to go back home. It was not long after, she received the horrific news that her husband, Chuck, had been killed by a suicide bomber trying to enter their Military post in Mosul while he was on guard duty. Of course, Deb and her two kids were devastated.

A huge celebration remembering Chuck's life and service was held at the Sheboygan Armory. The reception line was overwhelming, reaching far out the Armory entrance door. Representatives from every branch of service, and state and local government officials attended this service. Many of them spoke words honoring Chuck's life and service. The news media and TV cameras were there. Deb was also asked to speak on T.V. It was an incredible experience. I had never experienced anything like this. When I finally got to express my sympathy to Deb at this service, her words to me were – "We have work to do". Deb's courage, strength, and commitment to help others was remarkable. I told her to let me know when she was ready.

Deb and I grew closer through all of this. I knew that now she and her two children would be in need of the support of our Rainbow Kids program to help them deal with the death of their loved one. It was so good that Deb and her children had already met new friends through the Silver Linings group. These women and their children became supporters for Deb and her family through this difficult time of loss.

Deb's next request for me was to provide workshops for the families who had lost a loved one serving their country. Twice in the next couple years, Rainbow Kids facilitators did workshops that supported Wisconsin Gold Star Families of Fallen Soldiers with their loss. The first workshop was held in Madison, WI, and the second was in Appleton, WI. We worked hard on preparing materials that would be beneficial for the families who were grieving the loss of their loved ones – Fallen Soldiers who had sacrificed their lives serving our country. Five of us Rainbow Kids Facilitators provided the three hour workshops for the groups of adults, teens, and children. We felt both honored and blessed that we could provide this knowledge and support. Our efforts were well received by the families of the fallen soldiers. God blessed all of us in a phenomenal way. Words cannot express how grateful we were for this opportunity to bring help and healing to these families who sacrificed so much for our freedom.

At the next Enrichment Training I attended in Colorado, I shared our Silver Linings experience with RAINBOWS Directors from many of the United States and foreign countries as well. At times it was too hard to hold back my tears. At the conclusion of my presentation, Laurie Olbrisch presented me with a certificate and a beautiful crystal heart paperweight that reads – Rainbows State of the Heart Caring Award. This was an unexpected, special honor.

It was with sincere humility that I also received the Vatican II Award from Archbishop Timothy Dolan in 2006, for "Service to Families" because of my work with Rainbow Kids. I was invited to dinner at the Cathedral of St. John the Evangelist in Milwaukee with Archbishop Dolan and other award recipients. Ernie was my guest at this event. After the dinner, my picture was taken with Archbishop Dolan and Bishop Sklba. I was allowed to invite additional guests for the service in the Cathedral and the reception that followed. My son Jeff, daughter-in-law Debbie, brother Gerald, and sister-in-law Audrey attended this special event. Beautiful music was sung by a large choir, a homily was given by Archbishop Dolan. One of my cherished memories was when we sang one of my favorite songs – "Soon and Very Soon, We are going to see the King". I will never forget the beautiful smile on Archbishop Dolan's face as he walked down the aisle of the cathedral. Our eyes and smiling faces met while we were both joyously singing this awesome song. After this, Archbishop Dolan presented all the award recipients with a large, beautiful, crystal, engraved plaque. Mine reads:

Archbishop's Vatican II Award
2006
Service to Families
Judie Meise

Because I am a Protestant, I felt particularly honored that I would receive this recognition from Archbishop Timothy Dolan. In all honesty, when I received the letter of invitation, I thought there had been some mistake, as I was not a Catholic. Some of the questions on the questionnaire that I was asked to answer had reference to the Catholic faith. I did make a call to Archbishop Dolan's office in Milwaukee to verify that this recognition was really to be for me. I was told it was not a mistake. The Archbishop truly intended for me to receive this award. What an honor and awesome blessing it was to meet and spend time with Archbishop Dolan. Since that time, he has moved on to become a Cardinal serving in New York City. It is so good to see that God is blessing the service of this Godly man.

It was decided that it would be best to have me move into our Rainbow Kids office in 2008. My grandsons, John and Jesse were a great help in moving me out of my home office and then getting me set up in the Rainbow Kids office. This was located at 824 Superior Av. several miles from our home. For so many years, these two guys were my technical and construction helpers. They were the best. It was a very good decision for me to be in the office. At that time, my title was changed to Rainbow Kids Executive Director.

In 2011, Suzy invited me to be her guest at RAINBOWS Canvas & Corks, black tie fundraiser in Illinois. Again, Ernie was my invited guest. He looked so handsome in his tuxedo. Suzy recognized me for the work being done with Rainbow Kids, Inc. in Sheboygan at this dinner. A heart shaped stone with the word "Hope" was gifted to me. It was truly an honor to be recognized at this event. I was grateful our son Scott, worked and lived in Illinois at that time. Scott and his wife, Debbi, escorted us to the Country Club in Arlington Heights for this event. They were invited to attend the reception and dance that followed.

There were so many opportunities to teach the benefits of our Rainbow Kids program and to bring grief education to those in need. Countless numbers of college, high school, middle school, elementary school, and even pre-school students were taught. Members of charity organizations, our 30 Sheboygan County supporting churches, United Way Affiliates, and even many people from churches outside of our county gained the knowledge, support, and blessings of Rainbow Kids, Inc., and RAINBOWS, International. People chose to come from other counties to attend my training of the RAINBOWS program. At times, I was asked to teach other Registered Directors from around the world who were at the RAINBOWS Enrichment Trainings about how our Sheboygan program was operating.

There were live radio interviews, local cable TV interviews, Milwaukee Channel 58 TV filming's, a State Farm Insurance filming done by an incredible crew from Illinois, and many interviews by newspaper reporters and other people from our community. Every year we hosted a Volunteer Dinner honoring the years of our cherished Rainbow Kids volunteer's service. Believe it or not, I was even allowed to present the homily at Blessed Trinity Parish in Sheboygan Falls. What an honor this was. I would never have thought that I would ever see a large picture of myself on a billboard in Sheboygan. One year, United Way did make that happen. Amazing!

One of the very best parts of being the Rainbow Kids Executive Director came from hearing the response of our participants. Hearing words of sincere appreciation helped me to know that God was working. I knew right from the start that this was His ministry. People who were hurting were being healed. Many participants expressed that they didn't know what they would have done if they hadn't found the help and support from this program. They were ready to give up on their lives. They didn't think they could go on. So many times I heard the words, "Thank you so much for what you are doing. Never stop doing this." I was so grateful that our groups were being held in churches. This was God's work, His ministry.

One teenage boy in a group that I facilitated said to me, "I just want to thank you so much for what you are doing. I don't feel like broken glass or a dead bug anymore."

To this statement, the peers in his Rainbow Kids support group responded with these questioning words – "Broken glass or Dead Bug?"

He said, "Yes, that's just how I felt when my parents told me they were getting a divorce. I didn't think I could go on. I didn't come out of my room for two days. Now that I came to Rainbow Kids, I don't feel that way anymore. I feel so much better, and I know I can deal with this, and I can go on with my life."

Another teenage boy handed his facilitator a poem that he had written. He said, "Here, you can have this. I don't need this anymore." The poem he had written just before he got into the Rainbow Kids program was his suicide note. He had planned to take his own life. Now he had found his help and healing and was ready to move forward with his life. The stories that we heard were often heart-wrenching. The hurts were often so over-whelming. In my heart and mind, I would be reminded over and over again of the words of RAINBOWS Founder, Suzy Yehl Marta, who said, "It shouldn't have to hurt so much to be a child." The support received through this program brought the participants from their hurts, to receiving the support they needed. Their broken hearts were healed. Through the RAINBOWS program and Rainbow Kids, they found hope again for their future.

Parents and even teachers commented on the difference they saw in the children who attended the RAINBOWS program. Referrals came from counselors, teachers, the court system, Pastors, etc. I felt truly blessed to be the Director of this program, and I will be forever grateful to God for choosing me to be there to serve many thousands of people who were needing support through their loss.

The community support and love shown for our Rainbow Kids organization was fantastic. Backpacks from churches filled with school supplies, the Christmas time "Shop with a Cop" experiences, gifts and dinners with Santa, Kohler Company's Build a Bear experience, numerous donations of food and gifts for our annual Rainbow Kids picnic, and so many more blessings were received. Financial support from United Way, many churches throughout Sheboygan County, private and corporate donors, Sunday School offerings, V.B.S. offerings, money left in wills and memorial funds - all the contributions and gifts meant so much. Because of all the support, we were able to offer this program free to all the children. Our program participants were so grateful for what we were doing. What an incredible blessing it was to be a part of all of this.

RAINBOWS President, Suzy, and Vice President, Laurie always told me, "Sheboygan was the best." They loved the way we were operating. God was so gracious, and truly our work was blessed. So many lives were touched. My heart will forever be filled with gratitude to God for all He allowed us to accomplish through this ministry. Hundreds of wonderful, dedicated volunteers were needed to make this all possible.

Many people go to jobs they truly hate every day. That was not my experience. I especially loved facilitator training days. There was always a powerful feeling of spiritual blessings at the end of the training during the time of the Commitment Ceremony. I could always feel the Spirit of God's presence with us.

There are many stories of times I felt attacked on training days, but God always carried me through - even when I fell off a stage one morning while setting up for training at one of our churches. After I fell, I started to black out, and I had so much pain I couldn't walk. A girl working at the church had to call Ernie to come to pick me up. I did badly sprain my ankle and spent many hours in the E.R. that afternoon. I was told I couldn't put weight on that foot. I refused the doctor's offer of pain pills when they said the pills would probably make me feel groggy. I left the hospital on crutches. By the time training was to start that evening, I was determined and ready to proceed. I got the help that I needed and the next two nights of training was done from a wheelchair borrowed from that church. God provided for all my needs.

Training volunteers, and supporting and nurturing children and adults who were hurting became my life, my passion. My service was first and foremost for God. I definitely felt called to this position by Him. Once I accepted His call, God filled my heart with empathy and compassion for the children and adults who were grieving. He also provided me with much love for the volunteers and others who made this all possible. I know God blessed me with a job that I truly loved. I love the words that Suzy spoke to us when I was first trained to be a part of this ministry. She told us, "God doesn't call the qualified, He qualifies the called." That is so true. We all need to be encouraged by these words when we have doubts about our abilities.

After hosting the Rainbow Kids 25th Anniversary celebration at the Sheboygan Yacht Club, in October 2012, I retired. It was time to pass the baton and move on.

It was wonderful that RAINBOWS President, Suzy Yehl Marta; RAINBOWS Vice President, Laurie Olbrisch; and Laurie's husband, Bill, could come from Illinois to help us celebrate. It was also so special that our United Way CEO, Bill Weisert, could be in attendance. It wasn't long after our celebration that both Suzy and Bill passed on after their very short bouts with cancer. Suzy had become a special friend. God chose this divorced mom, who had been in the nursing profession, to author the international program called RAINBOWS, and with her efforts, God allowed her to make a huge difference in this world. Millions of people who were grieving a loss received help, healing, and hope. Suzy was a beautiful, strong influence on my life. Heaven received an awesome angel who was loved and admired by so many. Bill was a great and influential leader in our Sheboygan community. The affiliates of United Way, including Rainbow Kids, Inc., were greatly blessed by his efforts. Laurie and Bill Olbrisch retired from RAINBOWS shortly after Suzy's passing. New leaders have evolved.

Many changes continue to take place with new leadership. My prayer is that RAINBOWS, International, and Rainbow Kids, Inc. leaders, volunteers, participants, supporters and friends will forever be guided by, and be blessed by the love of our heavenly Father. This program was truly a gift from Him designed to help those who are hurting.

As for me, I will forever cherish the awesome memories and unmeasurable blessings experienced in my close to 25 years of service in Rainbow Kids, Inc. and RAINBOWS, International. To God be all the glory! Praise His Holy Name!

After the storms of life come, God provides beautiful rainbows. Along with this comes His promise that the sun will shine again, and there will be a better day.

May God let His light, His Rainbows, shine down on all His children who are grieving a loss. It is my prayer that each one of you will feel the warmth of His love, and be blessed with the knowledge that your Heavenly Father will never ever leave you, nor forsake you. <u>YOU ARE LOVED!</u>

Praying In The Mountains

It was a beautiful sunny day, Sunday, August 2, 1998. My bags were packed. I would be waking up on Monday, at 4:00am and heading to the Milwaukee airport. It would be my second trip to Colorado for another week-long RAINBOWS Enrichment Training.

But today was Sunday, so Ernie, and I would be attending our morning worship service at Bethany Church.

At some point during the service, Pastor Al paused to tell the congregation that all during the previous week, he felt God trying to convey to him that there was an urgent need to be praying for the people of Sheboygan to be saved. He felt that something big was going to be happening that week, but he didn't know what it would be. He felt the need to ask all of us to be praying for the people of Sheboygan that week.

After the service, Pastor Al greeted us as we exited the church sanctuary. As we shook hands, I told him that I was leaving early Monday morning, flying to Denver, Colorado, and I would be in the mountains for a week-long RAINBOWS conference. I told him that I would pray for the people of Sheboygan.

Every day, I remembered my promise to Pastor Al, and I did pray for God to save the people in Sheboygan.

Our classes started Monday morning, and we were busy every day. Most days we had meetings in the evenings as well.

Thursday morning, August 6, we were told that our classes would be starting later. After breakfast, I went back to my room, went outside onto my balcony, looked out over the beautiful mountains, and I prayed. I had a good amount of time to do this and found myself deep into prayer for the people of Sheboygan.

Saturday morning, I flew from Denver to the Milwaukee airport where the shuttle was waiting to take me back to Sheboygan. We were a few blocks away from my home when I noticed something unusual. Along the curbside, at every house, I could see a lot of trash piled up. I couldn't believe what I was seeing. I mentioned this to the shuttle driver. He said, "Didn't you hear? There was a big flood here on Thursday." I was totally shocked.

High up in the Colorado mountains at the St. Malo Conference and Retreat Center, we had no access to communicate to the outside world. Cell phones did not work, no television, no radios. We were pretty much cut off from what was happening in the world. I had no idea that there had been a flood in my own hometown.

Soon we were rounding the corner and pulling into our driveway. The first thing I saw was carpets that had been in our basement, lying on our cement driveway and on the floor of our garage. As I got out of the shuttle, Ernie appeared at the back door, with the phone in his hand. There were tears in his eyes. We embraced, and then he started to tell me the story. The flood that hit Sheboygan had occurred Thursday morning. The experience he shared seemed like a real nightmare.

We were actually quite fortunate as we only had a couple inches of water in our basement. Our son Jeff, and daughter-in-law Debbie, were not so fortunate. Ernie told me I needed to go to see their house. He said, "You won't believe it." Awhile later I did go to see what happened, and I heard their story.

Our grandson, Mark, who was nine years old at that time, had been in their basement. He saw some water come through the bricks from an outside basement wall. He put a bucket under the place where the water was coming in. Mark grabbed their large stuffed Cookie Monster animal and ran upstairs. Shortly after that, the basement wall collapsed, and the flood waters rushed in, filling their entire basement.

My daughter-in-law Debbie, was home with their five children, Ryne, Mark, John, Kelsey, and Kristin when this happened. After a while Debbie drove over to our house where she found our son Scott still sleeping. Scott had invited his friend Nick to sleep over for the night. Ernie had gone to work in Cedarburg early that morning, so he wasn't aware of all that was happening. Debbie woke Scott. She was amazed that he had been sleeping through this all. Then she called Ernie to come home from work, and the clean-up work began at our house. The guys carried the soaked carpets up from the basement and swept the waters down the drain. Only one large basement room was affected.

Jeff and Debbie's basement was filled with water up to the basement ceiling. Everything was covered in water and mud. Professionals were called in to shore up the area where the wall had given way until someone could come to rebuild the wall. The water and mud covered everything in the basement. The Salvation Army provided cleaning materials to help sanitize everything. All their appliances - washer, dryer, water heater, furnace and space heater had to be replaced. It was quite devastating.

The following Sunday morning after the flood, Ernie, Scott, and I were back at church. Church was filled so we had to sit in the front row. Pastor Al shared stories of the losses of people from our church. There were some homes that were totally destroyed. The soloist for that Sunday sang a touching song with words about our

God being the God in the mountains and valleys of life. Before too long, my tears were flowing uncontrollably. The reality of this all hit me hard.

When it was time to greet one another during our service, Pastor Al headed right over to me to shake my hand and ask me if I was all right. I told him we were fine, but that our son and daughter-in-law had major destruction. I remember the Pastor saying he wanted me to meet the couple that I was sitting next to, so with tear filled eyes, I met the visitors and welcomed them. I was definitely struggling with my emotions.

A few days had passed when I was sharing the story with our daughter-in-law Debbie of how our Pastor had felt the urgency for prayers for the people of Sheboygan, how I had picked up on this urgency, and how on the very day of the flood, I was really pouring my heart out to God as I prayed to Him in the mountains to save the people of Sheboygan. I think I was still trying to get over the shock of this all. After sharing my experience, Debbie said, "But Mom, it was so good you were praying. No one was killed. No one lost their lives in the flood."

She was right. It was true. I had seen all the pictures in our local newspaper showing rescue workers, some in boats, saving people from the ravaging waters. I had been told the story of how our grandson, Mark, put the bucket under the basement wall where he saw water coming in, grabbed Cookie Monster, and ran upstairs, just before that wall came crashing down. Praise God! It was amazing, but true. Yes, God had saved all the people of Sheboygan from a horrendous flood. We had so much to be thankful for.

Every time I read the stories in my Bible of how Jesus so often retreated to the mountains to pray, I am reminded of this story. Thank you, God, for hearing our prayers. Thank you, God for saving the people of Sheboygan from the flood, including our grandson Mark (and Cookie Monster too), and thank you, God, for allowing me to experience your closeness and love as I prayed in the splendor of your majestic mountains. Truly you are present, watching over us wherever we may be. Truly you are God. TO GOD BE THE GLORY! I LOVE YOU SO MUCH!

Preface

After I had been working for Rainbow Kids, Inc. for a few years, God gave me a special experience that turned out to be my favorite story to share at Christmas time. At the end of the 14-week peer support group sessions, one of my special duties was to participate in what was called "Celebrate Me" night. The sessions that I led were called the "Forgiveness and Closing Sessions".

This is the story that God led me to share that touched so many of our Rainbow Kids and Prism (adult) participants, and our volunteers as well.

T'was The Week Before The Night Before Christmas

This is a true story. This really happened at my house.

Twas the week before the night before Christmas, when all through my house not a creature was stirring – (that's because we were all in bed) - not even a mouse – (that's because we didn't have any mice living at our house. I was really happy about that.)

It was the week before Christmas, and I had been busy working on getting things ready for our special celebration of Christmas. Sometimes us moms try to do a lot of extra things to make the celebration of Jesus' birthday very special. It was after midnight, and I was really tired when I went to bed. I knew I had to get up to go to work in the morning.

I had just laid down and was just starting to relax, when I heard a loud noise. It kind of sounded like Whhhooossshhh.

My eyes popped open and I jumped up and thought to myself, 'What was that?'

*I hopped out of bed and went down the stairs, turned the corner, flipped on the light switch, and **there it was.***

(Question to the kids) *What do you think I was seeing?*

(The children's responses were usually – Santa. Other guesses were, Rudolph, St. Nick, Elves, deer etc.)

No, none of these. Remember, I said it was the week before Christmas. Santa wouldn't be coming for another week.

What I really saw was my crashed down Christmas tree. It was a big mess. Ornaments had rolled all over the living room floor. Some of them were broken. The lights flew right off the top of the tree. Water spilled out on the carpet. It was horrible. I was so upset and so tired. I felt like I just couldn't handle this.

(Question to the kids.) *So what do you think I did?*

(Children's responses – Cleaned up the mess. Got mad. Sometimes they guessed the right answer.)

I turned out the light, went upstairs, and went back to bed. I thought to myself – in just a little while my husband would be home. He was working second shift at that time. I thought – he won't be tired. He won't mind cleaning this up himself.

Well, I had a hard time going to sleep. I kept waiting to hear the garage door open. I wanted to know my husband was home. Finally I heard him coming in. I thought – okay, now I can go to sleep.

It didn't take very long, and I heard another noise. It sounded something like this. (With my two hands, I would pound on a table.)

It was my husband – running up the stairs and banging the bedroom door open. He said, "Wake up, quick. You've got to come down and see what happened."

I thought to myself, - Oh, no. I guess he doesn't want to clean this up by himself. To be honest with you, I really didn't ever want to see this mess again. I didn't want to deal with this, but I decided I'd better get my robe and slippers on and go back down to help.

The first thing my husband asked me was, "What were you doing when you decorated the tree. You must have been pushing or pulling on it that it would have fallen down."

He was blaming me for what happened.

I said, "No, I wasn't pushing or pulling on the tree when I was decorating it. It's not my fault."

Then the next thing I did was start blaming him. I said, "You should never have put that big tree in that little stand."

So there we were. Upset, tired, and trying to blame each other for what had happened.

The next thing I knew, we were both working - trying to clean up the mess. It was pretty obvious we needed to work together to get that big tree back up and in the stand again. We put the good ornaments off to the side and picked up all the pieces of the ornaments that had broken and threw them in the garbage. By then, it was really late and I was very tired, so I went back to bed.

The next day, I put the lights and ornaments back on the tree.

You know, what happened with our Christmas tree reminds me of what sometimes happens in our lives.

Sometimes things happen that we wish would never have happened. Sometimes we feel just like that crashed down Christmas tree. We feel like our lives have turned upside down and everything seems to be a big mess. Our hearts sometimes feel broken just like those broken ornaments. It seems like we can't deal with it. It's just way too much for us to handle.

Sometimes we feel like blaming other people for what went wrong. Sometimes we even blame ourselves.

That's when we need to stop and think. Just like my husband and I needed to do.

What we needed to do is forgive each other, forgive what happened, and stop blaming each other. Then we needed to work together to try to make things better. Sometimes that takes a while to do, but it's important that we try to work on forgiving so we can move forward and make things better.

(Question to the kids) *When I finished decorating our Christmas tree, did it look exactly the same as it was before?*

(Response from the kids) *NO*

You are right. Our Christmas tree looked different. It wasn't the same, but do you think our Christmas tree still looked beautiful?

(Response from the kids) *YES*

Yes, it was still beautiful.

With the divorce or death that happened in your families, your life looks different too. Someone may be missing from your family. It's not the same as it was. Your heart may feel hurt and broken just like those broken ornaments.

It was so good that you came to Rainbow Kids so you could work through your hurts with the other people in your groups. Remember to try to forgive the sad things that happened in your life, and work together with people who care about you so you can make your life special again. Your life may be different, but that doesn't mean that it can't still be beautiful. Always remember that you are God's special child, and that you will always be loved.

END OF STORY

This story that God gave me and encouraged me to share touched the lives of so many. A whole lot of the adults going through our program were touched to tears. Their gratitude was shown to me when they gave me a hug, and said, "Thank You" for the help, healing and hope that they received in the Rainbow Kids and Prism programs.

Thank you God for teaching us through life lessons, and for putting on our hearts, the importance of sharing what you have taught us so others may be blessed.

You'll Have To Take The Taxi!

It was a Tuesday evening in February around 7:30 pm. The parents and children participating in RAINBOWS peer support program were all saying good-bye and were heading for home. At the time this story took place, my position with this organization was Rainbows Registered Director.

It had been a beautiful day in Wisconsin with warm temperatures and sunny skies melting the snow. Now the temperatures had dropped. The conversation I was having with our volunteer Site Coordinators was interrupted with the call for help. One of our participants had fallen on the ice outside. Call 911, was the request.

Immediately, I got up, grabbed my jacket, and headed outside to the place where people were congregating. I found one of our RAINBOWS participants, a mom, (I will call her Sue), flat on her back at the end of the driveway. She was in a lot of pain, and not able to move.

I recognized Sue and her little boy, and knew they were residents in a home in our city which was set up for moms and their children who were in special need of temporary care.

First responders to the 911 call were the firemen. They attended to Sue and waited for the arrival of the ambulance and the paramedics. It was determined that Sue would need to be transported to the Emergency Room at one of our local hospitals. I instructed the RAINBOWS Site Coordinators to call the home where Sue and her son were residing and ask them to send someone to come to get the little boy. I told the paramedics I would go along to the hospital with Sue. They told me I should ride up front, and escorted me into the ambulance.

Sue was brought into emergency for care, and I was asked to go to the waiting room. This was not a new experience for me, as my husband's bone marrow cancer situation and accidents of my own had brought me in for emergency care many times in the past. I was aware that this would probably take some time.

I decided to let the people in supervision of Sue's residence know that we were now at the hospital, thinking there would be someone who would want to take over my position at the hospital. After several phone calls, I was able to retrieve the unlisted phone number of this residence.

It was now after 8:00 pm. I was informed that the little boy had been safely returned to the home. Then I was told that if Sue was not released from the hospital E.R. by 9:00 pm, she would have to take the taxi back home. From the waiting room, behind closed doors, a good distance away from the emergency treatment rooms, I was hearing Sue screaming with pain. I told the attendant on the phone, I didn't believe that Sue would be released that night. In the back of my mind, I found myself putting off any thoughts of how taking a taxi could even be a possibility. I decided I would stay long enough to see Sue through until she would be admitted and settled into a hospital room, and then I would be able to leave.

Time continued to go so slowly. Finally, I asked the receptionist at the desk if she could check on the status of Sue. She called back to the Emergency Room desk. They said they were getting Sue ready for x-rays and that I could come back to E.R. and be with her.

The attending doctor was at the desk. I was told that there was no way he would be admitting Sue. He said she would be discharged that evening sometime after the x-rays were taken – probably by 9:30 pm. He felt certain that the injury was muscular and surgery would not be needed.

At that point, I was really torn. How could I leave her? How could I tell her she needed to call a taxi to take her home? Who would be there to help her?

I decided I needed to call Ernie and ask him to have our son Scott take him to get our van, which was still parked at the RAINBOWS church site, and bring it to the hospital so I would have transportation to get home. The probability of our van being a better way of transportation for Sue than a taxi entered my thoughts.

I went in to be with Sue, and found her to be insistent that no x-rays should be taken. She just wanted to be able to get out of there and go back to her home. At her request, the order for x-rays was cancelled.

Little by little, with time in between, the doctor would raise the bed to help Sue adjust to getting up. Each movement was very painful for her.

Next came the excessive itching caused by a reaction to the pain medication. In the course of the next several hours, three injections were administered to counter the allergic reaction and relieve the itching.

When Sue and I were alone in the room, I listened to her strong desires to be able to get out of there. Her concerns were always for her son. Who would put him to bed for her? She longed to be with him, to be able to read to him, and tuck him in bed. She went over the regular night-time routine that they followed. Then her concerns were turned to who would be there to get him up for school the next morning, get him his clothes and breakfast, etc. Her anxiety was rising, and the itching would become worse.

She was blaming herself for having fallen on the ice. She felt it was because of her own stupidity. Her desires became stronger and stronger that she needed to be able to get out of that bed and go home so her son could be cared for.

I tried to assure her that what had happened was an accident. She didn't cause this to happen. None of us would deliberately try to fall on the ice. I also tried to convince her that others living at their home would need to help her out until she was better. I told her that sometimes people need to be there for each other. I said there could be a time that the others would need someone to help them too. I felt sure that she would care for others if they needed help. She agreed that she would be there to care and shared stories of times when she was able to be there to help others.

It seemed strange to me that at no time did Sue mention that a relative should be called to let them know of her situation. After a while, I asked if her parents were still around. She said they lived in another city approximately 40 miles away. No other conversation came up about them. I found myself questioning God why this had to happen to someone in her situation, and why it couldn't have been someone else. In all honesty, when I thought this out more thoroughly, God helped me to realize that had this been another of our RAINBOWS participants, we may have needed to find care somewhere for the children as well. Many of our single-parents in RAINBOWS were on their own. Sue's little boy had a home to be taken to where he could be cared for. So I thanked God for this provision.

At times I found myself wondering, how is this going to be possible for Sue to even get out of that bed? But she was saying, "I know I can do this, my guardian angel is here." I admired her courage and faith, and was grateful for her determination.

After hours had gone by, Sue told the doctor to help her get up. Slowly, she was worked into a sitting position. After adjusting to sitting awhile, she wanted to walk. The doctor helped her to a chair where she could sit, and then he left the room.

Sue said I should come and sit next to her, which I was intending to do.

In the course of our time together, I wanted to ask her if she would like me to pray with her, but up until now, the doctor and nurse seemed to be in and out so frequently that the opportunity had not come up.

Sitting right next to Sue, I was just about to ask her if I could say a prayer, when she asked me, "Are you a Christian?" I said, "Yes". We both had prayer on our minds. So as I held her hands, the words of my prayer for her flowed up to the God we both knew, trusted, believed in, and loved. She seemed to be so much more at peace after I prayed.

Occasionally, loud sounds from the monitoring machine that was hooked up to her would indicate that something was not right, and this would cause her to start feeling anxious again.

We talked about walking with Jesus, in a beautiful garden, with a gentle breeze blowing as they walked hand in hand, and she would come to a place of peace again. We talked about allowing Jesus' loving arms to be wrapped around her, and she could feel His presence and the warmth of His love.

After 10:30 pm, it was decided that she would be released. Three medications were prescribed. The prescriptions were written out and handed over to me.

I asked the nurse if it would be possible to give her enough of the medications to get her through the night. I thought surely they could do this for someone in Sue's condition. The nurse responded, "No, we don't do that anymore now that we have a pharmacy that remains open 24 hours a day in Sheboygan. You will have to go there to get these prescriptions filled."

Again, I found myself feeling, THIS CAN'T BE REAL! Why can't this be made easier for someone in Sue's condition? It's very late. She's in a lot of pain. We are tired, and just want to go home to bed.

I headed out to get the van, and the nurse brought Sue to the door. We got her in the van and proceeded to the pharmacy. It was now 11:00 pm. I was thankful for the drive-up window service at the pharmacy. We could stay seated in the warm van. The pharmacist took the prescriptions and told us to come back in 20 minutes. I was told I could not stay at the window as a buzzer alert would remain on if I did this.

While waiting for the prescriptions, I called home to tell my husband where I was. Not fully understanding the situation I was in, I found out that he was not too happy that I was not home yet. I know he was worried about me. He proceeded to tell me this was not my responsibility. Why was I doing this? I took a deep breath and calmly told him I would be home soon, said "Good-Bye", and hung up the phone.

A call came in on my cellphone from Sue's housing attendant. She was wondering how long it would be before Sue would be back. I told her the prescriptions would be ready in about ten minutes and that I would have Sue home soon after that. Sue had repeatedly expressed her concern that this person was going to be very angry with her for keeping her up this late. This caused Sue to feel even more anxious about what had happened.

In hopes that the order would be ready a little sooner, I drove back in for the pick-up, but was told it would be a little longer. Finally, the prescriptions were ready. A second check had to be made out as the first check Sue wrote was for more than the actual amount due. This was corrected, and we were now ready to take Sue home.

After assisting Sue into her residence, I headed for home. It was after 11:30 pm. I took a shower, went to bed, and read over the Bible Study lesson that I was to lead the next morning at our church.

Morning came fast, but another day was before me with schedules to meet. I felt a bit tired, but I felt much more than that. Somehow, the memories of all the circumstances and events that had transpired the night before seemed to leave me experiencing all kinds of emotions: stunned, troubled, saddened, upset, bewildered, grateful, etc. I felt so unsettled.

The Wednesday morning Women's Bible Study I lead was studying the book of 1 Thessalonians. We were on Chapter 2.

The Apostle Paul's feelings of being "torn away" from, and his concern for the well-being of the Thessalonians reminded me of Sue's emotions expressed while being away from her child, and the strong desire to be able to be brought back together seemed so similar to those that Paul was expressing. My mind & emotions continued to be wrapped up in Sue's story.

Early afternoon, my appointment took me to an acquaintance, who is a devout Christian man in ministry. He listened as I told him Sue's story, and his immediate response was, "You did what you needed to do. You did what was right. You were the "Good Samaritan".

The Good Samaritan – I thought about this and wondered – Who are the Good Samaritans? Who is really out there helping those in need when no one seems to care? Who is willing to step aside from their supposedly important, planned schedule for the day? Who is willing to realize that some things are just going to have to wait?

At one point in the hospital, Sue stated, "God puts people into your life just at the right time." Later she said, "I know that I am able to walk again and can go home only because of God. Only He could have made this possible." I told her I felt this to be true. Earlier, I would not have thought she would have been released that night.

I asked Sue what would have happened if she would have had to call the taxi, and she would have had to first pick up the prescriptions before going home. She said she would most likely have had to ask the taxi driver to take her to the pharmacy and drop her off. After the prescriptions were filled, she would have had to call another taxi driver to come to take her home. She would have had to wait outside in the cold at the pharmacy on her own.

I could not even fathom this. She was in pain, drugged with pain medication and antihistamines, and unstable on her feet. I could **not** fathom this.

It took this experience to help me realize that all of my life I have been tremendously blessed by being surrounded with loved ones who were always there for me. I have had family and friends to call on at any time of the day or night. I've never had to rely on a stranger to step in to see me through a crisis in my life. I think having loved ones always available for you is something many of us often take for granted.

I feel so grateful for the blessings I have received. To my family and friends, I want to say, "I Thank God For Each One Of You! You have always been there for me. What a blessing you are to me and to my life." Never in my life did I ever have to be told, *"You'll have to take the taxi."*

To all the taxi drivers in this world who have gone the extra mile, and have been "The Good Samaritans" to those who needed a little help from a friend, (or stranger), let me tell you how much I appreciate your kindness. I am so grateful to know that you are out there, just a phone call away, picking up the pieces when there is no one else to care. To you I want to say, "Thank you, and God Bless You."

RAINBOWS – the organization with which I was employed as a Registered Director for 23 years has been a true blessing in my life. I am reminded that, with that beautiful rainbow that God places in the sky following a storm, comes His promise. His promise to all of us is that He will always be there for us. He will care for us. My prayer is that God will help us to do all we can to care for one another. Our world is certainly in need of "Good Samaritans".

Remember - It's the right thing to do!

Christmas Past And Christmas Now - 2013

My memories of Christmas have always been special.

I grew up in a large family of ten children, and I was the youngest child. My older siblings would remember going through the years of the depression. I'm sure there were years when our family went through difficult times financially, but it would be my guess, that no matter what, Christmas time was always special.

On Thanksgiving, in the afternoon or early evening, our family headed to see the special Christmas display in the H. C. Prange Department Store windows. Sometime in October the first floor windows were covered to conceal the activity going on behind them. Starting in the year 1940, design crews created animated scenes in each of the 16 large window spaces. The windows were unveiled on Thanksgiving Day. The mechanical displays were a delight to the eyes of both children and adults. Everyone gazed with amazement at the animated figurines that danced with holiday delight, little elves assembled and packed toys for delivery, animated forest creatures "cooked" meals or popped up from tree stumps, and glittering snowflakes fell along the path to Santa's workshop. People crowded around the many windows and couldn't wait until they could get a spot right up front to see the new display. It was always so exciting to view this magical winter wonderland. There was excitement in the air. We knew Christmas was coming, and that meant Santa would be coming to Prange's. We looked forward to visiting him and telling him what we wanted for Christmas.

For me, there are special memories of always having a beautiful, real Christmas tree at our house. I loved the fresh, pine aroma that filled our house. We all helped hang the long, silver pieces of tinsel on our tree. This was not an easy task as each strand of tinsel was placed on the tree branch one at a time so the tinsel would hang down perfectly straight. Each branch held many strands of tinsel (tinsel was often removed from the tree after Christmas and used again the following years). The lights on the tree were the big fat bulbs that got very hot. We all learned not to touch those pretty, colored lights at an early age. If one lightbulb burned out, the whole set of lights went out. Sometimes it was hard to find out which light needed to be replaced. Some of the ornaments that trimmed our tree were purchased and some were hand-made. Besides hanging candy canes on the tree, we had what was called cherry candy balls. This was made up with two, red hard balls of cherry flavored candy that were connected by a thin wire that could be hung over the tree branches. They were very tasty. A brightly lighted star or a beautiful angel would grace the top of our tree. Since Santa did not bring our tree, it was up and decorated before Christmas day.

There was an awesome aroma coming from the kitchen when my mother was baking all those yummy Christmas cookies. She made several kinds of cookies that were formed into a long roll, wrapped in waxed paper, and put in the refrigerator to cool before they were sliced and baked. A huge assortment of candies, tasty breads, and stolen were made. Knowing we would get to eat all these delicious Christmas treats always brought great anticipation to the holiday season. Our mother was an excellent baker. She worked hard for days preparing all her Christmas specialties.

When I was very young, I did believe in Santa Claus. I remember writing a letter to Santa Claus every year and mailing it to him. Then I listened to our big, console radio every weekday to a program where Billy the Brownie and Santa would speak to the children. I sat on the floor right next to the radio putting my ear very close to it. Sometimes it was difficult to hear what was being said as static would make a crackling noise in the radio. Reception was not always good. I always hoped that Santa Claus would pick my letter to read on the radio. I wanted to make sure he got it, so I listened to hear him say my name. He was very wise in using first names only, and he always reminded us to be good boys and girls.

Every Christmas Eve, the Christian School children had a program at our church that took place early in the evening. We all participated in this program through 8th grade. This was always a very special night. We dressed up in our best clothing. My Mother always bought me a pretty dress to wear for this occasion. We sang special Christmas songs, and recited the Christmas piece that we memorized. Sometimes we took part in a skit or play. After our program, each child received a bag filled with wrapped, flavored hard candy, nuts - still in the shell – (we needed a nut cracking devise to open these), a wrapped popcorn ball, an apple, and an orange. We were delighted with this gift.

Santa always visited our house while we were at church performing in the Christmas program. Before we went to church, we put out cookies, milk, and a letter to Santa. We were always anxious to get back home to see if Santa had come. We could hardly wait to find out what he had brought for us. He always drank the milk, ate cookies, and answered the letter we left for him. There were always gifts for all of us.

Even after some of my siblings married, they all gathered at my parent's home on Christmas Eve in the evening. Coming from a musical family, we loved to sing, so we began our time of celebration with singing Christmas carols. My sister Rachel played the piano, and the rest of us became a beautiful choir. Our voices blended together in awesome harmony. Then our gifts were exchanged.

After my older siblings married and had children, our family became quite large. It was decided that we would draw a name and purchase a gift for just that one person. My parents always gave us younger kids who were still at home extra gifts, and sometimes, the married siblings bought an extra gift for us too. Christmas was a happy time, and I always felt special.

On Christmas Day, we went to church in the morning. This was followed by a delicious Christmas dinner which was served around noon time. I remember my mother getting up early in the morning to put the big turkey in the oven.

The thing that made Christmas so special was that throughout the holiday season, we celebrated the birth of our Lord and Savior, Jesus Christ. From little on, we knew and experienced the great love and joy of this holiday. Our family always felt blessed as we came together and worshipped Jesus, our Savior and King. At home, school and church, we were taught that the true meaning of Christmas was really all about Jesus' birth.

One of the best memories I have of the Christmas season was when my mother took me and my two sisters, Rachel and Diane, and my Aunt Esther took her three sons, Karl, Peter, and Robert, to Milwaukee on the train. We boarded the Chicago Northwestern train in Sheboygan; and when we got to Milwaukee, we walked several blocks to the Boston Store and Gimbels Department Store. The store windows were decorated with many mechanical Christmas displays that were eye-popping and breath-taking to a child. We felt like we were in a magical Christmas winter wonderland. The Boston Store was known to be the best. Another big thrill was when we got to ride the Christmas train (monorail) which was suspended from the ceiling of the Boston Store basement. The monorail train rode around above the toy department which covered the entire store's basement. It was so exciting for us kids to experience this incredible view. We also visited with Santa while we were there. This was such an exciting experience for us little kids. I also remember eating at a restaurant. It was a cafeteria so we took our trays and went down the line to pick out the foods we wanted to eat. When we were finished eating, we took the trays to an area where there was a mechanical dumb-waiter that took the dirty dishes on the trays down to another level where the dishes were washed. This was so fascinating to me. Sheboygan didn't have anything like this. I'm really not sure how my parents could even afford for us to make this trip, but my mother must have saved enough money for my two older sisters and me to go on this wonderful adventure. I'd say we were quite fortunate to have made this trip more than once in the 1940's when I was quite young.

My husband and I raised our four sons celebrating Christmas pretty much the same as we had been raised. We still went to see Prange's window display on Thanksgiving Day. Our children were always excited to visit Santa to tell him what they wanted for Christmas. Some of the department stores put out Christmas catalogs, so our kids had a lot of fun checking out all the toys that were available. They found toys on every page that they hoped Santa would bring them. After a big fire in 1983, that destroyed the H. C. Prange store, the new building was built with fewer windows, so the Christmas display became a lot smaller, but the children still loved visiting every year.

Ernie always went to buy our freshly cut Christmas tree, and we all helped decorate. We all loved the fresh, pine scent of a real tree. We did skip putting tinsel on the tree. Yeah! Colorful streams of garland, ribbons and bows were used instead. The big, fat, hot tree lights were eventually replaced with the small, energy efficient, LED lights that were not hot to the touch. Many of our tree ornaments were given to us as gifts, some were handmade, and some store bought.

Our children's Christmas program at church was held on the Sunday evening before Christmas Eve. Many churches found that Christmas Eve was not a good choice for the children's program as many families were traveling out of town to be with their families on that night. Our boys participated in the children's program by singing Christmas songs, reciting Christmas pieces, and taking part in skits or plays. At times, they had the leading part in the play. They received a gift bag of Christmas candies, fruits, and sometimes a wrapped popcorn ball after the program. This was always a special time that we all looked forward to. It was a time to celebrate Jesus' birth, and that was important to all of us.

Before we left home to attend the Christmas Eve service at church, the boys set out a plate of Christmas cookies, glass of milk, and a letter telling Santa that they had been really good that year. After we came home, the first thing our kids did was look under the Christmas tree to see if Santa had been there. They could never believe how many cookies Santa had eaten. They felt they understood exactly why he was so fat. Even after our older sons didn't believe there was a real Santa, they had a difficult time figuring out how the presents arrived under the tree, how all those cookies and milk could disappear, and how there was always a note for them from someone named Santa. Uncle Mike did a great job keeping this a mystery. We always took pictures in front of the tree while everyone was dressed in their best clothes. We sang some favorite Christmas Carols. Then we had our gift opening. Special Christmas foods, many that I had made, were enjoyed throughout the evening. I still made some of the cookies and breads that my mother did, but I didn't make as much. Really, I didn't have as many people to serve.

We stopped getting a real tree in the year 1998, after Ernie had been diagnosed with Multiple Myeloma. Our youngest son, Scott, was 17 at that time and the only child living at home. That Christmas, we decided it might be easier to get an artificial tree. Ernie also went out to buy an electric train and the start-up pieces to our Christmas village. Each year, we added more pieces to our village so now we have a beautiful, lighted display beneath our Christmas tree.

In 1984, the second year we lived in Tennessee, I took a ceramics class and made a nativity set. This nativity is set out every year and continues to bring special meaning to our celebration of Christmas. When I tell people I painted all the people and animals, they are shocked. All I know is God was so present with me while this was coming together. This is a special Christmas treasure to me.

Because all four of our sons are now married, and two of them live in Tennessee, we have had to celebrate our Christmas gift giving at different times of the year. Last year, our son, Todd, Denise and their two girls, Kaitlyn and Madeline from Tennessee needed to come in October, so we celebrated with them at that time. Our son, Tim, Lisa, and their sons Micah, and Jared from Tennessee could only come for Thanksgiving, so we celebrated Christmas with them the day after Thanksgiving. Tim and Lisa's daughter, Nicole, flew here from Tennessee to spend Christmas time with us shortly before Christmas. Our son, Scott, Debbi, and their two sons, Orion and Barry from Mequon, Wisconsin, and our son, Jeff, Debbie and their children, Ryne, Brittany, and our great granddaughter, Emma; Mark and Audrey; John, Lauren, and our great grandson, Mason, from Oshkosh, WI; Kristin, John, and Kelsey from Franklin, WI, were either here on Christmas Day for dinner or soon after. No matter when we celebrated, we generally sang some favorite Christmas Carols before we opened gifts, and after our gift exchange, we enjoyed some special Christmas foods that I had made. Christmas music is played a lot starting at

Thanksgiving time through December in our home, and while traveling in our van. I love the Christmas carols, and every year I cannot seem to get to sing them and listen to them enough. I really love so many of the songs, but I like to include, "Joy to the World", and "Silent Night! Holy Night"!. When our grandchildren are with us, we always include, "Away in a Manger". "Angels We Have Heard on High", and "Cantique De Noel" - "Oh Holy Night!" are more favorites.

Some of our Christmas traditions have changed, and some are still the same.

My husband and I still go to church every Christmas Eve where we attend a beautiful candle-lit communion service. After the service, we come home and exchange gifts. Special Christmas foods – cookies, candies, and breads, are always a part of our celebration. Ernie's favorite cookies are Chocolate Balls and Chocolate Chip. I love Maraschino Cherry cookies, Pecan Crescents, and my mother's Wheaties cookie, and so many more. Anything with chocolate, cherries, and coconut are high on my list of favorites. My favorite candy recipe is Toasted Almond Truffles. Yes, some favorite recipes that my mother made are still being used, although I think I am the only one of our family, who still makes her Boston Brown Bread recipe.

Now our decorated artificial tree has small colored LED lights, a pretty star on the top that lights up, and lots of beautiful colored ornaments (many of these were gifts). Two eye-catching, lighted Christmas villages (one under the tree and one on a table), our train, the nativity set I made, beautiful centerpieces, candles, and some treasured decorations made by my mother many years ago now decorate our home at Christmastime. One small artificial tree that I set on a table displays many hand-made ornaments that my mother and sisters – Florence, Lois, and Rachel, made for me. These hand-made decorations from the past bring special memories that continue to warm my heart each year.

Every Christmas, I make a delicious dinner for anyone that can join us from our family. At times, special guests are included. The dinner guest number ranges from the teens to the twenties. Dessert generally includes a special birthday cake for Jesus which I tell more about in the next chapter, "Traditions."

"Thanks be to God for His indescribable gift of Christmas." (NIV) II Corinthians 9:15

Traditions, Traditions

All families seem to have them. Whether we like them or not, traditions become a part of our life.

Some of my childhood memories of traditions were that we always had turkey, pumpkin pie, mashed potatoes, gravy, and cranberries along with other vegetables and salads on Thanksgiving. Easter dinner we always had ham, mashed potatoes, gravy, hard-boiled, colored Easter eggs, vegetables and salads. My mother was the cook. Christmas Eve was always the night my family got together in the evening to exchange gifts. My mother always made lots of delicious cookies, candies, and breads. Boston Brown Bread was one of my favorites. (This bread was made in cans that were yellow-lined. One batch would make seven breads – seven cans. The bread has raisins, walnuts, brown sugar, and cinnamon added to make a very tasty round bread.) The guys in the family all received a pair of socks from my parents, and the women usually received something that my mother made – like jewelry, beautiful tree ornaments, or a centerpiece that my mother created. My sister Rachel played the piano, and we all sang Christmas Carols. Coming from a family with ten siblings who loved music, the beautiful harmony that filled my parent's home was awesome and continues to be a treasured memory.

Once my parents had passed on, we started our own family traditions.

Something that has always been important to me is that we take the time to remember what the true reason is for our celebrations.

Having worked in a church for many years with children and women's ministries, I came across some pretty good ideas to make our family celebrations special.

For Easter, we have our traditional ham dinner with mashed potatoes and gravy, vegetables, sweet potatoes, home-made apple sauce, salads, crescent rolls, and a special Easter dessert. Usually I make something in the form of a cross. While we are eating dessert, we have our special family time of celebration. I put together a large basket lined with green Easter grass, and I added 14 different colored plastic Easter eggs. Inside each egg I placed an item that reminds us of the Easter story. The basket is passed around to the members of our family. They each select an egg and place it in front of them. When I call out the color of their plastic egg, they open the egg, remove the item inside, and place the item in front of them. I would then pass a piece of paper with the scripture that tells the story that coincides with the item in their egg for them to read. What are some of the items inside the eggs? There is a little ceramic donkey, a little wine glass, a seamless piece of cloth, 30 silver coins, a rooster, a small crown with thorns, a small leather whip with sharp objects attached, a cross and a nail, some dice, a sponge, a piece of linen, a small bottle with perfume, and a stone. The last egg that is opened is empty – representing the empty tomb. In this way, the Easter story is told and discussed with scripture and visual objects incorporating family participation. Our gratitude for the gift of God's Son, Jesus, who sacrificed His life on the cross so we can be free from the burden of our sins is expressed. There is no greater joy than the celebration of Easter. Jesus' great love conquered sin, and death, and hell for all of us who believe. We can rejoice knowing that Jesus is alive! Praise God!

For Thanksgiving, after we have had our turkey dinner, with stuffing, mashed potatoes and gravy, vegetables, sweet potatoes, cranberry sauce, crescent rolls, etc., we have our special celebration.

As I serve each person their pumpkin pie with their choice of ice cream or whipped cream, we each go around the table and share what we are thankful for. Everyone in the family participates with giving thanks to God for His love and special blessings received that year.

For Christmas, we celebrate Jesus' birthday. I make a special round cake – which represents the world. The cake has three layers. The bottom layer is brown – (chocolate) – representing our sins. The middle layer is red – (strawberry or cherry) - representing Jesus' blood that was shed for a complete remission of all of our sins. The top layer is green – (white cake with green food coloring) - representing the new life that we have received through God's gift of grace in the death and resurrection of His Son Jesus Christ, our Lord and Savior. The cake has white frosting representing Jesus' purity and holiness. Each one of us receives a small (birthday cake size) candle. A large white candle representing the "Jesus" candle is placed in the center of the cake. The large candle is lit and our family sings, "Happy Birthday to Jesus". Then we sing the song, "Away in a Manger". We talk about the importance of each one of us being the light in this world and that we need to receive our light through Jesus. We light our individual small candles from the lit Jesus candle on the cake and place our small lit candle into the cake. Then we sing, "Joy To The World". The lights are turned down, and we close our celebration with singing, "Silent Night! Holy Night!" around the candle lit birthday cake. Again, scripture is read to bring out the significance of Jesus' birth.

We do exchange gifts with one another, but one of the most fun things we do comes after our gift exchange. I call this, "The Blessing Bag" time.

Throughout the year, Ernie and I receive gifts from different charity organizations for donations they receive from us. As I receive these items in the mail, I place them in a large bag. At Christmastime, I let our children and grandchildren reach into the bag and pull out an item. They are not to peek inside the bag. They are asked to pull out the item they first touch. When they bring out the gift item and unwrap it, they have a choice to make. They can either keep the gift for themselves if it is something they could make use of, or they can give the gift away – "blessing" another person from the family. If someone "blesses" you with a gift, you are expected to keep it, and just say, "Thank You". One year, our Jack Russell Terrier, Toby, saw one of these wrapped gifts that our daughter-in-law, Denise, had set under her chair while waiting for her turn to open the gift. None of us saw Toby go under the chair and open the package. He picked it up in his mouth, and delivered it to our teen-aged grandson, Mark. It was a candle in a small, square, white ceramic container. The cover had a cute little ceramic Christmas mouse with red ribbons on it. I guess Toby, who was so loved by our family, wanted to have some fun playing this "blessing" game with us too. Toby was pretty special. Our kids were older now, so we all put our gifts under the tree before we went to church for our Christmas Eve service. Of course, there were always wrapped gifts with treats for Toby. It was amazing that Toby did not go under the tree and open his gift while we were at church. He waited till we got back from church and then he was ready. He knew exactly which gift was his and without hesitation, he pulled it out from among the many packages and opened it.

For some reason, this ritual, or tradition of the "Blessing Bag", has become the most talked about fun time for our family – young and old alike. There are always a lot of items in this bag including fleece blankets, patriotic t-shirts, jackets, calculators, gloves, colorful bags, books, toys, jewelry, etc. Sometimes I add some pretty serving plates, etc. that I no longer am using. Every year we get more than enough calendars for the coming New Year, so everybody gets to take home a calendar. This "Blessing Bag" activity seems to bring out a whole lot of joy and laughter. When all is said and done, everyone has been "blessed" with something.

I don't recall how old I was when I was allowed to stay up until midnight for the New Year celebration. I do remember that we opened up the front door of our house. Being in Wisconsin, it was very cold out there. Most generally, snow covered the ground. Off in a distance, we heard church bells ringing in the New Year. Some people would bang on pots and pans and shout out, "Happy New Year". Ernie and I still stay up until midnight, and I still open up the front door, but it's generally quiet out there. I will share more about our New Year celebration in the next chapter, "What's Your Secret?"

Our grandchildren are remembered on Valentine's Day, Halloween, Easter, and Christmas with special treat bags that include candy, cash, and sometimes a special card.

These are some of the traditions that we have been enjoying in the Meise family for many years. I'd have to say, our family traditions have been bringing smiles, happiness, and blessings to all of us. Maybe some of these traditions will be continued on by future generations. God already knows, and time will tell. TRADITIONS! May they forever be – Happy Memories.

What's Your Secret?

Years ago, the theme song written for the 1970 movie "Love Story", was entitled, "Where do I Begin".

When I first thought about writing a book, these are the words that kept coming into my mind – "Where Do I Begin." Somehow, I felt my book needed to be a story of love.

February, to me, is the month of 'Love'. I love that it's short, and I love that it is filled with so many celebrations. Ernie and I have birthdays for three of our children, four grandchildren, one brother, one sister (February 14), (a second sister born in February passed on), one brother-in-law, and two good friends. To top all that off, I get to celebrate Valentine's Day with the love of my life. This summer, July 2016, we celebrated our 56th Anniversary. We dated three and a half years before we married so we have a lot to celebrate.

Every Valentine's Day I look forward to a dinner date with my husband. I know he will be encouraging me to order lobster at the restaurant. I know, I know, I'm pretty spoiled – or I should say blessed. Ernie will choose to have a steak dinner. Then, as always, I will be sharing some lobster with him, and he will be sharing steak with me. To top this dinner off, we share a delicious dessert. Rupp's downtown – Rum Cake. Yummm.

For my 70th birthday, my husband planned a surprise party for me. He had surprised me with birthday parties before that were held at our son Jeff, and daughter-in-law Debbie's, house, but this time, the dinner party was at Klemme's Wagon Wheel. I had been told we were going to dinner with just two of our sons and their families. I was shocked when we entered the restaurant, and there were close to 70 people smiling and shouting, "Surprise". It was wonderful!

I was told later that one of our grandson's girlfriend heard one of the female guests make this comment to her husband as they left the restaurant – "I'm so jealous of their love."

At an outdoor worship service at our church, Ernie and I were sitting on folding chairs set out on the church lawn. A woman who was sitting behind us later said to me, "You can just tell how much your husband loves you." She was in awe.

In August 2013, Ernie was at Morningside Nursing Home recovering from surgery of a broken femur bone. After he had been there for about a month, I was called into the office of the head Social Worker. I was quite amazed when this young, pretty woman (probably in her late 20's) asked me, "What your secret, Judie? You and your husband seem to have an incredible love for each other. How do you do it, what's your secret?" In our conversation, she told me that she was dating, and she seemed to want to make sure that the man she was planning to marry would be her "Mr. Right". I guess she was insinuating that's what I had done.

In each of these situations, I found myself wondering, how did these people come to their conclusions about Ernie and me. What did they see? What were we doing that others would be commenting about our incredible love?

I searched my mind, but I really couldn't come up with anything concrete. In the case of the young single girl at the nursing home, my mind wondered if it was because she knew I was coming there to visit Ernie at least two and sometimes three times a day. Or was it because all the women staff were commenting about how good it smelled in Ernie's room. They all wanted to know the name of the cologne I had been purchasing for him. (Swiss Army, it's awesome.) Or maybe it was because of something I said or did when I called for a meeting shortly after Ernie was admitted to the nursing home. Was that it? Did she see my love in the way I was passionately fighting for my husband, determined to change the flaws in the system with the transition of patients from hospitals to nursing homes?

Ernie had knee replacement surgery less than a year before he fell and broke his femur bone. Recovery from the knee replacement was at another nursing home. Ernie went through a devastating time when he arrived, and he could not get the pain medication he needed. He had been on pain medication at the hospital and even before that at home. He called me at home around 9:30 pm in a lot of pain. He was in tears. The nurse had told him she couldn't give him a sleeping pill nor a pain pill. He was so frustrated and in so much pain. He actually told her, he was going to call 911 if she didn't give him the medication he needed. Instead he called me. I immediately called Dr. Matthews, who has been so much more to us than Ernie's Oncologist. Dr. Matthews called the nurse in charge and shortly after, Ernie received his medication.

Now, less than a year later, Ernie fell outside in our backyard and broke his femur bone. I had made up my mind he was not going back to that same nursing home where we were not pleased with his care. I took the time to visit other nursing homes. I asked the question if it would be a problem for him to be able to get the medication he needed if he was admitted there for his recovery. I didn't want him to have to experience what happened when he had his knee replacement. Ernie had to be on medication for his Bone Marrow Cancer, Parkinson's disease, arthritis, gout, etc., etc. Now he was dealing with recovery from femur surgery. That would require pain pills. In all honesty, he hates taking pain pills and always takes as little as possible, but at times, he knows he needs a pain pill.

The day he was admitted to the nursing home for recovery seemed to go well. I felt comfortable that he would be able to get all his medications as they had promised this would not be a problem. Ernie and I had been invited to a wedding that day. So after he was settled in, I told him I was going to attend the wedding dinner and that I would check with him a little later. When I got home, there was a message on the answering machine. I couldn't believe what I was hearing - Ernie was in pain and in tears. He told me that the nurse would not give him any pain medication. I immediately called the nursing home, and after a lot of hassle, I was told she would give him something for his pain. Sunday morning I went to church and when I returned, I saw there was a message on our phone. Again, it was Ernie, in pain and in tears. This was more than I could take, and I was upset and angry. This made no sense to me. Again, I had to battle to pull some strings to get the nurse to give him a pain pill.

Monday morning, I was in the nursing home office. An appointment was set up for me to meet with the head Social Worker, the young, pretty girl I spoke of earlier.

Two other staff people also attended the meeting. I came to that meeting prepared to get my questions answered. I wanted to know how this problem could be fixed, and I had no intention of leaving that office until I knew what had to be done. It had happened twice now, that Ernie had been put through undue suffering, and I wanted to know why. It was with much passion, I pleaded his case as I was determined to find out why this was happening. The Social Worker reminded me several times that I was beyond my appointment time allotment, but I didn't care.

In my quest, I found out that nursing homes cannot dispense any narcotic drugs unless they receive a hand-written prescription from the doctor. This was the requirement.

Believe me, with this knowledge, I was on a mission. Every doctor involved with Ernie's care got the message. When I told the surgeon, he said he had written on Ernie's transfer instructions what pain medication he was to be given. This was not good enough. I told him that I had been told that he had to provide a hand-written prescription for the pain pills as they were narcotics. I didn't stop there. Ernie's Oncologist, his Kidney Specialist, everyone heard the story. They were all shocked that this was happening. Ernie has excellent doctors, but in this case, I really loved Dr. Johnson's reaction. He is always so thorough and caring with his patients. When he heard this story, he immediately got up from his chair and boldly stated, "I am going to take care of this right now." Then he left the room.

I trust that the communication between hospitals and nursing homes concerning patient care and narcotics has been rectified. Praise God! Lesson learned – never leave the hospital and head to a nursing home without a hand-written prescription from the doctor for any narcotic drugs that you need to be taking. Amen!

Getting back to my being puzzled by the comments made concerning the love between my husband and me, and then being asked that mystifying question, "What's your secret?", I started to wonder – could it be that sometimes love has the ability to just flow from the depth of our hearts and souls naturally – without any effort or hard work on our part? So we don't even have to think about it, it just happens, and yet, it's inevitable, it's visible, and people can clearly see it? I wonder.

Love is an amazing thing. Everyone wants to be loved. Some people believe love is expressed in giving expensive gifts. For some it means intimacy. Then there is the song that seems to be trying to warn us that some people may be, "looking for love in all the wrong places." Hmmmmm!

In every marriage, I truly believe there will be times when you and your spouse will not agree. At times you will be upset with one another. Ernie and I have our differences, but one thing is sure, we never stay angry very long. We've learned that it is okay to disagree, but it's far better to forgive and get along. Life is so much better when we work together.

Ernie's cancer diagnosis put a whole new perspective on our thinking. Life became far more precious. We learned that some of the differences that we may have had in the past were really "picky" and "petty", and they didn't mean a thing. Cancer taught us to value each new day that we still have together. Each day became a gift – a blessing to enjoy. The journey battling cancer is so tough, but when there is love and support, that journey becomes tolerable.

I love this story about a little boy showing love:

A four year old child whose next door neighbor, an elderly gentleman, had recently lost his wife.

Upon seeing the man cry, the little boy went into the old gentleman's yard, climbed up onto his lap, and just sat there.

When the little boy's mother asked what he had said to the neighbor man, the little boy said, "Nothing, I just helped him cry."

Now that's love. Sometimes all we need to do is just be there.

One of my favorite stories of our love came into my life many years ago. On New Year's Eve, when Ernie and I were younger, we went out with friends for a steak dinner and then we went to a dance. We put on party hats, and at midnight, we shouted "Happy New Year", blew toy horns, and shook and rattled noise makers. We embraced and danced together into the New Year while the band played, "Auld Lang Syne". Now that we are older, our New Year's Eve celebration has changed. We generally eat a steak dinner at home, and then we watch T.V. We watch the ball come down in New York Times Square, and we wish each other a Happy New Year. After midnight, we eat some crazy foods such as: Ritz crackers and herring, and Miesfeld's ground round (raw) topped with salt, pepper, and onions on Johnson Bakery's Berlin Rye Bread. Then we enjoy some left-over Christmas cookies and candy, and of course, there is always a champagne toast. Then comes the best part.

For many, many years now, after we bring in the New Year with a kiss and hug, Ernie renews my contract. Yes, that's right. He renews my contract. He tells me, "I've decided to renew your contract. I'm going to keep you for another year." Oh, yes, now that's love! He's a keeper! I guess in his eyes, so am I.

What is love? What's your secret? Remember these awesome words from the Apostle Paul, "Love is patient, love is kind. It does not envy, it does not boast, it is not proud. It is not rude, it is not self-seeking, it is not easily angered, it keeps no record of wrongs. Love does not delight in evil, but rejoices with the truth. It always protects, always trusts, always hopes, always perseveres. Love never fails." (NIV) 1 Corinthians 13:4-8a

Jesus showed us what love is all about when he laid down His life for all of us while we were yet sinners. There is no greater love than this.

Thank God for His incredible gift of love through the sacrifice of His one and only Son, our Lord and Savior, Jesus Christ. This is God's ultimate gift of "LOVE" for you and for me. It's really no secret – **YOU ARE LOVED!**

Path Of A Princess

For years our Bethany Women's Ministry Team planned Women's Retreats in our area. We invited guest speakers in to do the presentations. We held these on Saturdays starting in the morning, serving the women lunch, and ending the retreat mid-afternoon. The women from our church were encouraged to invite guests to join us for this day of inspiration.

In 2009, God put it in my heart to be the speaker for the retreat. I had enjoyed many speakers in the past and felt called to take a turn leading a retreat. I invited my sister Diane to come. She brought her keyboard and accompanied us when we sang. My sister Rachel, and daughter-in-law Debbie, were also there for my presentation. We often chose to hold the retreat at Camp Y-Coda, an area just West of Sheboygan. This was a beautiful setting with hiking trails, beautiful areas of water, woods, grass, wild flowers, birds, etc. A wonderful spot to relax and enjoy God's creation, have quiet time, and be inspired. This was our plan for the retreat, but what was God's plan?

(Some of the information in my presentation has been told in previous chapters in this book. I chose to include the entire script so you know what God had planned for us to experience at that retreat. You may choose to refresh your memory by reading all of my script, or you may choose to scan through the first part of this.)

The title of my presentation given on Saturday, September 19, 2009, was called, "Path of a Princess".

Our guests were welcomed, and then I offered a prayer.

I continued with a brief introduction: I am married to my wonderful husband Ernie. We have four sons, Jeff, Tim, Todd, and Scott. We have three daughters-in-law, Debbie, Lisa, and Denise, and we also have ten grandchildren. I work part-time as the Executive Director of Rainbow Kids where we provide peer support groups for families who are grieving a loss due to death, divorce, separation, or abandonment.

I am going to invite you to come along with me on a journey – on the Path of a Princess. Before we get started, I want all of you women to know that each one of you is a Princess. Our Father in heaven is the King over all of us, and as His child, you are His special, precious Princess.

Sit back, relax, put aside your cares and concerns for a while, and spend some special time as you walk with our Father God, the King.

The Path Of A Princess

Once upon a time, there was a little girl, who was born on a beautiful, summer day in July. Her family consisted of her parents, five sisters, and four brothers. So if you are doing the math that made this little girl, child #10. From the very beginning, this child felt she was loved and cared for. She had a wonderful dad who read to her every day from a special book. On Sundays, the little girl and her family all went to church together in the morning and again in the evening. The little girl heard the Pastor read and tell stories from a special book. When she turned five, the little girl walked to school with her two older sisters. The pathway to their school was long. Every day at school, her teachers read and told stories to her from a special book.

In the Fall, the little girl had fun shuffling her feet, kicking up the beautifully colored leaves along her pathway to school. In the Winter, she plodded on through the cold, blustery winds and drifts of freshly fallen snow. She loved wearing her rubber boots and splashing in the puddles of rain in the Spring.

Some folks may have looked at this little girl, and thought – Poor Little Girl. They may have wondered why this little girl smiled so much, and why she always seemed so bubbly and happy. What they probably didn't realize, was that from the day this little girl was born, something special was happening in her life. Not only did she have eleven people in her family to love and care for her, she also had the blessing of being read to from that special book – at home, at school, and at church. What she was hearing, were messages from God's Word. She learned that she had a very special Father in heaven, and that her heavenly Father loved her so much, that He sent His only Son, Jesus, to die for her on a cross so all her sins could be forgiven. Because of Jesus' great love, she knew she would be able to live with her heavenly Father forever and ever. The little girl was so happy, she bubbled over with joy because she knew that her heavenly Father was the King. She knew that she was His precious child, a special little princess. She knew how much He loved her and that she belonged to Him.

So the heavenly King and the special little princess lived together happily ever after.

You probably all remember being read fairytales when you were little. Although, I'm sure you never heard the one I just told you.

We loved hearing those stories over and over again, probably because they always ended on a happy note with those special words, "and they lived together happily ever after."

If we recall the fairytales that we were taught, the pathways of the main characters were not at all very smooth.

Something was missing from the fairytale that I just told you. Where was the big bad wolf, the wicked witch, the evil stepmother, the absent father, the abusive siblings, the poison apple? Where were the struggles and scary times in this story?

If you could write your own princess story, what would it be like? What was the path that you have been on like?

We all know, there will be trials, temptations, and troubles in our lives. Why do tough times sometimes come along on the pathway of a Princess?

James 1:2 & 3 says, "Consider it pure joy, my brothers, whenever you face trials of many kinds, because you know that the testing of your faith develops perseverance." (NIV)

James 1:12 says, "Blessed is the man who perseveres under trial, because when he has stood the test, he will receive the crown of life that God has promised to those who love Him." (NIV)

1 Peter 1:6 & 7 says, "In this you greatly rejoice, though now for a little while you may have had to suffer grief in all kinds of trials. These have come so that your faith – of greater worth than gold, which perishes even though refined by fire – may be proved genuine and may result in praise, glory and honor when Jesus Christ is revealed." (NIV)

So the Bible tells us there are times we will be put to the fire – to be refined and purified like gold. At times, our faith will be tested, but when we remain strong in the Lord, the results will be phenomenal. We are promised "The Crown of Life".

How do we deal with the challenges in our lives? Where do we get our strength from when times are tough, and we need to fight the fight and carry on?

Some of us can't really pinpoint any dramatic story of a conversion experience. From my story, you can tell that from the time I was born, I was surrounded with the knowledge and love of the Lord. This truly was an awesome blessing.

I came from a family that was sometimes referred to as a "musical family". Christian music has definitely influenced my life. It may have influenced yours too. I'd like you to go back with me to childhood days. We are going to sing some of the songs that I learned when I was very young. For me, these songs were sung at school, at home, and at my church.

The first song we sang was 'This Little Light of Mine'. I loved that song. It taught me that even though I was only a little girl, I could let my light shine for Jesus. This song taught me that Satan was going to try to stop me from shining for Jesus, but I could decide to be strong and continue to shine for Him no matter what was going on in my life. I had decided that is what I wanted to do, shine for Jesus.

Next we sang, 'I'll Be A Sunbeam". Now wouldn't every little girl love to be a shining sunbeam for Jesus? I really loved that idea. In all of my life, wherever I was, I could be a shining sunbeam for Jesus. That would be so awesome.

I was blessed to learn so many wonderful children's songs. 'Jesus Loves Me'; 'I Have the Joy, Joy, Joy, Joy Down in My Heart'. I loved singing them all. They filled my heart and life with the Joy of the Lord.

One of my favorite things to do in the summertime was go to Vacation Bible School. There was a small brick building on Erie Avenue between 7th and 8th Street where Zion Church held V.B.S. Because our church did not offer V.B.S., my sisters, Rachel, Diane and I loved going to Zion's V.B.S. The influence this had on me was carried out throughout my life. I will always have a special heart for

Vacation Bible School. As an adult, I've continued to teach children in Vacation Bible School for over twenty years. One of my favorite songs that influenced my life that I learned in V.B.S. is the next song we will sing together.

At this time, we sang the song, 'Make Me a Blessing". I'd have to say the words of this song instilled in my heart the direction that God had for my future. I truly wanted God to help me to be a blessing to those who were struggling with difficulties in their lives. My prayer was that God would allow me to be a blessing to others as I let my life shine for him. I had a strong desire to tell the story of Jesus and His love, and I wanted everyone to know His power to forgive us. More than anything, I wanted God to make me to be a blessing so others would see Jesus' love in the things I said and did.

So life was great. My childhood was very happy. In my heart, I felt that I truly was a Princess. I believe the reason I was so content was that I knew that I was loved by my heavenly Father, the King of kings. Let's sing together our next song.

Next we sang the song, 'I'm A Child of the King'. Think about that, we are children of a King. It doesn't matter if we are rich or poor. It doesn't matter what possessions we have, God is preparing a mansion in heaven for us, His children. We belong to Him. He is our Father, and our Father is a King. Glory to God!

In all honesty, my family most likely would have been considered poor by the world's standards. Going through the depression with twelve mouths to feed had to be a difficult time. We may have been financially poor, but I truly never felt poor.

I know, I was too little to remember the days of the depression, so to this happy little princess, I guess I always believed, I had it all. In so many ways, I really did.

The greatest gift that we can possess as a child of the King, is that we can know that we can trust in the Lord, our Father, and believe in Him and His gift of salvation which has been given to all of us who truly believe. I had this blessing right from the start. I had and have this gift of grace.

Moving on –

When we become a teenager, what do most princesses start thinking about? Well, for me, I started thinking about searching for my "Prince Charming". I met mine pretty early in life. I was a sophomore in high school, and I was only 15 years old.

After dating for two and a half years, this princess thought – "This was the one." We were in love, so when I graduated from high school, I received my engagement ring. We planned to get married the following year.

I don't know your Prince Charming story, but I have to be honest with you, I probably was the only one who thought this was the right Prince Charming for me. Everyone around me felt I was making a big mistake. My family, my friends, and even my Pastor tried to tell me – this was not a good choice.

After meeting with our Pastor for pre-marital counseling, my Pastor hit me with some pretty thought-provoking words. These words were a warning from scripture that definitely got my attention. (II Corinthians 6:14 NIV) "Do not be unequally yoked together with unbelievers." The King James Version says, "Be ye not unequally yoked together with unbelievers."

Whoa! That was pretty tough stuff for me to be thinking about.

While it seemed like everyone around me felt like I was not making a good choice, to be honest with you, my Prince Charming's Mother didn't think her son was making a good choice in choosing me either. (I believe she thought this princess may have been too religious).

So, the logical thing for us to do was to listen to the concerns of everyone around us and break off our relationship. Right?

Well, being the intelligent, we know it all, teenagers that we were, we chose not to listen to them. In our fairytale world, I was thinking this was my Prince Charming, and I was his Princess. So we went ahead with our plans and got married.

When talking to our son, Scott, who was seventeen at the time, I said, "You probably never knew that everyone was thinking that dad and I shouldn't get married."

Scott said to me, "No, I didn't know that. Well, what did they know anyway?"

I responded, "Yeah, if we had listened to them, I guess you would never have been born, and that wouldn't have been good at all."

If you had to make a list of the most significant events that happened in your life that brought you to the point you are today, I think all of us who are married (or have been married) would certainly list "Getting Married" as one of those significant events.

Our pathway in life changes a lot once we become married. For most of us, following marriage, another significant event would be the birth of our children. We have four healthy sons for which we are very grateful, but along our journey, we also experienced the sadness of loss through experiencing two miscarriages.

When I was a child, my dad was the strong Christian leader in our family. When I got married, God called on me to stay strong in my faith. I needed to take on the role of being the Christian role model for our family. Many times my Christianity, my faith, was ridiculed and put down. At times, this was very hurtful. So the big bad wolves – or the trials and temptations suddenly started creeping into my life and my pathway became a bit rocky and rough. Some of you have had this experience. This is a time when we need to remember to "Trust in the Lord with all your heart, and lean not on your own understanding." (NIV) Proverbs 3:5

I was 30 years old when my dad passed away, and 12 years later, my mother passed on, the day before my 42nd birthday. We always wish we could have more years with our loved ones, but I was very grateful for the years that I did have, because both of my parents were very influential in my life. My memories of them are definitely special.

Many people are dealing with a job loss at this time. In our married life, Ernie experienced three plant closings. After the first one, we were transferred from Wisconsin to Tennessee. This meant leaving our oldest son, Jeff, who was a senior in college behind.

Our second oldest son, Tim, was already struggling with drug and alcohol abuse. This had started when he was in 8th grade and continued on through his high school years. Frequent visits from the police, and trips to the courthouse with our son were not really the pathway that I would have liked to be on.

Our move to Tennessee in 1983, became a blessing, as this got our son away from his drinking, drug using friends. After a while, Tim got over his bad habits and turned his life over to the Lord. Now he shares his experience in an effort to help others.

Moving 650 miles south was a great learning experience for me. I thought the move would be very easy. We would still be in the United States where most of the people speak English. Except for the temperature being warmer, I thought life would be just the same in Tennessee as it was in Wisconsin. (So I thought).

Many times while I was living in Tennessee, I was asked where I was from. My northern accent was noticed easily every time I spoke. Sometimes people would ask me what foreign country I came from. There were times I found myself feeling so far away from home, family and friends, and I would start singing this next song that we will sing together.

Our next song was, 'The King's Business'. My home in Sheboygan, Wisconsin, sometimes felt so far away. I admit, I may have felt like a foreigner at times, but it was clear to me that the message of the last line in the verse of this song was why God had brought me to Tennessee. I was here on a mission for my Father, the King. God had work for me to do in Tennessee. There was no doubt in my mind that God had planned our pathway in life to include time living in Jackson, Tennessee.

I found a church home shortly after we moved there and got involved. I taught Vacation Bible School every year we were there. I became active in the Women's Bible Study group, used my bookkeeping skills serving as the Women's Society Treasurer, played on the church volleyball team, and worked as a church secretary the last six months we lived in Tennessee. God truly helped to make me a blessing to others as he allowed my life to shine brightly for Him. A beautiful, Christian, elderly woman in our church stated to me just before we left to move back to Wisconsin – "You surely have left a mark on our church." I was grateful to God for allowing me to let my light shine for Him, in what at times may have seemed to be a foreign land.

We had been in Tennessee four years when the plant Ernie was working at closed. This was the second plant closing loss he experienced.

God put us on the pathway back to Sheboygan, Wisconsin, but with this move, our sons, Tim and Todd chose to stay behind in Tennessee. Tim was through college and had a good job, Todd had just started college.

Todd likes to tell this story, "Most of the time when kids go off to college, they leave home. When I went to college, my parents were the ones who left home."

This was another difficult move for our family. After tears and hugs, we departed and, once again, headed out on the pathway that God had planned for our lives.

Ernie had found employment at Tecumseh in Sheboygan Falls. We had decided I would not get a job for at least a year. Scott, our six year old, was enrolled at Washington Elementary School in kindergarten.

God had been working on me to visit several churches in Sheboygan when we got back. After several months of searching, he made it very clear to me which church we should attend. Shortly after, the Pastor of that church asked me if I would be willing to apply for a staff position that was opening at the church. He encouraged me to do this, but after I applied, I had second thoughts. I started thinking that I would not be qualified to do this work.

I went to the first interview with the attitude that they really should just pick the other girl who was applying. I had heard that she had a college degree in Christian doctrine. She would be the better choice. In the back of my mind, I thought it would be better for me to go back to the bank where I had worked before we moved to Tennessee. At the interview I mentioned something about doing this. That was my plan.

A second interview was called, but before that happened, I was talking with my sister-in-law, Audrey. When I expressed my insecurities about my qualifications for this job, she challenged me. She felt that I had everything that I needed to do this job. As she encouraged me, she pointed out many things that I had done in the past.

After Audrey's encouragement, I found God working on my heart. I realized that if this was His will, I needed to trust Him knowing that He would provide all that I needed to serve Him.

If there is anything we can learn from trusting God, it is the fact that our God is faithful. All He asks of us is to be willing to step outside our comfort zone for Him, and He will provide all that we need. Words that have become special to me that I learned from the Founder of RAINBOWS, Suzy Yehl Marta, are these: GOD DOESN'T CALL THE QUALIFIED, GOD QUALIFIES THE CALLED.

After the third interview, I was told that I was selected for the job. My title was - Church Life Coordinator. The Pastor often told me that if I had not made the move to Tennessee, he didn't feel I would have been right for that position. God had me on a mission to serve and touch the lives of others in Tennessee, but He also was preparing my heart for the work He had prepared for me to do when I returned to Wisconsin. I worked with children's and women's ministry at the church. Pastor Gary was a huge influence on my life. He encouraged me to get into leading women's Bible studies, and he also encouraged me to go through training with the Rainbow Kids, Inc., program. For over 20 years, God provided so many blessings in these ministries.

Back in Tennessee, our son, Tim was doing fine. For two years our two sons Tim, and Todd, lived together. Then Tim was offered a good job in the Nashville area. He continued his education and received a degree as a Certified Public Accountant. He became a volunteer in the Big Brother's program. He shared his experience with drugs and drinking with teens encouraging them not to make the same mistakes he had made.

Todd dropped out of college after just two years. After that, he struggled for many years not really knowing what employment he wanted to pursue. During this time, Todd experienced poverty, homelessness, hunger, and living in areas where roaches and rats were prevalent. Yet, he always remained close to the Lord. At times his stories were sad and frightening. Many times I told him to just come back to Sheboygan and live with us until he could get his life back together. He told me later that he was very close to doing that a couple times, but then God would always provide a way to keep him in Jackson, Tennessee again. After five years of struggles, he was in a bad car accident. His car was totaled, and he had some injuries. A drunk driver had hit the rear end of Todd's car which sent him down into a ravine. The car hit a cement culvert below, and Todd blacked out. He said he felt that he had died. When he came to, he heard people on the roof of his car trying to get him out. After a very long time of treatment and physical therapy, Todd finally recovered.

Pastor Gary, who was now serving a church in Florida, came to our home for dinner when he was visiting in Sheboygan. In our conversation, he asked how Todd was doing. I shared the struggle that Todd was having finding direction for his life. I told Pastor Gary that I always thought Todd would be a good Christian Counselor. He seemed to have the perfect qualifications for doing this.

Five days later, I received a letter in the mail from Todd. It read: And now, the news you have all been waiting for – Drum Roll Please – I have enrolled in Union University, and I intend to get my degree in Social Work. The tears flowed down my face. This was truly an answer to prayer. Then God spoke to me saying, "Now your son Todd will be ready to be an excellent counselor. He will be very understanding of the needs of the people he will be serving."

We need to remember to trust in the Lord with all our hearts always. As parents we want to protect our children, and we forget that these kids, first of all, belong to God. He is working in their lives, grooming them to be who He created them to be. Todd's wife, Denise, doesn't like it when I talk about how I tried to get Todd to move back to Sheboygan. She always says, "No, if he would have done that, we never would have met." So true. That would have been terrible. It was definitely in God's plan that Todd and Denise and their two precious girls, Kaitlyn and Maddie would someday become a family. What a blessing they all are.

Several years later, Ernie experienced a third job loss. This time he went down to receiving his last unemployment check, but God, in His perfect timing, provided a job in Cedarburg at Amcast. This meant traveling 45 minutes each way in all kinds of weather on the freeway, but he was grateful to be employed again as a Plant Supervisor.

In 1997, pain in Ernie's neck warranted his making an appointment to see the doctor. Ernie had felt quite certain the pain was from stress with his job. After several more doctor visits for more testing, we were told the devastating news. He was diagnosed with Multiple Myeloma – Bone Marrow Cancer. We couldn't believe this was true, and we were in total shock. I kept thinking in the tests they had ordered for him, they would find out they were wrong. I was so in denial. All the tests confirmed that it was cancer. His Oncologist, Dr. Matthews told us if he went through chemo treatment and had a Bone Marrow Transplant, he could probably live another five more years.

At the consultation, Ernie was told that if he didn't have a religion, he should get one, because he would need this to get him through the treatment and transplant.

September 1997, the treatments were started and the battle began. More than ever, God called on us to trust in the Lord with all our hearts. Just before the transplant, Ernie's good white stem cells were collected to be transplanted in him later.

Any of you who have dealt with cancer know the battle. I trust that you also know the importance of and the power of prayer. We've learned so much from dealing with cancer. We have definitely learned to understand how precious each day is that God gives to us.

Life seems to take on a whole new meaning when you feel like you are dealing with a death sentence. Far too often in our relationships, we get hung up on picky, petty things that truly have little or no significance. Cancer often seems to help you put life back into perspective, and the power of prayer becomes so significant.

Ernie's first transplant experience did bring him to a closer relationship with God. He saw the power of prayer working in him and learned to trust in God for his care and healing. He was at death's door many times, and time and time again, God pulled him through. From everywhere, he was hearing the words, "I'm praying for you," or "We are praying for you."

I really couldn't even think about counting down the five years we were told he would have. For most of that time, he was battling sickness and pain.

Several years before Ernie's diagnosis with cancer, my doctor told me that in time, I would need to have a hysterectomy. In 2001, the doctor said that it was time to go ahead with having this surgery. I thought about it and decided, I'd better set this up. Ernie still had insurance that would cover my health care, and that would be very important.

When I called our son, Todd, to tell him of my plan, he said, "Oh good, Mom, I was going to tell you that you should be doing this." I was puzzled at his remark and asked him about it. I wouldn't have thought that he even knew I would need this surgery. He told me he would explain another time. He didn't want to talk about it. I had the surgery in February, and in May we took a trip to visit Todd in Tennessee. I had all my materials along that I would be using to teach V.B.S. I showed Todd what I was working on, and he asked me when V.B.S. was going to be. I told him in June. Then he said, "Oh...that's why." I asked him what he was talking about.

Todd told me that on January 1, God had spoken to him and had told him he needed to tell me I should set up an appointment to have my hysterectomy now, so that I would be healed by June. We both thought this was a pretty awesome revelation that God had given him.

Well, June came, and I had an awesome week teaching V.B.S.

Right after VBS ended, Ernie started having extreme pain in his back and down his leg. There was a spot on the end of his spine that the doctors couldn't figure out what it was. They were prescribing the strongest painkillers possible (OxyContin, Oxycodone, Morphine, along with Valium). At times, the pain was still so bad that I had to call 911, and he had to be hospitalized and be put on I.V. painkillers.

The next months were awful. At one point, I actually told God that if it was His will, He should just take Ernie home to heaven. I couldn't bear to see him in this terrible pain any longer. The doctors decided to try an Epidural injection. They had to wean him off the blood thinner medication he was on first. He was kept sedated most of the time. His snoring was so loud, you could hear him far down the hospital hallways. Finally, they were ready to do the Epidural. The next day, he was sent home from the hospital. The following morning, his temperature went up to 104.9. I had to take him back to the hospital. After several doctors checked him out, he was diagnosed with Spinal Meningitis. We were told that one in a million people would ever get this from an Epidural. Ernie was the one in a million. That afternoon, Dr. Matthews ordered a very strong antibiotic I.V. that he sometimes referred to as Dynamite. I decided to stay with Ernie at the hospital through the night as he was so sick, he wouldn't have been able to call for help even if he needed it.

At 10:00 pm that night, our Pastor Ted and his wife, Bette, came to see Ernie at the hospital. We talked awhile and then we formed a circle around Ernie's bed, held hands, and he prayed over Ernie. Our daughter-in-law Debbie was there with us. Shortly after they all left, Ernie started sweating profusely, and the fever broke. He felt so good, he wanted to watch T.V. I was so stressed out and tired, I decided it would be best for me to just go home and get some rest. The following day he was able to return home. God pulled him through another tough battle.

After seven months of dealing with this horrible pain and the doctors being puzzled by the strange object on his spine, the pain finally went away. I asked the Doctor, "What did you do to get rid of Ernie's pain?"

He said, "We didn't do anything. You'll have to talk to the man upstairs about that."

I said, "Thank you for telling us. We have been talking to the man upstairs, and now we know where all the credit is due."

God had performed a miracle of healing.

It was years later that I realized, this had been year five for Ernie's cancer. I also came to realize why God had spoken to Todd, and I had been encouraged to have my hysterectomy earlier that year. It may have been so I would be healthy enough to teach V.B.S. in June, but more than that, I think God wanted me to be ready to help Ernie get through the seven months of terrible pain and suffering that started the week after V.B.S. – in June.

Ernie passed the five year mark and started to do so well. Year six passed, then year seven, eight, nine and ten, and then came year eleven. When he hit eleven years of remission, we were told his counts were getting too high. In January, we were told a second transplant was necessary. He had been doing so well. I really didn't want to face this again. I had a lot of concern that this would be too hard on him. I was hoping God would somehow stop the process. What I think I was doing was a lot of wishful thinking.

I asked the Doctor if they could just do the chemo treatments for a couple months and skip the transplant. I was concerned Ernie was too old for this. The answer was that it was important for him to have another transplant.

The transplant date was set for May 26, 2009. Shortly before that, I had heard the news on T.V. that someone who had contracted the Swine Flu – H1N1 Flu, had passed away at one of the Milwaukee hospitals. That news really bothered me.

When I talked with the nurse who gave me instructions for Ernie's admittance, I asked her, "Are you still going to do this with the Swine Flu being in Milwaukee?"

I really didn't know which Milwaukee hospital had reported the loss as the news reporter didn't specify which one.

The nurse said, "Oh yes, we will still be going ahead with transplants. That won't be a problem."

So I wondered why I was feeling so concerned.

When we were first told Ernie needed another transplant, the recollection of the first transplant haunted me, and my fears and worries had to be dealt with. He had faced death so many times that I dreaded thinking about doing this all over again. I truly was concerned about his age as well. When I thought about another transplant for him, I often found myself in tears. I made up my mind not to even let thoughts go to the possibility of him having another transplant.

Pastor Ted and Bette visited us at our home and Pastor Ted wanted to know more details about the transplant. After we had talked a long time, he asked me, "Don't you ever cry?"

I said, "Yes, sometimes I cry, but I try not to think about this a lot, because if I do, I'm going to be too sad, and I really don't want to waste time and miss the joy that God has planned for us in each day. We still can find so much in our lives to enjoy."

I do know that at times, we need to just stop whatever we are doing and allow ourselves to have a good cry. Maybe I don't do that enough. Sometimes I feel like I am crying so hard on the inside. I do know it's okay to cry. Even Jesus wept when He was sad.

Another of my favorite songs is 'The Warrior is a Child' sung by Twila Paris. We sang this together.

This was another song that spoke to my heart. Many times we have battles that we have to face in life. With God, we know we will always be the winner. This doesn't mean that we will not suffer and be wounded in the fight. Many times I've been told by others that I am strong. The truth of the matter is that many times I am crying on the inside, and so often, I try to hide my tears. When I am knocked down, that's when I run home to my Father. Sometimes I need to drop my sword and just cry. That's when I know, I am His child, and I need to find rest in His love at His feet. His armor is the best, and He is always waiting with open arms to hold us up through the battles in our lives.

At an appointment with Dr. Hari, Ernie's Oncologist at Froedtert Cancer Clinic, I asked, "Will you be giving Ernie a lesser dose of chemo because of his age?"

The doctor said, "No, I will be giving him the normal dose that we give to everyone."

Ernie was told that he would be in the hospital for at least four weeks, and then he had to stay in the Milwaukee area for another two weeks.

I popped out the words, "I'm not going to take him to some dirty motel." I really thought I'd rather have him home where I could care for him the best.

On the day Ernie was admitted, I was quite amazed when the doctor on duty came in and told us they were going to give Ernie 10% less of the normal dose of chemo. Hummmmmmm? I wondered where that idea came from.

For one hour he ate the big glasses of ice to help him ward off mouth sores that are a side effect of having a transplant. He did this while the huge injection of chemo was injected into him. He was complimented on doing so well eating the ice. When the nurse asked him if there was anything else he needed, he told the nurse he could use some de-icer. She laughed and said that was the first time she heard that request.

Driving home from the hospital that day, I started to cry just thinking about the tough journey ahead. I cried out to God telling him how I wished Ernie wouldn't have had to go through this again. Over and over again, I kept on saying, "It's too hard, it's just too hard, Lord". I knew very well there was no turning back. The huge shot of chemo was already in him. Then I started praying,

"Lord, please, please help him through this." Now it was time again for me to put my trust in the Lord. Immediately, I felt God's love encompass me. My tears were dried, and I felt at peace.

The next day, Ernie's good white stem cells that they had collected and preserved 11 years prior to this transplant, were now injected back into his body. Amazing! I found myself praying that they would be sure they had the right stem cells for him. Again, trust in the Lord with all your heart.

Ernie shared the precautions they took to make sure they had the stem cells that belonged to him. They were unthawed and injected all at the proper time. We were very impressed with all the precautions they were taking in this process.

We had been told that days six through ten would be the toughest. Ernie would be very sick at that time. Every day I went to visit, he was up, dressed, and eating well. In about a week, I was told I had to wear a gown, mask, and rubber gloves. Every day I expected Ernie to get very sick. One day he had a little diarrhea a couple hours after he ate his meals, but it wasn't a big deal. After that day, he was fine, so I stopped thinking about him getting sick, because it most likely wasn't going to happen. It didn't.

I was totally shocked when Ernie called me on Day 17 and said he could go home.

While the nurse was giving us instructions before his release, I noticed a little bit of a rash on his arm. I asked her about this and was told that she would give him some Benadryl before we left, and I should get some more at the pharmacy when I picked up his other prescriptions.

I got Ernie settled in at home and went to pick up his prescriptions. By the time I got back, he said he needed some more Benadryl. A couple hours later, the itching and burning got worse, so I told him he better call the hospital number that they had given him if any concerns or problems came up. He called the doctor at the hospital and was told he had to come back as soon as possible.

His suitcase was still packed, so we got back in the van. Our daughter-in-law, Debbie, drove us back to Milwaukee to the hospital. This was not an easy drive for her. She was hoping nothing bad would happen before we got there.

That night was the most difficult for us. When I left him, he looked so sad. He told me he felt so miserable. He was back in the same room in the Bone Marrow Transplant Unit, but the walls that had been decorated with cards and other special gifts were now bare. It was heart-breaking having to leave him there. That night, I felt like I needed to drop my sword and just cry, as the words of the song say. The night was long and hard to be alone, but I knew God was with both of us, and I could share all my sorrow and concerns with Him.

I could hardly wait for morning to come. Ernie called fairly early to tell me how bad the rash had gotten. He described his whole body to be fire engine red, and his skin looked like a red alligator. He said the burning and itching were so bad, he could hardly stand it. The doctors didn't know what to do for him. They didn't know what this was. They had put in a call for the Dermatologist to see Ernie and were waiting for her to come. She was still in a meeting.

After we hung up the phones, I immediately went to my computer and put in a request to our Prayer Warriors – family, friends, and church prayer chain.

About one and a half hours later, Ernie called and said, "You won't believe what happened." He sounded so excited. He said, "I was just sitting here in my room on the chair in my pajamas waiting for them to let me take a shower, and all of a sudden, a warm feeling came over my body. It started at the top of my head, and went 'ppphhhssss', like a washing feeling going down through my body."

Then he continued, "I looked at my skin, and I was totally healed. The rash was completely gone. I called the nurse in, and she couldn't believe her eyes. She ran for the doctors, and when they came in, the one doctor who had been with me all night, saw what had happened to me. He gasped, and jumped backwards letting out a scream. He was so shocked. He said he wanted to see my whole body, and he checked me over and saw that the rash was totally gone. The doctors asked me how this happened, and I told them it had to have been "Divine Intervention".

Wow! Divine Intervention! Truly that is what it was. The doctors had not done anything to make this go away. They were at a loss as to what they should do. So God took over and performed a healing miracle right before their eyes. All I could say was, "Praise God, Thank You, Lord! I was so anxious to get to see this myself. When I got to the hospital, his skin was beautiful. Not one speck of rash remained. Amazing!

They kept Ernie in the hospital one more night to make sure he was all right, and then sent him back home. Still way ahead of schedule. This was only Day 19. His counts had rebounded beautifully, and he didn't get any mouth sores. The doctors were so impressed with his recovery. The nurses became our friends and wanted to say, "Goodbye", and tell us Ernie deserved the "Best Trouper Ever Award" for being their best ever patient. They all loved him.

Several weeks later, we had an appointment with Dr. Hari at the Cancer Clinic at Froedtert in Milwaukee. Dr. Hari was full of smiles when he saw Ernie knowing that he had done so well. That is when he told us the news that about took our breath away. Out of the 12 Bone Marrow Transplant patients that were there at the time Ernie was, Ernie was the only one who did not get the Swine – H1N1 Flu. Eleven of the patients were infected with this deadly flu. He told us that at that time, three of them had already died. He told us that it is pretty much impossible to save a transplant patient through a battle with this flu. Ernie, the oldest patient there, was the only person who escaped getting that flu. Not only did he escape once, he even wound up going back into that unit for another two nights when he had that terrible rash, only to see God perform an incredible miracle of healing. WOW!

I have to tell you, we walked out of that clinic feeling numb. I felt like a zombie. It felt like my feet weren't even touching the floor. I was totally in shock, in awe and amazement, and I was totally thanking God for caring for Ernie and blessing him so richly. How great is our God!

*None of us know about our tomorrows, but we have right now - today.

Wherever our path will take us, we can know that our Father, the King of kings, is right there beside us, guiding us, loving us, and blessing us in so many ways. All He asks of us, is to trust in Him.

I hope that through my life stories, you could see that sometimes, we may be in the midst of tough struggles for a very long time, - sometimes for years, but I also hope that you can see that God is always in control. He is always working out something very special to fulfill His purpose in our lives. Over and over again, He just asks that we trust in Him with all our hearts.

The sign outside at our Bethany Church reads, "Turn trying times into trusting times." We all need to remember to do this.

At the conclusion of the morning session of our Women's Retreat, I said, "We are going to take a break now and spend some time alone with God. You can go outside and find yourself a quiet place. Take along a handout that I've prepared to guide you in your devotions. We'll meet back here for lunch at 11:30."

When God Calls

Path of a Princess (Part two)

During our break time, I decided to sit outside and go over the handout that I had prepared for the women. I stayed close to the Johnsonville Lodge where I was giving my presentation.

Some of the women from our ministry team who were in charge of lunch got things ready. It had been decided that Amy's husband, Pastor Lyle, would pick up the Sub sandwiches and bring them to the retreat location so that none of us would have to leave the site.

By 11:30, the women started coming back in to the lodge for lunch. We had been eating for a while enjoying conversation with those around our tables, when Christi came into the lodge and called out, "Does anyone here know CPR? You need to come quick."

It didn't take long to find out that one of the women who had been at the retreat had not returned to the lodge. Christi had gone out to see if she could find her. Luanne was found slumped over in her car – unresponsive. 911 was called immediately.

Several of the women responded to the request for CPR assistance. My daughter-in-law Debbie was one of them.

Most of us went outside to do what we could to help. By the grace of God, Pastor Lyle was still there with us. Luanne's cell phone provided numbers of her family. Her husband was not answering our calls.

Many of us were together in a circle holding hands and praying. At times I was off by myself praying. I wasn't sure what God wanted me to do. The afternoon session of the retreat was still before me. Would I be able to bring the women back for this? How well would they be able to focus? What was the proper thing to do? I prayed to God for His guidance.

The women who were working on Luanne were not seeing success. It seemed to take a very long time for the responders to arrive. All we could do is wait and pray. Once they arrived, our women attending to Luanne stepped away and let the responders take over.

The women who tried so hard to bring life and breathe back to Luanne were shaken. Debbie told me she felt it would be best for her to leave. This was a very traumatic experience.

After quite some time, Luanne's husband Ted was reached. The ambulance team was taking Luanne's body to the hospital. Ted was able to meet them there.

After the ambulance pulled away, Pastor Lyle stood with all of us in a circle and said a prayer. By that time, I knew I had to go on as best I could. There was a conclusion to this presentation, and God would want me to present this.

Before I continued on with my prepared script, I felt the need to speak to the women. This is what I said:

I've been hearing so many of you blaming yourself for not being able to do more for Luanne. I'm hearing a lot of "I wish I would have", or "If only I would have" statements. I just want you to know that your feelings are very normal, but please allow yourselves to work through this, and don't blame yourself for what happened.

We have to realize that this was the exact place and the exact time that God had planned to take Luanne to be with Him in heaven, and there was nothing that any of us could do to change that. God is in control.

You all need to know, you did an awesome job trying to help her. That's just what I do when I see my husband is in trouble. Our first instinct is to fight for the lives of those we care about. We don't want them to leave us. But God knows exactly when our time on this earth will be over, and when the day comes that He has planned to take my husband to heaven, I will not be able to do anything to keep him here. I know that someday I will need to let him go.

Today, God called His Princess Luanne to come home to live with Him, and we can know, she will be living happily forever after with Him. We all need to accept this, and know that God knows all things. We need to trust Him.

Path of a Princess (Continued)

I read John 20:24-29 (NIV)

After Jesus rose from the dead, His disciple Thomas didn't want to believe Jesus had risen until he saw the wounds on Jesus' hands and feet. So Jesus came to Thomas and showed him his wounds, and the greatest story ever was revealed.

Let's sing together – 'Because He Lives'.

The words of this song bring so much hope into my life. Knowing that God sent His Son into this world to love us, heal us, forgive us, and conquer sin and death and hell on the cross so one day we can live in heaven in eternal glory can bring such peace to our lives. We can face tomorrow knowing that our future is in His hands and that one day life's war with pain and sorrow will be over. With calm assurance, we can know the victory will be ours, because Jesus lives. Praise God!

I had the opportunity to speak to the Oostburg Kiwanis Club, and a man who was a Rainbow Kids Facilitator was there. He knew Ernie was having the Bone Marrow Transplant, so I told him the miracle rash healing that we experienced. When I finished telling this story, Tom said, "You know what you have to do now, don't you?"

I said, "What's that?"

He said, "You need to tell everyone that story."

I told him, "I am. That's what I am doing. I want everyone to know, God performs miracles. A lot of people don't believe. I love sharing Ernie's story with everyone I can."

All too often, we try to hide our wounds. We try to cover them up. We don't want anyone to know about our scars. All too often, we don't tell our stories of painful situations. That's not what Jesus did. Jesus revealed His wounds. He shared His story.

Behind our wounds, we too have a story. My story will not be the same as yours. That's because God has a special plan for each one of us. He has us all on a different pathway. Your life story is every bit as special as mine, because in God's eyes, you too, are His Princess. Never forget – You belong to Him. You are a child of the King.

At this time, I had the women get into small groups where they could share their thoughts on the questions that they worked on for their time of devotion. They were told to feel free to share their stories of how God had touched them in their lives. I read these words from 1 Thessalonians 5:11 (NIV) "Therefore, encourage one another, and build each other up."

After the time of sharing in small groups, we had a session on forgiveness. The women were asked to bring their worries, concerns, feelings of anger, pride, jealousy, or whatever burdens they were carrying and to give them all over to God. They did this by squirting food coloring into a bowl of pure, clean water. The food coloring represented their burdens and concerns. They were told to say a little prayer asking God to help them with whatever struggles they were dealing with.

When this exercise was complete, I stirred the water and said, "When we hold on to all these burdens, we feel pretty yucky inside – just like this water looks like now. We don't have to stay feeling this way. God wants us to find forgiveness through Him."

I have a jar with a couple cups of bleach in it to use for this exercise of forgiveness, as I pour this bleach into the bowl of colored water, I refer to it as God's forgiveness.

I stir the water and say, "God tells us to cast all our burdens on Him. He cares for us. He forgives all our sins and takes them from us. When He does this, we can be free to live our lives shining brightly once again, for Him."

The bleach (forgiveness) will take all the dark color from the water and the water will look clear and bright again.

Closing –

Take these words with you -

Trust in the Lord with all your heart, and lean not on your own understanding. In all your ways, acknowledge Him, and He will direct your paths. (NIV) Proverbs 3:5 & 6

Let's sing together 'Trust and Obey'.

Oh those two little words. How important they are for us to remember. This song tells us that there is no other way to be happy in Jesus. We need to trust and obey Him. Walk by His side, have fellowship with Him, sit at His feet, go where He wants you to go, do His will, and know that He will take care of your burdens, doubts, and fears. All He asks of us is that we 'Trust and Obey' Him. Remember these two little words.

I concluded our retreat with prayer.

My work was not done. After packing up my materials and helping our women's ministry team clean up, I could focus on what I needed to do next.

I drove directly over to the home of Ted and Luanne. By the time I got there, Ted was already home from the hospital. He was home alone. Ted and Luanne were not only church friends, we were also friends because they both had trained to be Rainbow Kids Facilitators. We had worked together helping kids and adults through their loss situations for many years. Ted's first choice was always to work with adults who were grieving a loss due to death. I felt the need to spend time with Ted. He would appreciate my company. I shared all that had happened at the retreat, and allowed him to ask questions. He was so at peace knowing that Luanne went home at the women's retreat. She was there spending time being close to her Lord when He came to call her to her heavenly home. She had a heart attack and was taken quickly. Ted said that he hoped that his final time here on earth would be that special.

A short time later, a time was set up where Ted and one of his sons could meet with me at Camp Y-Koda. I shared the message from the presentation that I had given, and they both had some time to ask questions and get some closure to the loss of their loved one, Luanne. Ted wanted his son, who was struggling with his faith, to know the details that surrounded his mother's passing.

We can plan our lives and think that we have everything under control, but we truly never know when God will take us on another pathway. One thing we can count on is that wherever He leads us, God will always be there to show us His will, His way, and His love.

Before the women at the retreat went outside they picked up the guide for their time of devotion. These were the questions used for their time of reflection. I am sharing this with all of you. I hope you will be blessed as you read the scripture and answer the questions below on your own. God Bless You!

List the most significant events that have occurred in your past that have influenced you to be the person you are today.

Read Psalm 23 several times and let these words of scripture speak to you.

What promises can you claim from these verses?

What does Jesus warn his disciples of in John 16:33b

What does Jesus promise here?

What does James 1:2 & 3 tell us about facing troubles and why?

Read James 1:12

What has God provided to guide us in times of trouble? Read Psalm 119:105

Read Philippians 4:4-7

There will be times of trial in our lives, what does Psalm 120:1 tell us? Read Psalm 121

In John 14:1, Jesus tells His disciples not to let their hearts be troubled. What are they supposed to do instead?

What does God promise in Isaiah 41:10&13?

Our journey in life needs to be a walk of faith trusting in the Lord. We have the opportunity every day to let our lights shine for Him. Our lives are like a letter being read by all those around us. The Holy Spirit lives in our hearts. The things that we do and say should be Christ-like. How can you let your life be a "Letter of Recommendation for Christ Jesus"?

Read Galatians 3:26-29; Read John 1:12 & 13; Romans 8:16 & 17; 1 John 3:1-3

If you could tell others about your "Path as a Princess" (as a child of the King), what would you like them to know?

In I Timothy 6:15, Paul refers to God as the blessed and only Ruler, the _____ of _____ and Lord of lords. In Revelations 15:3, John writes, "Great and marvelous are your deeds, Lord God Almighty, Just and true are your ways, _____ of the ages." What words did Pilate have fastened to Jesus' cross? Read John 19:19

Read John 3:16

Because of God's great love for you, you can claim the promise that when your journey on this earth is done, and you have put your trust in our heavenly Father, the King of kings, YOU, (yes, YOU, His special princess) will live happily forever after in eternity with Him. Praise God, and thank Jesus for His saving grace!

Enjoy some special time drawing closer to your Heavenly Father, the King of kings.

Surprise!

It was July 18, 2016. Just a couple weeks before, I had told some of my family and friends that I had completed my last story for my book. I was really feeling good about that. Then ten days later, another chapter seemed to evolve that I felt needed to be included.

When I first started thinking about writing a book, I kept wondering how I should begin. Where should I start? Now my question is, when should this book end? I do believe this will be the last chapter.

When we - Scott, Debbi, Orion, Barry, Ernie and I traveled to Lebanon, Tennessee, for Easter, we had several days to spend with Todd, Denise, Kaitlyn, and Maddie, and also with Tim, Lisa, Nicole, Micah, and Jared. We all had a wonderful time. It was special celebrating Easter with three of our sons and their families.

Saying good-bye to the ones you love is never easy. We were at Todd's home when Tim's family was saying good-bye to us. I overheard our granddaughter Nicole tell our daughter-in-law Debbi that they were probably coming to Wisconsin this summer. That got me thinking. I wondered if they would be coming at the time of my birthday. I was hitting the ¾ century mark. The big 75 years old. Nobody said anything to me that they were coming to Wisconsin, so I just put Nicole's comment in the back of my mind.

While we were in the van on our way back to Wisconsin our grandson Orion said, "Jared said they are coming to Wisconsin this summer." Orion's Mom, Debbi, was trying to hush him from talking about this. So again, I just put this in the back of my mind, as nobody seemed to be talking to me about the plan.

I did get the feeling that Debbi was going to be scolding Orion for saying that Jared was coming in summer, so after a little while, I told Debbi that she shouldn't be too harsh with Orion, because I had already heard Nicole bring up this subject.

On Father's Day, Ernie always receives a call from our out-of-town sons. After he talked with Tim for a while, Tim asked if we would like to talk with Nicole. When we were about to end the conversation, Nicole said she was excited that they were coming to Wisconsin in two weeks. A bit puzzled, I asked, "Does Grandpa know about this?" I looked at Ernie, and he didn't say anything. He just shook his head, "No". I could hear Tim and Lisa speaking up to Nicole in the background. Then Nicole started making excuses like, she had this wrong. She said that they were going to meet some of the family at a waterpark.

Again, the wheels in my head starting rolling, as I tried to make sense of what was seemingly going to be a surprise.

Ernie had told me the two of us were going out for dinner at Rupp's Restaurant on my birthday which was on a Saturday, July 9. Jeff and Debbie were going to be in Wisconsin Dells vacationing, and they wouldn't be back home until late Saturday. Debbie had said we could come to their house for a birthday celebration on Sunday. Our son Scott asked what we were going to do for my birthday, so I told him he should check with Debbie. I was sure they would be invited to the party at Jeff and Debbie's home too.

Scott did tell me they were going to the Dells for a few days and planned to meet up with Jeff and Debbie's family.

I had a lot of guesses going on in my mind. Would Ernie and I be asked to go to the Dells too? Were Tim and Lisa and their kids just going to the Dells and not coming to Sheboygan? I knew Todd, Denise, and their girls, Kaitlyn and Maddie had just traveled to Atlanta, Georgia, to Six Flags for their vacation. Todd's family generally came to visit us in Wisconsin once a year in October, so I didn't think any more about any possibility that they would be coming in the summer.

Two weeks from when we had talked with Nicole would have been the weekend of July fourth. Scott, Debbi, Orion, and Barry planned to come to Sheboygan for the day. They went to the parade in the morning and had lunch and a steak dinner at our house. In the evening, we went to the fireworks along with our grandsons, Ryne and John and their families. We all had a great day.

The rest of that week I kept very busy. Friday I did my usual tasks - getting groceries, getting meat at Miesfeld's, and then I cleaned our house.

After our evening meal, both Ernie and I sat in our recliners and fell asleep. A little after 7:00 pm, I woke up when the doorbell rang. I went to the front door and when I opened it, there on the front sidewalk stood, Tim, Lisa, Nicole, Micah, Jared, Todd, Denise, Kaitlyn, Maddie, Scott, Debbi, Orion, and Barry. They had a big sign saying, "Happy Birthday". They all shouted out, "SURPRISE".

WOW! They did it! I was definitely surprised. Even though I had suspicions of what might happen, I would never have guessed they would all be there that night. After hugs from everyone and a picture with all of us along with their big "Happy Birthday" sign, we went in to wake up Ernie.

I was told that Ernie had been planning this surprise since February. He told the boys that they had to be here for my birthday. He said he was booking the GrandStay Hotel for three nights for them, so this expense would be paid.

I was also told that we needed to be at Fountain Park for a family photo shoot at 4:00 pm the next day. Debbie's Aunt Elaine would be coming to take the photos. We were all to wear a black top and khaki bottoms for the family photo. After the photo shoot, the birthday dinner was planned for 5:30 pm at Rupp's Restaurant. Lisa said she and Nicole were coming Saturday morning, and we were going to get a pedicure together.

I went to bed that night, but sleep was hard to come by as I was so excited. I had a very hard time settling down after the surprise, and I knew a lot more excitement was coming the following day, which was my actual birthday.

The pedicure was my first, so I really didn't know what to expect. Lisa and Nicole helped me out with what I needed to do. I picked out my polish and got up onto the chair. I think Nicole turned on the massage feature on my chair. The first thing I said was, "Oh, I think someone is really whooping me on my back." I was getting some pretty good pokes. That started it. I think from then on, everyone in the place knew this lady (me) was going to put a lot of smiles on their faces. A lady getting a manicure didn't take her eyes off of me. Every time I looked her way, she had a big smile on her face. Before everyone left, they were all stopping to wish me a "Happy Birthday". My ignorance and silly questions about what was going on was rather funny to them. We did have a fun time. It was a great way to start out my special day, and my toes never looked prettier.

After lunch with the kids at our house, we got ready for the photo shoot and party. It was a beautiful day, so outdoor pictures went very well. We have 28 people in our family, and everyone was there.

Elaine did an awesome job. From there, some of us went to change our clothes for the dinner party. Ernie had given me my birthday gifts that morning. He had shopped with Debbie and bought me a dress, three tops, shorts, and two necklaces. I had tried on the dress early in the afternoon when the kids were at our house. It fit perfectly and looked so nice, we all thought I should wear this dress for the party (my pretty toes matched perfectly with the dress and jewelry).

Ernie had set everything up for the dinner at Rupp's. They prepared a menu just for our family with no dollar amounts listed. Ernie also ordered a beautiful floral table arrangement from Hoffmann's and a birthday cake from Johnson's Bakery. Our oldest son, Jeff, offered a prayer before our dinner. He referred to all of us being together was like a "miracle". I was nodding my head in prayer – "Yes". It had been six years since we could all be together. I truly didn't think it would ever happen again. This was so special. What a blessing!

There were eight entrée choices. Lobster, tenderloin steak, rib-eye steak, and ribs were the choices that were offered. I'm the lobster lover. Ernie loves the tenderloin, but then we always share a bit with each other. Some of our kids did the same. Every one of us had a delicious dinner. Our daughter-in-law, Lisa, prepared a special video of many family pictures from the past. She also prepared an album with family pictures. She had each one of the family write a special note in this book before she presented it to me. This is now a real treasure. I had received two other floral arrangements, one from Scott and Debbi and one from some special extended family – Rob and Laura Miller. I received other gifts of money, gift certificates, and a special gift with teas, and a unique brewing cup. It was an extremely happy time. More than I could have ever imagined. I would have to describe it as -"Over the top".

After dinner, we spent some time at our house. Then everyone headed out. I got to bed and slept a bit better than the night before, but I was still so excited with all the family being together. The happy memories kept flooding my mind.

Sunday morning, Todd, Denise, Kaitlyn, and Maddie, joined Ernie and me at our church. At noon, we all met at Jeff and Debbie's home for a delicious chicken dinner that Ernie had asked Debbie to order from Shuff's Restaurant. Most of us were able to be together for this dinner. We had a light supper that evening at our house which was topped off with fresh picked strawberries that Tim had picked up the day before.

Scott, Debbie and Jeff all had to go back to work Monday. Tim and Lisa's family had to head back to Tennessee Monday morning. Todd and Denise and the girls stayed an extra day so we had one more day to enjoy with them. Our great-granddaughter, Emma, came to play with Kaitlyn and Maddie for one last time that afternoon.

So much happiness and fun was jam-packed into that weekend. I said to Todd, "I am so spoiled." Todd shook his head and said, "No, you're not spoiled." I thought about it, and decided that he was right. Then I said, "I guess what I should say is that I am so blessed." Todd agreed.

I watched my four sons, Jeff, Tim, Todd, and Scott, and their wives, Debbie, Lisa, Denise, and Debbi, and saw how well they seemed to get along and enjoy being with each other, and that day I felt that God had truly blessed me. Knowing that all of them loved and served the Lord has always meant so much to me. When our children were ready to start school, we had made the choice to send them to public schools. I'm not exactly sure why, but it may have been that the school was so close to our home, or it may have been the difference in cost. Ernie had gone to public schools. I had gone to Christian grade school and a public high school. Whatever the reason for our choice, the task of teaching religion to our children now had to come from the education they received at home and at church. This was important to me. Two of our sons, Tim and Todd, chose to go to a Christian College in Tennessee for a couple years and gained Christian education there. As best as I could, throughout their lives, I tried to teach them the importance of loving and serving the Lord by my example. It is now a tremendous blessing to see our children carrying on this tradition in their lives.

I watched my grandchildren, Ryne, Brittany, Mark, *Audrey, John, *Lauren, Kelsey, Kristin, *JB–John, Nicole, Micah, Jared, Kaitlyn, Maddie, Orion, and Barry, and our great-grandchildren, Emma and Mason, and that weekend I saw how well they seemed to get along and enjoy being together, and I truly felt that God had blessed me beyond measure. (* - soon to become family)

I saw my husband, my Prince Charming, the guy who so many thought was not the person I should be marrying, and all I can tell you is, they didn't know what God knew all along. They had no clue as to what God had planned for our future together.

Over the years, I have seen my husband's faith grow. This means everything to me. It's amazing how our love for one another continues to grow even after 56 years of marriage.

For those of you who know Ernie's physical condition, you know the tremendous effort that he has to take to even go out shopping to purchase gifts for me. For all of our family, we are amazed and in awe at how hard he worked to show his love not only to me with this special birthday party, but also his hard work in making special provisions for our kids and grandchildren as well. To say it was "Over the top", is probably putting it mildly.

Right now, July 2016, Ernie has begun his third bout with fighting his cancer. He just started chemo once again. He has been a 19 year cancer survivor, and our family and I are so proud of the tremendous courage he has had through this very difficult battle. He has been an incredible role model for all of us. His courage, positive attitude, and amazing drive have been so commendable. He has taught us all so much, and we are loving every day that God has continued to bless us with having him in our lives. To God be the glory!

I know some of you reading this book are married. At times you may have wondered if you did the right thing, - that is, if you married the right person. Some of you may be concerned that your spouse is not a believer, and you wonder whether your spouse will receive eternal life in heaven. In I Corinthians 7:12b, 13, 14 & 17a, you will find these encouraging words: "If any brother has a wife who is not a believer and she is willing to live with him, he must not divorce her. And if a woman has a husband who is not a believer and he is willing to live with her, she must not divorce him. For the unbelieving husband has been sanctified through his wife, and the unbelieving wife has been sanctified through her believing husband. Otherwise your children would be unclean, but as it is, they are holy." Verse 17 says, "Nevertheless, each one should retain the place in life that the Lord assigned to him and to which God has called him". (NIV)

There is no marriage that doesn't experience difficult times. We experienced challenges. We have had our differences. We did not always agree, but we learned to respect each other. We learned to forgive. We always remained faithful to each other. We know that we have so much to be grateful for. One thing we can be sure of is that God has blessed our marriage, and we will always love each other, and that is not a surprise.

Thank you, God, for blessing our marriage.

I love these words from the Heidelberg Catechism that were part of my Christian Education at my church. In the days of my youth, these words were memorized:

What is your only comfort in life and in death?

That I, with body and soul, both in life, and in death, am not my own, but belong to my faithful Savior Jesus Christ, who with His precious blood has fully satisfied for all my sins, and redeemed my life from destruction, and so preserves me that without the will of my Heavenly Father, not a hair can fall from my head, indeed, that all things must work together for my salvation. Wherefore, by His Holy Spirit, He also assures me of eternal life, and makes me heartily willing and able from this time forward to live eternally for Him.

(I have seen these words written in many different ways. To the best of my knowledge, this is close to what I had to memorize when I was young.)

When I decided to write this book, most of all, I felt I wanted it to be a love story. It is my hope that – first of all, I have been able to share God's incredible love for me. I hope that I expressed my special love for Him. I also hope that I have portrayed my love for my family, for my neighbor, and for all those who God brought into my life. I pray that this book will be a source of help and encouragement to many. Of greatest importance, I pray that this will be for God's glory.

In closing, let me remind you that this is what we have been commanded to do.

"Love the Lord your God with all your heart and with all your soul and with all your strength and with all your mind and, Love your neighbor as yourself." (NIV) Luke 10:27

May God be with you and bless you now and through eternity.

Great grandfather Jacobus Pieter Vercouteren &
Great Grandmother Magdalena Kamerik

Back Row – Grandpa
Gerhardt Otte; Grandma
Flora (Buteyn) Otte
Front Row – Peter; John
(my dad); Mary

Back Row – Magdalena (my
mother; James; Catherine
Front Row – Grandpa
Karel Vercouteren; Govert;
Grandma Dina (Kamerik)
Vercouteren

Back Row – Gerald; Lois; Florence; Carl; Ruth; Bob
Front Row – Judie (me); Diane; Magdalena
(mother); John (dad); Donnie; Rachel

Ernie – 1957; Judie – 1959

Judie; Ernie – 1958

Ernie; Judie – 50th Anniversary – July 2010

Back Row – Jeff; Tim; Todd; Scott
Front Row – Ernie; Judie

Front Row – Emma; Mason; Kaitlyn; Maddie; Barry
Seated – Ernie; Judie
Standing – Brittany; Audrey; Lauren; Kelsey; Debbie; John
(J.B.); Jared; Kristin; Lisa; Nicole; Micah; Debbi; Scott; Orion
Standing Back Row – Ryne; Mark; John; Jeff; Tim; Todd; Denise

Special Thanks

I would like to acknowledge some special people that took the time to help me put this book together.

Kevin Gesch, thank you for your willingness to edit my writings at a time when you were very busy yourself. I appreciate your input and kindness in helping to make this all possible. I hope that your dream of writing your own book will become a reality.

Laura Miller, you have been wonderful. You put so much time and thought into doing a second edit on this book. I love your many suggestions, and I appreciate your encouragement in getting me to stretch a bit. You are awesome. Thank you so much for your help. You know how much I love you.

Thank you to my cousins Pastor Karl Vercouteren and Jim Vercouteren for providing information and photographs from my mother's ancestors.

Thank you to my brother Gerald Otte for providing information and photographs from my dad's ancestors.

I truly appreciate all of your help in putting this book together. Thank you, and God Bless You!

Most of all, thank you God for the life you have given to me. You have given me a story to tell, and I pray that my story will be a blessing to many.

Printed in the United States
By Bookmasters